P9-AQY-324

Monograph 58
THE AMERICAN ETHNOLOGICAL SOCIETY
Robert F. Spencer, *Editor*

*

The Library
St. Mary's College of Maryland
St. Mary's City, Maryland 20686

VISUAL METAPHORS:

A Formal Analysis of Navajo Art

Evelyn Payne Hatcher

with an Introduction by Anthony F. C. Wallace

WEST PUBLISHING CO.
St. Paul • New York • Boston
Los Angeles • San Francisco

COPYRIGHT © 1967 By Evelyn Payne Hatcher
COPYRIGHT © 1974 By Evelyn Payne Hatcher
All rights reserved
Printed in the United States of America

Library of Congress Cataloging in Publication Data

Hatcher, Evelyn Payne,

Visual Metaphors: A Formal Analysis of Navajo Art
Bibliography: p.

1. Navajo Indian—Art. 2. Indians of North America—Southwest, New—Art. I. Title.

E99.N3H35 709'.01'1 74-20691

ISBN 0-8299-0026-8

Hatcher–Navajo Art

To any reader who is irritated enough by this essay to try and do better.

*

Introduction

The anthropology of art is a peculiarly difficult domain in which to work, and for a particular reason, in which it resembles the study of religion. In both cases one must always be torn between the effort to be objective (i. e., to use categories of observation and description that others can replicate, and standards of proof comparable to those employed in other branches of science), and the effort to be appreciative and empathic of the whole (i. e., to read the meaning of myth and ritual, to get beyond the mechanics of analysis, to understand the relation between art and social structure).

An extreme objectivity characterizes the old classic in the field, Boas's *Primitive Art*; it is so spartan a catalogue of forms as to discard meaning almost entirely. On the other extreme, psychoanalytic and Lévi-Straussian interpretations sometimes approach the subject in a mystical and intuitive way, arbitrarily asserting meaning without involving analysis or proof, almost as if the meaning were visible for any fool to see, somehow explicit in the symbol rather than implicit in the persons using it.

Evelyn Hatcher's methodological study is an effort to resolve some of these difficulties. On the one hand, she insists on describing art style in objective and formal categories (which are probably usable cross-culturally). Her descriptive schema is probably far more detailed than any other in use in anthropology. But she seeks also to regard the style not merely as expressive of a personality type, or a world view, or what have you, but as a more or less deliberate effort by the artist (or craftsman) to communicate something to his audience (which may be a sick patient, a concerned family, visiting neighbors, or whoever). This relieves her of the need to view art only as symptom, expressive of personality in the same sense as any neurotic compromise is, and permits her to relate her interpretation of meaning directly to the social situation in which the artist is communicating.

The art form she presents and analyzes most thoroughly is Navajo sand paintings. They are produced in the course of a shaman's performance of a ritual sequence ("chant" or "way") as an accompaniment to formal recitation. The purpose of the ritual is to restore health to the individual and solidarity to his group by a renewal of commitment to the values of power, vitality, order, harmony, and balance. Anxiety, fear, and conflict are not expressed. It is no surprise to her, then, that the formal qualitites of the paintings "express" precisely these values, since this is just what the artist-therapist wants (quite consciously) to get across. But it is also no surprise to her to find that other art forms, used in different settings (e. g., watercolors made for sale to Anglos), have somewhat different formal qualities, because they are intended to convey other messages to other people.

Dr. Hatcher very kindly makes reference to my youthful effort to contribute to this field. The paper on Maya art is dear to my memory because it was the first anthropological paper I read to a scientific audience. The International Congress of Americanists was meeting in New York in 1949, and, as an aspiring graduate student, I thought I might try my wings. With his encouragement (I got an A for it), I spruced up a term paper I had written for Linton Satterthwaite's course on Middle American cultures. It was received ambivalently by the discussant, Géza Róheim, who felt that I failed adequately to recognize the role of one of the mechanisms of defense (displacement, perhaps). The Congress declined to publish it but it quickly found a haven in the psychoanalytic quarterly *American Imago* where an expanded version appeared.

After all this time I naturally am pleased to see someone take up the enterprise which I abandoned so many years ago. Her methodology is essentially the same as mine but much more thorough both in the classification of formal qualities and in the collation of authorities to whom she has turned for hypotheses about the meaning of such qualities. But, with the advantage now of greater experience, I would have to agree with her that a communication model is probably more productive than a merely projective one. Undoubtedly defense mechanisms are present in the forms of art but they can be analyzed more fruitfully, I am sure, in the context of a communicational transaction.

Such a view also would help to develop the insights of Margaret Mead on the role of art forms in the socialization of a child. I recall somewhere in her writing a recognition that the formal qualities of the arts and crafts of a culture convey the same values, the same world view, as do myth, and the homilies of parents. Art, in effect, both in religious usage and outside it, is an effort, sometimes self-conscious and sometimes implicit, to effect or to block certain transformations of mood, health, awareness, sentiment, or value and world view felt to be important by the artist in his relation to other members of his community.

Anthony F. C. Wallace

Preface

When I realized that my efforts were to appear in print, I began looking to see what sort of thing I would be expected to write in a preface. I could find very little that really sounded very much like my experiences. I put the whole thing off thinking that at the last relief would be so great that gratitude would flow in the proper fashion, but here I am, and it does not. I'll have to tell it like it was.

It all started with irritation because I couldn't find the comparative studies, couldn't find the field work, couldn't even find the definitions that ought to be available to back up the sweeping statements in all the introductory textbooks concerning the many significant relationships between art and culture, art and society.

Then I read the article by J. L. Fischer. I thought "now we're getting at something," but the whole thing irritated me greatly; in assumptions, definitions, statistical techniques, and especially the data, and I went around muttering, "Damn it, if one is going to do this sort of thing one ought to at least . . ." The "least" turned out to be more work than I bargained for, but after some years I think I have made a start. The one time I met Fischer and asked him about some of the things I questioned he said the article was "purely heuristic." At the time I thought this was a pretty weak cop-out. Now I know that anyone who can get so much work out of me has achieved a heuristic triumph. Every time I bogged down, somebody would reprint his article, or worse, quote his conclusions, and I would go back to work. So I can say in all honesty that if it had not been for J. L. Fischer this work might not have been started and probably would never have been finished.

Then we have all those persons who read one's manuscript with patient loving care and make all kinds of valuable suggestions without any goofs. E. Adamson Hoebel read this back in the 1967 dissertation stage, and I thought he was pretty great *not* to make a lot of suggestions but to let me work it out in my own way. R. F. Spencer found a mistake in the bibliography, and later said that he thought the effort would be suitable for an A. E. S. Monograph. This was gratifying, as I have always admired the Series, but I wish I'd said "no" and used the time for the next, more exciting step in my investigations. Still, that's not his fault, and I suppose I should thank him. Hoebel, Spencer, M. E. R. Nicholson, and

C. T. Shay who all gave me so much in the way of encouragement during the thesis period would probably have given the considerable amount of time and effort to make specific suggestions for this rewritten effort, had I but asked them. As it stands, I am grateful for their intangible support, but bear the full responsibility for any and all shortcomings; no one can fault them for not pointing out such shortcomings—I didn't give them a chance.

It is irritating to think of the number of interesting publications on art, particularly in the realm of cross-cultural esthetics and in perception that I have read since this was originally written, and that do not even appear in the bibliography, but they would not affect the basic job I have tried to do. Worse is the thought of the pertinent works I have probably missed entirely.

When I wrote to A. F. C. Wallace asking him for an introduction, I got a speedy reply with the introduction enclosed. This sort of thing is hard on the ego. A flash of insight reveals that perhaps one's own lack of eminence is largely due to procrastination when one would prefer to blame sexism or cruel fate. The fact that he thought the work worth adding his name to, however, does wonders for the morale, which almost compensates for the insight, and I appreciate it.

I suppose I'm grateful for the editorial work done by various persons, but who can really enjoy having all one's mistakes pointed out, and having one's beautiful copy marked up with blue pencilled question marks and variations on the question "What does *this* mean?"?

Writing for permission to reproduce illustrations was a big fat headache. The publishers listed below were very decent about permission of reproductions of published material, but in some other cases I had to make hasty substitutions because the amount of credit insisted upon was so great as to foul up the visual definition pages with their advertising copy.

My husband J. B. Hatcher did all those traditional spouse-of-the-writer things such as typing and retyping and putting up with my irritability and retyping and living on sandwiches; but then he likes sandwiches. He also pointed out the inconsistencies which my various inspirations inflicted on this appallingly systematic treatment, and frequently interrupted my intellectual endeavors with questions about the sizes of illustrations and picky little matters like proofreading, and the index, and omissions in the bibliography.

Preface

I am forced to admit that the people at West Publishing have on the whole been pretty patient with an author who has to have a lot of drawings exactly placed within the text, and a representative who objects to Old Style type face without ligatures. We have been at least as irritating to them as they to us, and all anthropologists know that reciprocity is the tie that binds.

Admiration for Navajo art forms goes as far back as my memory, because my parents, Elsie Palmer Payne and Edgar Payne, took me along when they painted in the Navajo country. So the over-intellectualized analysis often seemed, and seems, not merely inadequate but idiotic. And yet the lag in the study of art in an anthropological way as compared to other aspects of culture irritated me more. It implies a lack of respect for art, treating it as a kind of minor decoration on the real concerns of human life, where any generalization could be tossed off without regard for the standards of scholarship required for other fields. Furthermore, to my surprise, when I emerged from the long discipline of putting stupid little tally marks on numerous sheets, I found that I looked at all kinds of visual art with new and increased enjoyment and understanding. Still, I feel apologies are due Navajo artists for so much that is left out.

Evelyn Payne Hatcher

St. Cloud and
Minneapolis,
November 1974

*

Acknowledgments

Permission to reproduce published material has been obtained from the following; their cooperation is gratefully acknowledged.

- Basic Books, Inc., for material from

STRUCTURAL ANTHROPOLOGY by Claude Levi-Strauss, © 1963 by Basic Books, Inc., Publishers, New York.

- Dover Publications, Inc., for material from

DECORATIVE ART OF THE SOUTHWESTERN INDIAN by Dorothy Smith Sides, Dover Publications, Inc., New York, 1961.

DESIGN MOTIFS OF ANCIENT MEXICO by Jorge Enciso, Dover Publications, Inc., New York, 1958.

PRIMITIVE ART by Frank Boas, Dover Publications, Inc., New York, 1955 reprint of 1927 edition.

- Holle Bildarchiv, Baden-Baden, for material from

AFRICA, THE ART OF THE NEGRO PEOPLES by Elsy Leuzinger, © 1960 by Holle and Co. Verlag, Baden-Baden, Germany.

THE ART OF ANCIENT AMERICA by H. D. Disselhoff and S. Linne, © 1960 by Holle and Co. Verlag, Baden-Baden, Germany.

THE ART OF THE SOUTH SEA ISLANDS by Alfred Buehler, Terry Barrow and Charles P. Mountford, © 1962 by Holle & Co. Verlag, Baden-Baden, Germany.

- Payne Studios Inc., for material from

COMPOSITION OF OUTDOOR PAINTING by Edgar A. Payne, Seward Publishing Company, Los Angeles, 1941, Copyright renewed 1969 by Elsie Palmer Payne.

- Pitman Publishing Corporation, New York for material from

COMPOSITION: THE ANATOMY OF PICTURE MAKING by Harry Sternberg, Pitman Publishing Corporation, New York, 1958.

- Princeton University Press, for material from

NAVAJO RELIGION by Gladys Reichard, Bollingen Series XVIII (© 1950 by Bollingen Foundation) published by Princeton University Press.

- University of California Press for material from

ART, FORM, AND CIVILIZATION by Ernest Mundt, University of California Press, Berkeley, 1952 by permission of the Regents of the University of California.

- University of Washington Press for material from

NORTHWEST COAST INDIAN ART by Bill Holm, University of Washington Press, 1965.

Contents

Contents

†

VISUAL METAPHORS:
A Formal Analysis of Navajo Art

1

Concepts and Methods

ART AS COMMUNICATION

Anthropologists often state that art reflects the values of a culture, or that the function of art is to perpetuate the values of the society, or that it in some way serves social needs. If art has these social functions in addition to whatever individual psychological functions it may have for the artist, then what the artist puts into his productions must be in some way communicated to the other members of his society. If we are concerned with art not merely as a psychological expression of an individual, or as individual creativity, but as a sociocultural phenomenon, we are faced with a problem in communication. To regard art as communication is by no means new or unusual. Bohannan says:

> All art can be said to have two sweeping characteristics: it embodies a message within an idiom of communication, and it arouses a sense of mystery—a feeling that it is more than it appears to the intellect to be. (Bohannan 1964:141)
>
> Art is of the essence in analyzing culture because it supplies the media in which some of the most perceptive and original thinkers in any society communicate their experience. (ibid.:142)

Although given lip service, the view that art is a form of communication has not been explored in cross-cultural contexts to any extent, nor has its implication for ethnological theory been developed. As long as art is considered basically as a personal expression, the social aspects are secondary, a kind of reflection that can be seen as a minor embellishment of little importance to the serious study of sociocultural behavior. But when art is considered primarily from the point of view of communication, art is revealed as having an important role in the processes of culture.

To consider art as a problem in communication immediately involves the investigator in a whole series of problems which are not relevant when it is considered only as a kind of reflection or individual projection. One asks not only about the artist, but about the audience; i. e., who communicates to whom. One asks what is communicated under what circumstances. One asks by what means a work of art conveys something from one person to another.

The focus of the investigation reported here is on the last of these questions: the means by which visual art, in this case in the graphic form, can convey some kind of meaning from one person to another. But it is a premise of the investigation that such communication cannot hope to be understood without reference to the circumstances in which the communication takes place, and the nature of the communication appropriate to the circumstances.

The whole idea of art as a category is a construct in our own culture, and while it may be a useful and legitimate one, it may need to be enlarged and redefined to be useful in cross-cultural context. An excellent contribution to this end has been made by d'Azevedo (1958). For our purposes here, the best definition would seem to be a very broad one: Art is viewed as the esthetic component of any human activity; the extra quality of the form which gives pleasure and satisfaction. Thus art can be seen as the enhancement of any activity, forming an additional channel of communication in the social setting in which the activity takes place, and reinforcing the function of that activity.

Within this framework, it would seem inescapable that the various functions of art may operate in different circumstances, express different needs, communicate different messages in different situations. Does it follow that, at least within a given cultural tradition, different functions are related to differences in stylistic expression? Do differences in use and technique relate to differences in function and show differences in perceptual form? Implicit in most of the discussions of art is the idea that form follows function—that somehow the style itself has meaning—that art does not fulfill its function simply by activity and a generalized esthetic satisfaction.

> When we speak of the "forms" of visual art, we have in mind the physical (that is to say the visible and touchable) *signs*

> through which artists realize ideas and express feelings. What are these forms? They are the lines, spots and shaped surfaces, the solid masses and volumes of air space, the textures, tones and colors which we find in architecture, in sculpture and painting. Just as verbal language is made up of sounds which we interpret as words (that is, meanings), visual art is made up of material forms which can take on definite meanings. They are the vocabulary of art. Without forms—audible or visible signs—there can be no communication between men. (Eitner 1961:38)

These forms are sometimes called the formal qualities of art as distinct from its content. When speaking of specific types of form in this sense I use the term *form-quality* because the term "form" by itself has such a wide range of meaning as to be frequently ambiguous. Eitner says these forms are the vocabulary of art, but we are not provided with a dictionary of the meanings of form-qualities which would give specific *form-meaning* (a term that is used by Longman 1949) for each form-quality.

Most students of art are very dubious concerning the usefulness of such compilations because of the importance of the totality of interrelationships or the gestalt of the individual production. Students of art stress the individual production as an indivisible entity. Langer terms such a work "the expressive form" or "art symbol," which has "import" (i. e., "presents a feeling for our contemplation") rather than meaning. No verbal analysis or interpretation of the elements that go to make up the "art symbol" can ever convey the import of a work of art because the communication is of a different order from that which can be conveyed by discoursive symbols. This does not mean that any extraphysical or mystical means are employed, but only that the arrangement of formal qualities (and content) are too complex, subtle, and unique, as well as of a different order, to be put into words.

The fact remains that these form-qualities are the only means at the artist's disposal by which to convey import, and the only means by which the viewer (or listener) can get the message. As a matter of fact, the way a person in our society is trained to receive the import of an art work is to have some of the form-meanings pointed out to him in regard to each work until he perceives a gestalt that has import. The idea of the artistic whole which alone conveys import seems on examination to be exaggerated. The well-known cliché that "nothing can be added and nothing taken away" really adds up to, "you can't change the art form without changing the import," and this is not the same as saying that any change destroys all meaning. If this wholeness is indispensable to import, what is the sense of playing the *Leonore Overture* or singing an aria in the concert hall? How can art books be illustrated by hunks of the Sistine Chapel ceiling torn from context? In Langer's book *Feeling and Form* there is a reproduction of a painting by Matisse without color. Does it have no import at all? Then why is it there? If a work is reproduced in such a form, it is because by examining some of its properties the viewer can receive some of its import. There is no reason why the examination of some portion of the qualities of a work cannot convey a portion of the meaning. As a matter of fact, the form-qualities of art forms are frequently interpreted within one context or another.

While it has often been stated that the formal qualities of art are ineffable, that the message cannot be put into words, such a statement is more often than not followed by an attempt to do just that—to interpret the stylistic qualities in words, relating them to a variety of social and psychological characteristics. Not all the interpretations of form-qualities in art are phrased in terms of feeling and emotion; they may go directly to the circumstances that give rise to the feeling, or, put another way, certain form-qualities may be related to specific values, psychological symptoms, or world views, or they may be seen as the reflection of social organization.

Ideas as to form-meanings of art in particular depend on the analyst's idea of the function of art in general. Thus persons who consider the function of art in general in terms of the expression of the ideal discuss the particular stylistic qualities in terms of the expression of more or less specific cultural ideals. Persons with a different orientation regarding the function of art may interpret the same stylistic features in a different way. For example, where art is conceived as an expression of the ideal, symmetry is said to be an expression of order, stability, harmony, and serenity. Where art is considered an expression of the social order, symmetry may be considered a reflection of an egalitarian society. (cf. Lévi-Strauss 1964, and also Fischer 1961). Where art is considered an expression of the dynamics of personality, people who like symmetry are considered to be "constrictive, depressive, hypochondriac, or highly conventional" (Schmidl-Waehner 1942) or suffering from "depression and fixation" (Bell 1948). These interpretations are very confusing. Are not the stressed ideals of order and stability usually associated with hierarchical societies? Are egalitarian societies made up of constrictive hypochondriacs?

If, however, we consider art not so much as an expression but as a communication, then its function depends on the situation, involving not only the artist but also an audience with needs which the communication helps to meet. Instead of interpretation on the basis of the specialization of the investigator—the ethnologist looking for signs of values, the social anthropologist for analogies to social structure, the historians for Zeitgeist, the psychologists for projections of one kind or another, and so forth—a more promising approach might be to look at the art in terms of the situation in which it is made and used.

The more that is known about the circumstances in which an art form plays a role, and the reaction of the people to it, the more can be inferred as to the "message" which is being transmitted. If a reasonable inference can be made as to the meaning of the message in general, hypotheses concerning the meaning of its component parts (form-meanings) can be supported insofar as they are consistent with overall meaning. For example, the meaning of Navajo chants for the people has been rather extensively explored; the message of the sandpaintings which are part of the ceremonies should be consistent with the function of this activity as well as with the premises of Navajo culture as a whole.

But the question still remains as to how the interpretation of form-qualities as individual projection is related to the use of such qualities as sociocultural communications.

RELATION OF ART TO PSYCHOLOGICAL PROJECTION

Art is traditionally looked at as something *expressed* through the individual artist. There is considerable difference of opinion as to what is expressed, and still more difficulty in understanding how the mechanisms of projection, which would presumably be the operating means, can function to produce culturally standardized forms. Studies that have been made of the expressive aspects of graphic forms can contribute to our understanding of the communicative means of such forms, once the relations between the two functions are clarified.

If the artist is striving to communicate, and is not simply a kind of medium through which various things are expressed, he must in some way select what is to be communicated at a particular time. Expressing one's concepts or feelings in such a way as to be understood is a difficult and demanding task in any medium, and to regard art simply as a psychological projection because it sometimes and in part functions in this way is on a par with considering language in the same light. The relation between art and self-expression has been stated very clearly by Susanne Langer:

> Now, I believe the expression of feeling in a work of art—the function that makes the work an expressive form—is not symptomatic at all. An artist working on a tragedy need not be in personal despair or violent upheaval; nobody, indeed, could work in such a state of mind. His mind would be occupied with the causes of his emotional upset. Self-expression does not require composition and lucidity; a screaming baby gives his feeling far more release than any musician, but we don't go to a concert hall to hear a baby scream; in fact, if that baby is brought in we are likely to go out. We don't want self-expression.
>
> A work of art presents feeling (in the broad sense I mentioned before, as everything that can be felt) for our contemplation, making it visible or audible or in some way perceivable through a symbol, not inferrable from a symptom. (Langer 1957:25)

But an artist of any kind—playwright, actor, or painter—is aware of the ways people do express feelings as simple self-expression, as symptoms. Many of these symptomatic expressions he uses quite consciously as symbols to convey feeling. This is certainly usually true of content. But he may also be aware of some such expressions without conscious analysis, and he may use them in his art. For this reason we may be able to use the interpretations that have been made from projective tests to enhance our understanding of meaning in the arts.

MUNCH

The artist, however, does not simply go around looking for symptoms. The painter, sculptor, or musician is much more immediately concerned with the form-qualities themselves; his interest in their meaning is always related to his immediate creative problem. He draws his "vocabulary" of form from what he has seen and uses whatever he thinks will look "right" or "nice" or "Hmmm" in the message. Studio lore seldom deals in generalities, but rather in terms of the needs of a particular work.

Arnheim (1954) sees no intermediary at all between forms and the feelings they convey; no associations with the self-expressions of oneself or others, no need to empathize or to formulate analogies is required. The human organism, in his view, responds in terms of feeling first, association and analysis later. He does not deal with the possibility of cultural relativity in this regard. Beam also assumes that the basic psychological responses are everywhere the same:

> Communiciation through works of art—sometimes between artists and observers who are separated by thousands of years of time—is only possible because certain psychological responses have remained relatively constant and can be discussed with a fair chance of agreement. If this were not so, any enduring communication would be impossible. If, for instance, a brilliant red-orange color had a soothing effect on the ancient Chinese artist instead of the highly stimulating effect it has on us today, there would be no continuing community of ideas on which we could count. But the ancient Chinese reacted to red-orange in about the same way that we do, and much as we do to such elements as line, mass, and texture. In that respect there is a univeral basis for visual communication. This predictable response to the various elements in art is exemplified by many familiar works. Our main points of reference will be vitality and repose, just as order and variety were in the study of the esthetic orientation of design. However, we shall find these universals in a unique combination of energy, emotion, idea, and design in each work of art. It is thus that art achieves simultaneously both universality and exactness of meaning. (Beam 1956:682)

As for my own views I am committed neither to complete cultural relativity in perception nor to the view that all human perception is fundamentally alike. My feeling is that the truth lies somewhere between, but that we know very little as to how the human, the individual, and the sociocultural are related. This is the underlying problem to be investigated, a very important one of which art is only one manifestation. By collecting the hypotheses concerning those feeling qualities of perceptions which are considered to be universal, and by examining their use in different cultural and situational contexts, we may gain some insight into this matter.

If, for this purpose, we assume that there is a basic vocabulary of forms and colors which universally communicate certain feelings, it follows that it is by the various combinations of these basic qualities that patterns characteristic of certain personality types, certain situational communications, and certain cultural configurations are conveyed.

In spite of their number, the assumptions concerning the existence of basic perceptual visual qualities have never been determined or defined in any but the most sketchy and scattered fashion. They are usually related to specific examples from our cultural tradition. Even if the form-qualities are fairly clearly stated, the interpretations are not in terms of feeling but in terms of diagnoses of configurations of interest to the investigator. That is to say, the form-qualities are interpreted in terms of the psychological symptoms projected, or the social values suggested, or the religious concepts symbolized. William Henry, for one, has discussed (1961) the overspecific culture-bound interpretation of perceptive qualities in the Rorschach Test.

In seeking to examine the basic vocabulary of the visual communication of feeling, specific interpretations may give clues to the underlying, more general ones. This kind of interpretation may be used in a cultural or sociological context as well as a psychological one. I should think that when and where and to whom an artist is communicating would indicate something about the more specific meaning. A form-quality suggesting order and system, when used by a person seeking psychological help in a clinic, might well be an attempt to communicate a symptom, and might well have reference to "constriction." In certain religious contexts, the communication might convey reassurance concerning the orderly quality of the universe in view of the chanciness of life. In another context, a message about order and system might refer to the value of maintaining a traditional kinship system.

The psychoanalytic approach to form-qualities can provide useful clues to generalized meanings, to the underlying feel of various qualities. Probably the more expert the artist, the more completely he controls the use and combination of these qualities to convey the import he considers appropriate to the statement in the context of the situation.

This does not rule out the possibilities of unconscious projections, which may account for some of the individual variations on cultural style. Such individual projections may become cultural innovations. I do not pretend to know how esthetic productions satisfy emotional needs, but the processes by which creative solutions become part of a culture are similar for esthetic and social innovations (cf. Wallace 1956).

Art and psychological projection both draw on the same vocabulary of perception and, presumably, form-meaning. It does not follow that all art is projection, nor all projection, art. Neither does it follow that the "vocabulary" is the same in all cultures. The extent of the cultural variation in this vocabulary is not known.

It should be clear that in this approach concepts of basic or modal personality are not immediately relevant, and that this is not, in fact, primarily a psychological orientation, but a sociocultural one, depending on the related concepts of communication and social function. Psychological interpretations play a large part simply because more applicable hypotheses have been put forth in psychological contexts than in any other, and because feeling and perception are considered somehow more "psychological" than cognitive symbols or ideas. Perhaps this is owing to the assumption that human beings perceive and feel in the same way even if culture makes them think differently, an assumption distinctly lacking in empirical verification.

METHODS FOR THE CROSS-CULTURAL INVESTIGATION OF FORM-MEANING

Aside from the scattered interpretive statements which are to be found in discussions of various forms of "primitive" art, there has been very little effort made to examine the formal qualities of art in terms of their possible cross-cultural meanings, much less to test the validity of such interpretations. Such efforts as have been made in this direction are all based on the interpretations of clinical psychologists, and take the position that art is a projection, through the artist, of the modal or basic personality of the society, even where these interpretations are phrased as values.

Wallace is very explicit about this in his study of Maya codices. He says:

> The basic assumption underlying this approach is that all kinds of human behavior are determined, among other factors, by the personality of the agent. All behavior is expressive of—is a "projection" of—the agent's personality; the technical problem is to isolate behavioral categories which can be directly correlated with psychological categories. (Wallace 1950:241)
>
> . . . a conventional art-style must contain elements which are aesthetically (i. e., psychologically) congenial to the large majority of the people supporting art production over continuing generations. The nature of what is aesthetically congenial is determined by the basic personality structure of the people. (ibid.:244)

The following excerpts summarize his methodology:

> In order to make inferences about Maya character, it is necessary first to describe the sample of their art in psychologically relevant terms. There is, unfortunately, no standard list of descriptive categories to be used automatically in the projective analysis of art products. Each worker in the field has a more or less individual system of description and interpretation because each worker uses slightly different kinds of data. Schmidl-Waehner handles spontaneously produced drawings and paintings; Machover asks the subject to "draw a person"; and so on. In the face of this welter of methodologies, it seems advisable to take an eclectic approach: to select any descriptive categories (with their interpretive meanings) that are applicable to the sample chosen for analysis. (ibid.:245)
>
> My initial procedure in making the blind diagnosis was, having a general familiarity with the categories employed by Rorschach, Machover, Elkish, and Schmidl-Waehner, to peruse the codices (using both colored and photographic reproductions) and to jot down certain features which seemed common to all or almost all and which had been used by one or more of the authors as interpretive criteria. I then matched these descriptive categories with the interpretive categories. This gave a disjointed list of personality traits. These personality traits were then studied and reorganized into a somewhat more structuralized personality portrait. (ibid.:246)

The interpretive categories Wallace uses are given in a table in the appendix of his paper. He used 27 descriptive qualities, twelve of which relate to content, chiefly the human form, and fifteen of which are formal qualities. Some samples are:

Descriptive	Interpretive	Source
Tendency to keep human arms close to body	Mild introversion	Machover 1949
Long human hands, feet, and noses	Ambition, phallic aggressiveness	Machover 1949
Frequency of black human figures	Aggression and depression problems	Naumberg 1947
Filling pages to margins	Ambition, initiative, good adjustment (often found with children)	Schmidl-Waehner 1946
Generally "compressed" design	Introversive, obsessive, compulsive	Elkisch 1945
Avoidance of blending colors	Careful control of emotional responsiveness	Alschuler and Hattwick 1943

The other formal traits used by Wallace are: tendency to avoid sharp corners and to emphasize rounded corners, lack of perspective, lack of background, ready use of color, tendency to outline form elements carefully in black, avoidance of naturalistic use of colors, avoidance of rigid geometric design, complexity of design, profusion of tiny form figures, tendency toward frequent combinations of red and black, preference for relatively small form elements, and avoidance of sharp points. These are taken as characteristic of Maya codices without consideration of degree, either quantitatively or qualitatively. No comparison is offered with other Maya art forms.

Wallace's conclusions are in the form of the personality portrait, and his test of the validity of the interpretation was to compare the personality diagnosis with Rorschach protocols of modern Maya, and with observations of Bishop Landa in postconquest times. Criticism of this work has been directed at the validation; the choice of a long-dead population for any kind of test relating to personality would seem an unfortunate one. However, as long as art is considered a projection, and the concept of basic personality is accepted, this is a technique with many possibilities, and it is surprising that it has never been carried forward in situations permitting comparison with other psychological analyses.

George Mills, in his doctoral thesis (1953) and the book based upon it (1959), employed very much the same technique with regard to Navajo arts and crafts; that is, he assembled from the literature a number of interpretations for the characteristics he found in Navajo art. Being more interested in art than in personality, Mills phrases his interpretations in terms of values; he pays some attention to iconography and very little to the portrayal of the human figure. The concept of basic personality structure is implicit rather than explicit. His work is best summarized in his own words:

> . . . I describe the styles of four Navajo media: drawing, drypainting, weaving, and silverwork. The section on Navajo values summarizes the premises of the culture as these have been described by various field workers. . . . If factors besides cultural values influence style, I must find some way of discounting their effects. Because little is known about determinants of style, I assume that stylistic traits appearing in three or four of the four media are culturally determined. . . . This recurrance of traits tends to cancel out the effect of more localized determinants.
>
> The culturally significant aspects of art that are representational, consciously symbolic, or iconographic, I relate to cultural premises by standard methods. . . . Formal traits (kinds of organization, addiction to particular forms, density of design) are more problematic. I compiled material from the psychology of art bearing on relations between forms and states of mind, e. g., circles represent a desire for protection and integration. Assuming that these associations of form and meaning are cross-culturally valid, I used them to develop the meaning of formal traits for comparison with the meaning of representational traits and cultural premises. . . . An interpretation of Navajo values emerges. (Mills 1959:1)

The formal traits Mills considers are: conception perfected before beginning work, outlining, curves, straight lines and angles, swastikas, zigzag, emphasis on center, context rather than isolation, movement, full but not crowded use of format, expansion, ability to use large formats, radiation, carefully structured designs, compositions as varied organization of similar elements, repetition, balance, contrast, psychical distance; and the following pairs of traits: carefulness-casualness, expansion-containment, fixity-variability of patterns, and restricted-liberal use of color.

He summarizes his discussions of the various interpretations in a table, from which some examples are given below. The table does not do justice to Mills's sometimes perceptive analysis, but it indicates the kinds of relationships he finds, which are not structured in terms of either values or basic personality, but are a collection of interpretations that seem applicable.

Trait	Cue Value	Meaning
Outlining	Insecurity; inturned emotions; emotional tensions; simplification and clarification	Navajos are strongly emotional with tendency to turn inward. Desire for clarity of artistic situation
Full but not crowded use of format	Balance of freedom and discipline, dynamism and control; vitality and spontaneity	Navajos enjoy a healthy balance of dynamism and control, their vitality is unimpaired, and they recognize external conditions and are able to adapt to them
Balance	Balance is more favorable than symmetry which expresses rigidity and constraint. Hieratic art tends toward symmetry	Symmetry is more common in crafts than hieratic sandpaintings. The importance of balance suggests that Navajos accept chance and change as well as their desire to master the conditions of life

The discussion of balance and symmetry, in the more extended form as well as in this summary, brings out one of the difficulties in Mills's treatment. To find a discussion of Navajo art that considers sandpainting lacking in symmetry is startling to anyone at all familiar with this art form and its elaborate use of various types of symmetry. Navajo sandpainting rarely employs bilateral symmetry, which is presumably the type of symmetry to which Mills refers; such confusion points up the need for defining the terms used.

Mills's study has the merit of discussing the art forms separately and considering a cultural style on the basis of such characteristics as are shared, rather than making any a priori assumptions concerning the existence of a cultural style, although the descriptions are very generalized except for the children's drawings. As with the Wallace paper, the form-qualities are simply stated as being characteristic, without any accounting or itemization of the works analyzed or the frequency or degree to which the qualities are to be found.

A fundamental difficulty, of which Mills is quite aware, is the problem of cross-cultural influences on the artist:

> The weaver or silversmith finds that the trader controls the market. The trader, in turn responsive to his customers, makes demands upon the craftsman. Perhaps this is what Reichard had in mind when she wrote that it is impossible to study the style of Navajo weaving because too many of the designs have foreign sources. Are the bordered style of weaving, brash dyes, and the commercial style of silverwork no longer indicative of Navajo emphases? Are these opportunistic rather than expressive products? How does one distinguish ordinary diffusions from those that break the ties of style and culture?
>
> Adair's statement that the arrow and swastika forms, suggested by traders, appealed to the Navajos and became part of the native style indicates the complexity of the problem. Since the same process may have produced the bordered blanket and riotous colors, these aspects of style must be assigned to the limbo of traits whose bearing on cultural values is uncertain. (ibid.:103)
>
> If the values of an alien culture are expressing themselves in Navajo weaving, I err in drawing conclusions about Navajo values from this art. (ibid.:63)

This is part of the more general problem of interpreting the qualities shared by several art forms of a culture in terms of cultural values: what do the qualities that are not shared mean?

Another study of form-meaning is that of Barry, who uses a cross-cultural statistical approach. He describes his method in regard to the art data as follows:

> Thirty non-literate societies were selected from the list of 76 on which Whiting and Child gave socialization data. These 30 societies comprised all those from which the investigator was able to find at least ten works of graphic art, either exhibited in museums, or as illustrations in ethnographic reports. If 10–20 works of art were available for a culture they were all rated; if more than 20 were available, representative ones were picked at random. In all, 549 works of art were rated.
>
> Each work of art was rated on 18 criteria of art style, using a 7-point scale. Since the score on most of the variables was influ-

> enced by the materials used, the art works of each culture were compared with those of other cultures in the same material, e. g., weaving, woodwork, wickerwork, and pottery. The culture was designated as above or below the median on each variable, combining its score in the different materials but comparing its art in each material only with the art of other cultures in the same material. (Barry 1957:380)

The undergraduate honors thesis (Barry 1952) upon which the article is based gives the full rating scale used in the description of graphic art, "design on any kind of a surface." Barry used 18 characteristics of style, 11 of which are used in the analysis. These characteristics were selected for three attributes:

> 1. Objective, able to be rated on a quantitative basis, and minimizing the influence of the rater's subjective feelings.
>
> 2. Universal, able to be scored on the same basis in all varieties of works of graphic art.
>
> 3. Expressive of essential features of the aesthetic process. (Barry 1952:4)

The characteristics chosen are considered to be polar, and Barry constructed a seven-point rating scale for each. For example:

> Design Simple-Complex
>
> 1. Design simply organized, all features constantly repeated, and a fairly small number of figures.
>
> 4. Design showing some complexity in basic organization; a fairly large number of figures, but much repetition of them.
>
> 7. Design elaborately organized, with little repetition of figures and a large number of them. (ibid.:Appendix A)

As in the case of Wallace and Mills, most of the qualities were drawn from the psychological literature, but in this case the rating scale provides the necessary definitions and the useful concept of degree.

The weakness of the study lies in the sampling. While the claim is made that the nature of the material was taken into account, the lumping together of various media cannot fail to affect the ratings. For example, the rating of Maori art as being characterized by the predominance of straight lines is particularly surprising, as one usually thinks of Maori art in terms of the curvilinear carvings. Such a rating can only come from counting more examples of mats than of carving, rafter painting, or tattooing. This procedure is based on the unproven assumption that there exists a single style for every culture, regardless of

Maori Art

medium, even though Maori carving and Maori mats have no obvious features in common. Furthermore, when one is aware of the great variation within each medium in the art styles of tribal societies, the idea of a sample of 10 to 20 including several very different media seems remarkably naïve.

The use of defined terms along a scale is the strongest part of this study and is a needed step toward objectivity. It is unfortunate that interest in this work has been entirely in terms of further statistical use of its dubious results, as by Fischer (1961) and Robbins (1966) rather than by further use, refinement, and testing of Barry's descriptive scale. (The only new "data" used by Robbins were my offhand impressions; I was the "assistant" who rearranged the rank order of the cultures with regard to shape of line. Robbins published over my shocked protest.)

METHODS AND TECHNIQUES OF THIS STUDY

These three studies point the way to the kind of investigation that will be necessary to test the proposition that visual forms in art have meanings which can be analyzed and verbalized, and that some of these meanings are cross-culturally valid.

To carry out such an investigation successfully, the first need is for a "standard list of descriptive categories" such as is mentioned by Wallace, selected according to the criteria set forth by Barry, and carefully defined with due regard for usage by artists. Interpretive hypotheses, rather than being picked out of the literature to fit a particular case, should be collected and examined, and the terminology studied in order to relate the interpretive hypotheses to the standard descriptive list.

Second, descriptions of a number of art forms in these terms are needed. They should be separate for different media, and cover samples of adequate size. Cultural styles should be discussed only in terms of categories found in several of the media used by a culture, as Mills has shown.

Third, in order to relate these qualities to other aspects of society, culture, and personality, the contexts in which the art styles occur should be carefully examined. Cross-cultural comparisons are dependent on a number of such intensive studies.

Fourth, a broader conceptual framework that will make it possible to account for various factors that influence style, rather than merely to find ways to discount the effects of qualities that do not fit one interpretive theory or another, is a basic necessity. Such a framework must be able to take into account cross-cultural influence.

By exploring the idea of art as communication to some of its logical conclusions, I have, I believe, supplied a conceptual framework that makes it possible to encompass cultural, cross-cultural, and psychological determinants of style. In the chapters that follow, I attempt to supply in part the other needs mentioned above, with the idea of forging tools that may eventually be used to test the proposition that art means something. Not everything can be done at once.

The first objective of this work was the development of techniques in the description of formal qualities of graphic forms. My schema describing form-qualities has been limited in several ways, with the intention of providing a relatively complete, workable tool for one aspect of the problem before proceeding to others. Descriptive terminology is limited to formal qualities and does not consider content. It is limited to what one can see in looking at an object and does not consider the way in which the artist proceeded or, on the level of description, what he said about it. It is limited to graphic or two-dimensional forms, or to those that, being applied to a surface, can be treated as two-dimensional.

In my description of art styles, emphasis has been given to adequate samples of a relatively few forms, with separate treatment not only of different media, but of forms having different uses and functions. The Navajo have been selected as the focus of interest because of the variety of art and craft productions, the existence of both traditional and contact styles, and the wealth of data, comparatively speaking, on all aspects of culture, society, and personality.

At the core of the study is the collection of hypothesized form-meanings derived from a variety of published sources; these were used as a basis for selecting the qualities to be described. The study was conceived as proceeding according to the following steps:

1. The various literatures were examined for statements concerning the interpretation of formal qualities.

2. The qualities were defined by reference to the literature of art.

3. Examples of art reproduced in published sources were described in the defined terms, using a tally sheet for each different medium, style, period, or source.

4. The qualities found descriptive of each art form of the Navajo were compared with the form-meanings assigned to that quality.

5. The ethnographic literature was examined to determine which of the interpretations, if any, were consistent with the function of the art form and the sociocultural setting.

This procedure was actually followed in that sequence in what turned out to be a pilot version. Each step, however, suggested modifications or, more often, amplifications, of the others, and these modifications eventually meant complete revision. For example, descriptive tallying of the various styles soon showed the inadequacy of the early descriptive schema, and new categories were added. These new categories had to be defined, necessitating a new check of the art literature for accepted usage, a new search for interpretations, a re-tally of the Navajo material, and a new search of the ethnographic sources. Similarly, new possibilities were suggested in all facets and stages, requiring revision of all the others. Sometimes sheer logic forced an alteration of the schema.

The descriptive schema used for the Navajo art forms reported here was the fourth full revision, and the results are summarized in the Appendix. Since that time, a few additions that seems desirable have been made; they include consideration of the descriptive categories called for by Proskouriakoff (1958). On the following pages the existing revision of the tally sheets now being used is reproduced. Naturally the usefulness of the schema is strongly dependent on evaluation by others, and subsequent modification and improvement. Permission to reproduce the tally sheets in whole or in part is therefore granted for this purpose.

In the tally sheets the categories of my schema are given simple, outline-type designations (e. g., I.D.2) and a short title (e. g., Smallest Details). The category designations are used throughout the chapters that follow, being repeated in the sections on interpretations, definitions, and analysis of the drypaintings. The precise objective characteristics of each category so designated will be found under its definition, with perhaps a more formal or complete title. But, as will be clearly evident from the sections on interpretations, the different usages of words and their sometimes ambivalent meanings suggest that any word titles, either short or long, should not be trusted as precisely meaningful without a study of the complete word-and-picture definition; the alpha numeric designation serves for identification and ease of reference, and is not meant to imply specific interrelationships of specific categories beyond that inherent in the definitions themselves.

A second objective of this work is an attempt, by the use of these descriptive techniques, to answer the question as to whether, and in what way, it is legitimate to speak of a Navajo style that includes the various graphic media used.

And the third objective is to test the various interpretations of the meanings of form-qualities. This is done in some detail for drypaintings, which are made in a ceremonial context where the functions and symbolism have been extensively studied. Category by category, the hypotheses regarding the import of various form qualities are examined to see whether they make sense in terms of use and function and Navajo symbolism.

By________

Hatcher Art Analysis—Tally Sheet

Scale B ◆ Two Dimensional Works

Sample ______________________ **No. in sample** ______________

Medium ______________________ **Source** ______________

I. Layout

A. Shape of whole — ROUND | OVAL | SQUARE | RECTANGULAR | IRREGULAR | OTHER

B. Distribution of forms — CENTER | OFF-CENTER | INTERMEDIATE | PERIPHERY | WHOLE

C. Relation of figure to ground

1. Contrast	CONTRASTED	DISTINGUISHABLE	REVERSIBLE	POSITIVE	NEGATIVE
2. Ratio	EMPTY 1	2	3	4	5 FULL
3. Spacing	1	2	3	4	5

D. Measure (size) Actual size range of original art: ______________

1. Largest design units	1	2	3	4	5
2. Smallest details	1	2	3	4	5

II. Repetition, Balance, and Symmetry

A. Symmetry

1. Type

a. Bilateral	SIMPLE	BIAXIAL	RADIAL	ROTATIONAL	DYNAMIC REPETITION
b. Biaxial	BILATERAL	SIMPLE	RADIAL	ROTATIONAL	
c. Radial	BILATERAL	BIAXIAL	SIMPLE	ROTATIONAL	
d. Rotational	BILATERAL	BIAXIAL	RADIAL	SIMPLE	BIFOLD
e. Circular	BILATERAL	BIAXIAL	RADIAL	ROTATIONAL	SIMPLE
2. Degree	1	2	3	4	5

II. B. Repetition (Infinite Repetition and Rhythm)

1. Forms repeated — COMPONENT LINES — COMPONENT FORMS — ELEMENTS — DESIGN UNITS

2. Type of repetition
   a. One dimensional — b. Two dimensional

c.	STATIC 1	2	3	4	DYNAMIC 5
d.	PERCUSSIVE 1	2	3	4	CONTINUOUS 5

3. Variation of repetition

a. Degree of exactness	LOW 1	2	3	4	HIGH 5

b. Type of variation — ALTERNATION — GRADATION — COMBINATION — OTHER

III. Treatment of Lines

A. Component Lines

1. Linearity	1	2	3	4	5
2. Size					
a. Weight	LIGHT 1	2	3	4	HEAVY 5
b. Length	SHORT 1	2	3	4	LONG 5
3. Shape of Line					
a. Degree	STRAIGHT 1	2	3	4	CURVED 5

b. Type of curve — ARCS — EXPONENTIAL CURVES AND SPIRALS — MULTIWAVE LINES — FREE AND REVERSE

4. Relation of lines to each other					
a. Oblique	1	2	3	4	5
b. Parallel	1	2	3	4	5
c. Perpendicular	1	2	3	4	5
5. Relation of lines to edges					
a. Diagonal	1	2	3	4	5
b. Horizontal	1	2	3	4	5
c. Vertical	1	2	3	4	5

A. Component Lines

6. Line endings

a. Endless 1 2 3 4 5

b. Meet others 1 2 3 4 5

c. Terminal markers 1 2 3 4 5

d. Free ends 1 2 3 4 5

7. Meeting of lines

a. Use of points 1 2 3 4 5

b. Corners SHARP 1 2 3 4 5 ROUNDED

8. Simple Figures [OMIT]

B. Structural lines

H/V H=V V/H D/V D/H

V‖V H/D V/D D×D D‖D D

H‖H ∽ ⌒ O O+* *

C. Borders and Outlines

1. Borders NONE LIGHT MEDIUM HEAVY MULTIPLE COMPLETE INCOMPLETE

2. Divisions NONE LIGHT MEDIUM HEAVY MULTIPLE COMPLETE INCOMPLETE

3. Outlines NONE LIGHT MEDIUM HEAVY MULTIPLE COMPLETE INCOMPLETE

IV. Color

A. Emphasis	1	2	3	4	5
B. Number of Hues	1	2	3	4	5 & +
C. Intensity	1	2	3	4	5
D. Value contrast	1	2	3	4	5
E. Hue contrast	1	2	3	4	5

V. Perspective

A. Illusional	LINEAR	OVERLAPPING	SIZE	COLOR
B. Geometric	POSITIONAL		DIAGONAL	
C. Conceptual	MULTI-VIEW	SOCIAL	TOPOGRAPHIC	

VI. Composition

A. Complexity	1	2	3	4	5
B. Boldness	1	2	3	4	5
C. Tension	1	2	3	4	5
D. Movement	1	2	3	4	5
E. Formality	1	2	3	4	5

USES AND FUNCTIONS OF NAVAJO DRYPAINTINGS

While Navajo drypaintings are usually made in a therapeutic situation, centering about a patient, the patient is not the artist, and the paintings are part of the cure rather than part of the diagnosis. Even a very general statement of the context in which this art form appears shows a conceptual framework that sets limits to the nature of the communication to be expected.

"Sandpaintings," Reichard points out, "are not something of and for themselves, but they are part of a performance which continues for a period varying from one to nine days which is commonly referred to as a 'Chant' or a 'Sing'. These words simply mean a combination of many ritualistic acts carried out in a fixed order." (Newcomb and Reichard n.d. :6). Drypaintings are usually called sandpaintings, but, since other materials besides sand are often used, "drypainting" is technically the more correct term. These ceremonies are the principal means the Navajo have of coping with a dangerous world in those aspects not amenable to control by practical techniques.

Drypaintings are made on the ground, usually on the floor of a hogan. The background is "natural" earth color, preferably a pinkish tan sand brought in for the occasion and smoothed with a weaving batten. The main colors used come from seven basic pigments in the form of sand, and sometimes, in addition, the colors of symbolic objects which may be stuck in the sand, such as evergreen twigs. While the Navajo are by no means unaware of esthetic effect, the primary intention is the careful assembling of the appropriate symbols in proper relationship to each other. Hence some of the drawing may even be covered by other symbols and not show in the final work at all. Even errors are not erased, but are covered with sand of the ground color and redrawn over it.

There are standard paintings that go with each chant, each with several versions depending on the circumstances. Or it may be more exact to say that each rendition of the basic paintings that go with the chant must combine the symbolic elements appropriate to the occasion.

Sometimes the objective of the ritually required painting ("a prayer made visible") can be achieved by somewhat different paintings which may be alternate choices. For example, the painting may be done either in a simple version with few repetitions or in a more complex version with a greater number of repetitions, requiring a larger size and more workers.

The chanter is the one who knows the painting appropriate to each part of the chant of which he is the master, and the elements that are to be varied according to circumstances. He is also the designer in that he decides on each occasion how these elements are best combined in view of such practical circumstances as the space and number of painters available. He is seldom the actual painter, for he does little of the strewing of pigment, but rather directs others. It is he who is responsible for the ritual correctness of the performance, but the assistants are not mere helpers; all contribute their knowledge and make suggestions to assure perfection of the symbolism. The actual working together of people is part of the whole ceremony, part of the harmony sought and expressed in all the media that go to make up the totality of the "Sing."

According to the Navajo view, the dangers of the world are caused by lack of harmony; illness, unhappiness, and drought, for example, all result from disharmony. Rituals can restore harmony within the area where they are performed if the proper procedures are chosen to right the cause of the disharmony. The Navajo view of causation is rather mechanistic; all events are ordered and interrelated in a single vast system. But the system is not a tight one kept running by human will, like that of the Hopi. It is an extended system with a multiplicity of forces interacting within it. The proper rituals act automatically, if one can know which are applicable; neither human nor divine will is an important factor. According to our ethnocentric definition of religion, which requires a concept of supernatural will, such automatic procedures are classified as magic. The stress on ritual knowledge is a basic theme in Navajo myths; a drypainting is at once an illustration of an episode from some myth and an act of ritual learned by the hero of the episode. The compulsive power of ritual, including the songs, paintings, and prayers which are parts of the whole, brings everything in the vicinity into line, harmonious, under control, and therefore healthy.

Kluckhohn has analyzed the social functions of Navajo ritual, and his account can be considered as showing the basic functions of the paintings which are a part of the ceremonial:

> Almost all Navajo ceremonials (essentially every ceremonial still carried out today) are curing ceremonials. And this apparently has a realistic basis . . .. But there is also a great deal of uneasiness arising from interpersonal relationships, and this undoubtedly influences the way the Navajo react to their illnesses . . ..

> Here myths and rituals constitute a series of highly adaptive responses from the point of view of the society. Recital of or reference to the myths affirms the solidarity of the Navajo sentiment system . . .. Performance of the rituals likewise heightens awareness of the common system of sentiments. The ceremonials also bring individuals together in a situation where quarrelling is forbidden. Preparation for and carrying out of a chant demands intricately ramified cooperation, economic and otherwise, and doubtless thus reinforces the sense of mutual dependency.
>
> Myths and rituals equally facilitate the adjustment of the individual to his society. Primarily, perhaps, they provide a means of sublimation of his antisocial tendencies. It is surely not without meaning that essentially all the known myths take the family and some trouble within it as a point of departure . . . the chant myth supplies a catharsis for the traumata incident upon the socialization of the Navajo child.
>
> Thus "the working gods" of the Navajo are their sanctified repetitive ways of behavior. If these are offended by violation of the culture's system of scruples, the ceremonials exist as institutionalized means of restoring the individual to full rapport with the universe: nature and his own society. Indeed "restore" is the best English translation of the Navajo word which the Navajo constantly use to express what the ceremonial does for the "patient". The associated myths reinforce the patient's belief that the ceremonial will both truly cure him of his illness and also "change" him so that he will be a better man in his relations with his family and his neighbors . . ..
>
> Myths and rituals jointly provide systematic protection against supernatural dangers, the threats of ill-health and of the physical environment, antisocial tensions, and the pressures of a more powerful society. In the absence of a codified law and an authoritarian "chief" or other father substitute, it is only through the myth-ritual system that Navajos can make a socially supported, unified response to all of these disintegrating threats. The all-pervasive configurations of word symbols (myths) and of act symbols (rituals) preserve the cohesion of the society and sustain the individual, protecting him from intolerable conflict. (C. Kluckhohn 1942: passim)

There are variations in the basic function of ceremonials, and one would expect that if communication by means of art is achieved by form, this variation in function should be reflected in the forms of the drypaintings in the different ceremonial categories. This aspect of the subject was not investigated in great detail in the present study, but the chants from which the sandpaintings were taken were tabulated separately, and the differences in form-qualities and form-meanings among them can be seen. "Chant" and "way" are equivalent terms used with the names of the different ceremonials by different authorities, and I have retained the terminology of the author from whom I have chiefly drawn information on each "sing." Reichard favors "chant" as more accurate descriptively; Kluckhohn and Wyman favor "way" as a more accurate translation of the Navajo term. Chants are not completely independent entities, but are interrelated. Different categories of chants may be said to vary in purpose and function; standard variants of given chants are called "branches."

Paintings from four chants were separately recorded, and some differences emerged which are not discussed here. A thorough study of such variations requires that several factors be taken into account, such as the identity of the chanter, the district or school to which he belonged, the date, and the descriptive recording of many more paintings.

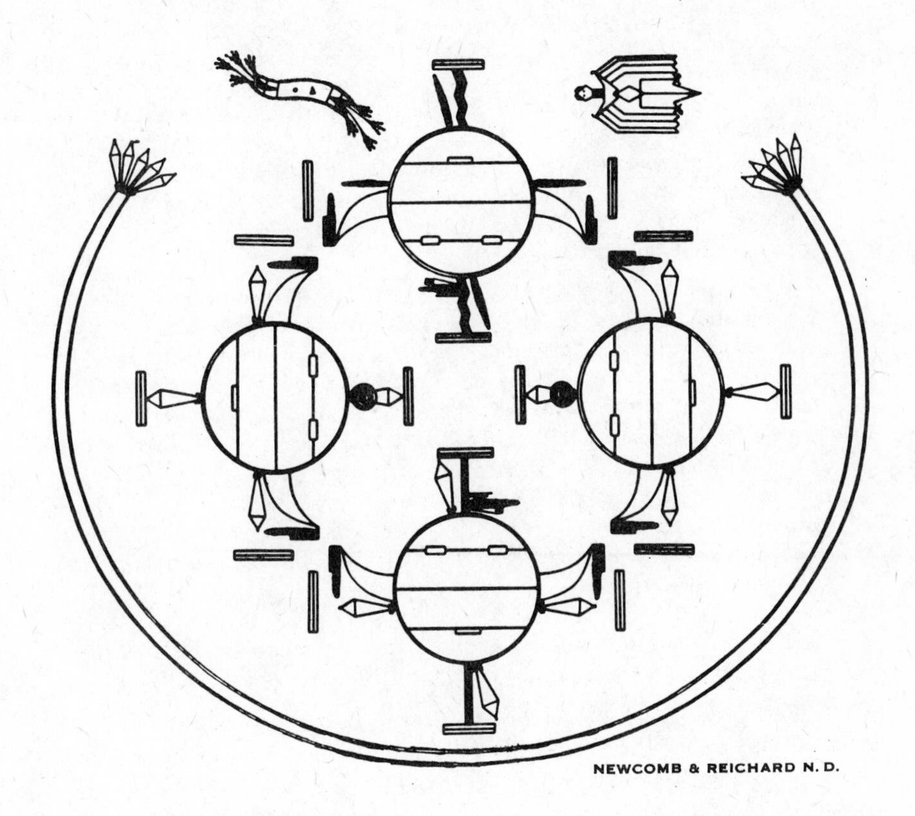

NEWCOMB & REICHARD N. D.

2

Arrangement of Forms in Space: Layout

An underlying assumption in many of the interpretations of the spatial relationships of the forms within the field in graphic productions seems to be the idea that such spatial relationships are somehow related to social relationships. In the psychological interpretations these are seen in terms of the individual's response to his social environment; in some anthropological and artistic interpretations such forms are seen as related to culturally patterned social configurations. It is assumed that in any society there are certain characteristic ways of patterning that reflect, underlie, and structure the way various aspects of life are seen; there are certain configurational postulates, so to speak. Lévi-Strauss for example (1963:265) refers to "organic wholes wherein style, aesthetic conventions, social organization, and religion are structurally related." In his actual examples, the stylistic features which he relates to social organization are spatial relationships (*ibid.*:245–268 and 1964:-178).

The chief difference between the artistic and psychoanalytic interpretation lies in the matter of control. Machover (1949:90) says: "It is probable that the size and placement of a figure are less subject to conscious control and variability than any other structural parts of a drawing." Artists and students of art, on the other hand, insist that the artist first of all controls the spatial arrangement within the pictorial field, a control that extends to awareness of the negative space or ground. Arnheim makes this very clear:

> Painters take care to verify the shape of interstices by forcing their eyes to reverse the spontaneous figure and ground effect. This requires training, because the naive observer sees such areas as shapeless parts of the underlying ground. He pays no attention to them, and finds it difficult and unnatural to do so . . . .. Even in Rorschach ink blots, in which the figure-ground reversal is facilitated by structural ambiguity, positive use of the interstices is said to suggest a diagnosis of negativism, stubbornness, doubt, suspiciousness and even paranoid trends. The artist controls such areas in order to assure the unity of the work in the frontal plane, and also to enhance the subtle interplay between the positive figures and the negative, half-hidden shapes, which, within their limits, contribute to the expression of the total composition. (1954:231)

Because of the artist's emphasis on control of space, many of the form-qualities interpreted by psychologists simply do not appear in discussions of art. One does not find "figures clinging to the edge" or "fussy details," and such a phrase as "irrelevant space" is, of course, meaningless. Artists may sometimes use extremes precisely for their disturbing effect, although always combined with quite controlled devices in other categories. For example, da Vinci's drawing *The Deluge* bears strong resemblance to examples of the drawings of psychotics. This was, however, a study for his own use and would have been combined with more controlling qualities in a finished work.

In any case, productions that are controlled in accordance with the esthetic canon of any culture will show it by conforming to a style, and we assume that art styles are largely learned behavior rather than coincidental expressions by persons of similar personality. Hence, in the matter of layout, if this order of interpretation has any meaning, and if the meaning is cross-culturally valid, one would expect the qualities that can be established as characteristic of a style to be related to social configurations and social values. Deviations from these stylistic qualities by individual artists might properly be regarded as individual projections—an inference that would be strengthened if such deviations from style were also deviations from the standards by which we distinguish "art."

For example, if a style is characterized by an ambiguity of figure and ground, we might suspect a tolerance of ambiguity in social relationships, rather than the oppositional tendencies suggested by psychological interpretations when such usage is not culturally encouraged. One can see the possibility of a relationship between projection and art, and of the role of the deviant in innovation. The originator of such an ambiguous form might do so out of oppositional tendencies, but the form might become a characteristic of style depending not on direct identification with such tendencies, but rather on acceptance of them, and a need to deal with social ambiguities.

In the cognitive and conscious realm, spatial relationships can be used to symbolize a variety of relationships beside the interpersonal ones. Geographical relationships are the most obvious examples; many peoples draw maps. Sometimes geographic relationships are incorporated into art forms, as in the sacred arts of the Australian aborigines and the Navajo. Dark suggests these broader possibilities:

> Do the spatial arrangements of the artist's design range model the cultural delimitations of interpersonal space relations, or of the spatial relations of man to his natural space, or of the intimacy of space between man and different kinds of objects? (1967:131).

According to the ideas expressed by Lévi-Strauss, these would be not so much alternatives as aspects (presumably congruent) of a culturally structured view of reality.

The cognitive role of visual forms is beginning to be recognized, and is becoming an important area for study. It will be interesting to see the extent to which cognitive uses of forms will be found to be congruent with the kinds of form-meanings examined here.

MEANINGS ATTRIBUTED TO QUALITIES IN LAYOUT

I.A. Shape of Whole

There are very few interpretive hypotheses concerning the shape of the design field as a whole, since this is usually regarded as simply a given condition for the artist. The shape of the field to be decorated is culturally determined and is closely related to what is decorated. The interpretive possibilities have not been explored.

Because the shape of the field is accepted as culturally standard, Waehner (1946), in a psychological study centering largely on adjustment as indicated by paintings, interpreted the selection of conventional or unconventional shapes as very important indications of social adjustment, or lack of it. She does not provide interpretations of specific shapes.

Slight clues are available in the works of students of art. Arnheim and Taylor discuss the effects of different shapes as pictorial fields:

> The baroque style offers many different examples of tension produced by distorted shape. Wölfflin points out that when the square yields to the rectangle, the favorite proportion of the rectangle is rarely that of the golden section, which was popular during the Renaissance because of its harmonious and more stable character. The baroque prefers the slimmer or squatter proportions, which contain more tension because they appear as compressed or drawn out versions of more simply proportioned oblongs. (Arnheim 1954:409)
>
> The geometrical shape of a circle has this peculiar property, that it remains visually stable, however one may rotate it in its plane. That would appear still to be its property as a possible pictorial field, that there is no rotation at which its stability as a simple symmerical shape is greater or less than any other. (Taylor 1964:14)

Most references to shape do not specifically apply to the design field, but to geometrical shapes as symbols; for example:

> The square (and often the rectangle) is a symbol of earthbound matter, of the body, and of reality. It is a representation of the "fourfoldness" motif, usually a symbol of completeness. (Jung et al. 1964:249, 289)

Longman (1949:9) presents us with form-meanings which could apply as well to shape of format as to design elements:

Form-meaning . . . b. Two- or three-dimensional shapes.

1. Simple and regular—restful and quiet.
2. Complex and irregular—restless and exciting.
3. Horizontal rectangle—calm and repose.
4. Vertical rectangle—strength and dignity.
5. Circle—completeness and finality, but instability because of a tendency to roll.
   Lunette less complete and more stable.
6. Crescent—vivacious and exciting, especially if axis is diagonal.
7. Triangle—active, energetic, incisive, abrupt, the most dynamic geometric shape; the isosceles resting on its base is the most serene because symmetrical.

8. Square—sturdy, rugged, plain, straight-forward, e. g. 'square deal' or 'square shooter'. Less distinguished than the rectangle because less variety. [Also note the current usage "a square," implying dull and conventional.]
9. Diamond—active, alert, restless, but less so than inverted triangle which is top heavy.

I.B. Distribution of Forms

Interpretations concerning this category are all psychological:

> The very large figure, placed aggressively in the middle of the page, is seen most often in the grandiose paranoid individual who possesses a high fantasy self-esteem. (Machover 1949:90)

> Some subjects place the figures in such a way that they seem to cling to the edge of the paper. This suggests the need for whatever additional support the environment can afford and a fear of coming out into the center of the stage in an independent, self-assured fashion. (Halpern 1951:335)

> An hypothesis worth checking against other factors in the record is that *de* [edge details] represent a fear reaction, comparable to Kipling's musk rat, who always crept around the edge of a room because he feared to venture out into the middle of the floor. (Alcock 1963:35)

In this kind of interpretation it is easy to see the dangers of indiscriminate application to any and all art forms. Edge design on a vessel such as a plate, bowl, or basket may well be meant to enhance the attractiveness of the contents, rather than signify a fleeing from open spaces. The total effect of the format when the object is in use cannot be ignored when the meaning is considered.

> However in those cases in which inadequate control can be eliminated as a factor, work all over the page seems to parallel and reflect a relatively outgoing, assertive, self-reliant personality. This association was particularly apparent among children who changed during the course of the observation from shy or repressed to outgoing behavior. In such instances, painting patterns repeatedly showed a parallel change from work in a restricted area to work all over the page. (Alschuler and Hattwick 1947:89)

According to Waehner (1946:65), "format filled up to the margin . . . with balance" indicates intelligence.

> Individuals with high n-achievement [need for achievement] tended to leave a smaller margin at the bottom of the page than those with low n-achievement. (Aronson 1958:252)

> The drawing of the 'highs' [those scoring high in n-achievement] are spread out all over the paper; those of the lows are confined to a relatively small area. (ibid.:264)

Interpretations concerning the right or left distribution of forms, or higher and lower, which are based on observations made in a literate society, would seem to call for particular caution in cross-cultural interpretation. This is true also of artistic analysis of "normal eye path" and the "point of strongest interest" in a drawing or painting. At the very least, the normal position of the art work in relation to the viewer must be taken into account; a painting made on the ground is not the same as one made or hung on a wall.

> If the figure projected on the page is towards the right, it is environment oriented, toward the left it is self-oriented, high up on the page, it is related to optimism, low down on the page, it is related to depression. (Machover 1949:89)

> The placement of the [small] figure is relatively high on the page, and often gives the impression that the figure is adrift in space. Lack of insight, unjustified optimism, a low level of energy, and, basically, a lack of secure footing, are some of the psychological correlates of this type of projection. (ibid.:90)

> [A] high percentage of center distribution . . . [may indicate] . . . infantile, flighty, regressive trends. (Waehner 1946:65)

I.C.1. Contrast of Figure and Ground

Some of the possibilities concerning the interpretation of the perception of figure and ground have already been indicated. Rorschachers use the symbol *s* to indicate responses to the white space; their position has been clearly stated by several persons:

> If we recall that the most general principle of perceptanalysis is that the individual's perceptual handling of the blot corresponds to his handling of interpersonal relationships, it is understandable why the selection of the white "space" should point to some kind of opposition. (Piotrowski 1957:94)

> Tenacity as a form of stubbornness is among the traits which high white space percentage projects. This is the more so when the *s* percept is a reversal of figure and ground . . . .. Contrarily, a low percentage of space responses or a total lack of them in a test record confirms findings of passivity. It may be a lead to suggestibility. (Beck 1952:61)

From an artistic point of view, Preusser (1965:208) emphasizes that: "Figure ground reversal . . . causes the spectator to actively participate by resolving the tension between positive and negative."

In looking at samples of art from other cultures in which there seems to be an ambiguity between figure and ground, we are faced with a problem in perception, since we do not know whether the maker and the viewer in that culture perceive the forms as ambiguous, or, if not, which they see as figure and which as ground. For example, in the pottery of Santo Domingo Pueblo there seems to be such ambiguity in the painted decoration. If the painting shown below is seen as positive, then the most characteristic forms are seen as sharp, thornlike, pointed figures. If, on the other hand, the painting is considered negative, the figures are seen as smoothly rounded forms. With or without knowledge of the perceptions of the makers, the interpretive possibilities are far from simple.

CHAPMAN 1936

I.C.2. Ratio to Figure to Ground

The interpretations are treated in I.C.3.

I.C.3. Spacing of Design Units

The basis for the interpretation of spatial relationships as related to interpersonal relationships is that figures are identified with the self and with persons interacting with the self. The use of figure in this regard means any kind of identifiable form, in the same sense as is meant by "figure and ground." Even in the case of the Machover technique of human figure drawing, the reference is not solely to the human figure, as is shown by Machover's reference to graphology in this connection. This is the case in Rorschach interpretation:

> Another approach to content interpretation is illustrated by Schactel who studied the dynamic aspects of perception involved in the Rorschach test, illustrating his point of view by analysis of the size of objects seen by the patient. He pointed out that size was related to the subject's own feeling of strength or weakness, his identifications, his sadistic tendencies and so on. (Bell 1948:130)

One hypothesis seems to rest on a different basis. Fischer (1961:81) has suggested that:

> Design with a large amount of empty or irrelevant space should characterize egalitarian societies; design with little irrelevant (empty) space should characterize the hierarchial societies.

His assumption seems to be that the figures represent the whole society or in-group rather than the individuals. I can find no other use of or reference to this assumption.

The psychological interpretations as to the relative emptiness or fullness of the space available concern the way in which the individual relates to his social environment:

> Empty drawings are made by rather unemotional, moderately communicative and undemonstrative individuals. Practically all subjects whose drawings show empty composition (not to be confused with Smallness or Constriction) tend to be orderly and lucid, but lacking in genuine warmth and spontaneity. (Kinget 1952:89)
>
> Ample covering (¾ or more of the space) is a sign of vitality and often a certain spontaneity. Combined with strong lines it may be regarded as a reliable indicator of actually operating driving force, of ardor and aggressiveness. (ibid.:90)
>
> The extreme form of dense covering is indicated as Compactness . . . .. Its basic diagnostic tendency is towards an excessive vitality and a need to excel and dominate which thwarts social adjustment and maturity. It may also be an expression of compulsiveness and overt aggressiveness. (ibid.:91)
>
> When crowding or actual overlapping of figures occurs, gross disregard for the limits of an entity can be inferred. This is found in individuals who are not sensitive to others, who have an aggressive, abrupt way of dealing with the environment. (Halpern 1951:334)

Mills (1959:159) says that the "cue value" of "full but not crowded use of format" is "balance of freedom and discipline, dynamism and control; vitality and spontaneity"; while Barry (1957:381) says that "crowdedness" in primitive art forms correlates (correlation coefficient .12) with "severity of socialization."

If the design field is to be seen in terms of social space, then emptiness or fullness may also be related to ideas or values about numbers and closeness of people.

I.D. Measure (size)

I.D.1. Size of Design Units

> Whole styles depend on the quality of measure. In ways which give us clues to their characters, individual artists and periods choose between the lean and fat, the thick and thin, the powerful and graceful, and reveal themselves through these conceptions of scale . . . ..
>
> Refinement and finesse are related in our minds to a small or at least not overly assertive scale. On the other hand, certain nations have felt compelled to assert their ambitions and their will-to-power through bigness . . . ..
>
> We subconsciously attribute characteristics of power, durability and ponderousness to that which, like an elephant, is large and heavy. Conversely, we compare a slender form with things we know from experience to be agile, graceful, and quick. (Beam 1958:688)

The interpretations of projective drawings are much more specific, being concerned with symptoms related to the concept of self.

> Very small figures would seem to reveal a tendency to pull back on the self and inhibit spontaneity and outgoingness. Such individuals fear to release their emotions and give them direct expression . . . .. [Very large figures] show a general lack of control and inhibition. (Halpern 1951:334)
>
> [Where] the self esteem is definitely not high . . . the figure is correspondingly small . . . .. Tiny figures may be seen in the regressed and vegetative schizophrenics as an expression of low energy level and as a shrunken ego. . . .
>
> Micrographic figures are also encountered frequently in the deeply repressed and neurotically depressed individual. . . .

> The large figure is not restricted to the overactive maniac, the grandiose paranoid, the fantasy infected individual. The aggressive psychopath may well give a fairly large figure, but it may be shifted to the left or introversive side, corresponding with the felt inadequacy that is expressed in other drawing indices of insecurity. (Machover 1949:90, 91)
>
> [Smallness is related to] an imposed state of restraint with accompanying feelings of inadequacy or frustration. Depressed subjects also produce fairly small drawings. (Kinget 1952:89)

When this psychological view of size is translated to the interpretation of what is perceived in the graphic productions of artists, one obvious implication is that the monumental portrayal of rulers and deities serves not only to awe the viewer, but to induce him to accept the personification of such power by identification with it. This supports the view, so forcefully expressed by Langer (1962:83) and Read (1955 in toto) that art is not merely a focus of projection for the viewer, like the Rorschach blots, but acts upon him to shape his view of himself and the world.

I.D.2 Size of Components

As compared with the size of figures, which are usually seen as associated with the concept of the self, components ("details"), as part of or in connection with such figures, are seen by psychologists as having to do with modes of action and interaction. Thus Alcock (1963:35): "*dd,* tiny details . . . in excess, their use suggests a fussy, over meticulous approach." And:

> Individuals who have a predominance of normal detail responses have been found to be preoccupied with the practical, common problems of everyday life—to think through the issues of life in terms of obvious and, at times, platitudinous ideas. A deficiency in the use of normal details may point to an inability to employ such common sense or to attend to the necessary practical routine of living.
>
> The presence of an excess of *Dd,* tiny or unusual details, frequently accompanies anxiety. Small details may be the result of quantity ambition, of excessive preoccupation with the minute, of fussiness and obsessive-compulsive tendencies, of overcritical characteristics, or of inferiority feelings. The quality of the *Dd* responses will affect their significance. A predominance of edge details, for example, may reveal an escape mechanism, an attempt

> to get away from the disturbing inner aspects of the blot, and, by analogy, from the inner aspects of the self; a preoccupation with details on the inside of the blot may indicate absorption in the inner life. (Bell 1948:121)
>
> Interest in small details [indicates] decrease in tension and anxiety with business . . . work the healer of sorrow . . . what appears to be purposeless activity or activity of insignificant importance from the viewpoint of the individual with many *d*, who is worried that he is not advancing in life, may be quite useful and purposeful from the standpoint of society. (Piotrowski 1957:87)

Waehner (1946:65) offers a hypothesis that seems to relate to a comparison of scale between design units and components when she says: "similar proportions between parts and whole of picture, including spaces between drawn and painted form" indicate "superior emotional balance."

The interpretations of Kavolis (1965:passim) relating to art styles are phrased in terms of values. Concerning layout, Kavolis includes five form characteristics, four of which have to do with the ratio of figure to ground, and one with the size of design units. (In order to maintain the original form of these hypotheses the tabular arrangement in which they appeared is maintained, except that the items are regrouped by form category, whereas in the article the categorization is that of Florence Kluckhohn's value schema):

Form Characteristic	Quality Suggested	Value Orientation
Small bottom margins	Intolerance of unused resources	Doing
Larger bottom margins	Tolerance of unused resources	Being
Colossalism	Immovable monumentality of power	Lineal
Little irrelevant space	Tendencies toward total control	Lineal
Much irrelevant space	Tendencies toward incomplete control	Collateral

PROPOSED DEFINITIONS FOR ASPECTS OF LAYOUT

In this and subsequent chapters each term and category is defined as specifically as possible, both in words and by illustration. For convenience in cross reference, the categories are given the same alpha-numeric designations used in the tally sheets (p. 22–5) and these designations are repeated throughout the text. (There are some terms of the schema for which no interpretations were found, and some interpretations can only be applied to two or more categories, and, as indicated above, some terms have been added as definitions since the original study, so that all of the categories may appear only in the definition sections.) In addition, some general terms, used in connection with the more specific form-quality identifications and categories are defined here.

Various terms have been used to refer to the arrangement of forms in the available space. The most usual are *composition, design,* and *layout.* The differences in meaning are more connotative than denotative. Traditionally the first has often been associated with the fine arts, the second with crafts, and the third with pottery decoration and commercial art, but they are often used more or less interchangeably. The distinctions implied by usage are followed here for the most part. *Layout* is used to refer to the spatial arrangement of elements in the more objective sense, and *composition* is used to refer to a more analytical description of the whole. This type of analysis by artists is often a kind of interpretation at a very low order of abstraction, and the terminology is often somewhat metaphorical. Composition takes all aspects of the work into account; the term layout usually refers to the main spatial relationships only. "Organization" and "structure" are sometimes used as synonyms for composition or layout.

Often employed in the analysis of formal design are some terms referring to parts and wholes which are defined here. It is usual to use a classification of forms based on levels of complexity, although the terms used for these levels are by no means consistent. Some such classification is necessary, however, in order to distinguish whether we are talking about a very small part of some larger element, the whole unit, or some other level. The terms used here are adapted from several sources, principally Shepard (1948), and Fontana et al. (1962). For very complex designs there are not enough levels; for simple ones there are too many; but at least some kind of consistency is provided through the use of the following terms.

Component, basic component: The smallest meaningful form, which may be curvilinear or rectangular, but is formed without the crossing of lines. The fundamental portion of symmetrical elements.

Design element: A simple constructional form made up of basic components.

Design unit: A combination of elements and/or components. Such a unit forms the repetitive entity in complex symmetrical or repetitive design, but may be used as the sole or central form. It may or may not be symmetrical.

Design field, field of decoration: A distinct area, especially of a three-dimensional form, such as the neck or shoulder of a vessel or the side or top of a box.

The *whole design, whole layout,* or *whole composition* must be defined for each work or group of works, as wholeness is not as obvious as one would think. The important thing is to specify where the item belongs in the hierarchy of wholes. (For example, what is the artistic whole in regard to dry-painting among the Pueblo? The painting itself? The construction of the whole alter? The series of such constructions for a particular ceremony? The whole ceremony? The ceremonial cycle?)

Motif (plural *motifs*) is best retained in the flexible usage in which it is widely taken to refer to a form favored and often used in a particular style; in this sense it may refer to any level of complexity.

Except perhaps for the first, these terms are relative. A more objective classification, based on a quantitative scale with the basic component as a unit, seems unduly cumbersome at this stage of knowledge.

The following illustration is taken from the analysis of Northwest Coast art by Bill Holm (1965). In this work he uses the terms "element" and "unit" somewhat differently from the way I am using them here, although his usage is very appropriate for the Northwest Coast style. A comparison of his usage with those of Fontana et al. (1962) and Shepard (1948) will show that however appropriate a usage may be for a particular style, much better standardization is needed to make cross-cultural comparisons. As usages in the literature are so various, I have no choice but to establish a set of terms which seems useful for a variety of different cultural styles, and to employ them as consistently as possible.

Parts and Wholes:

In this example the field of decoration is the side of a painted box. It can be considered as the design field or "whole" which is described in terms of layout or composition.

Components:

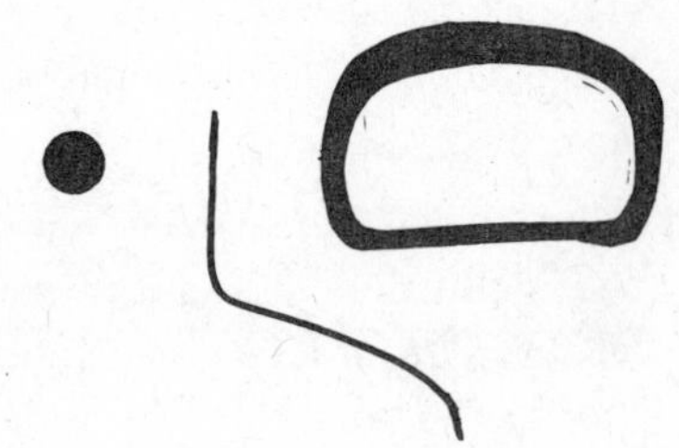

Elements:

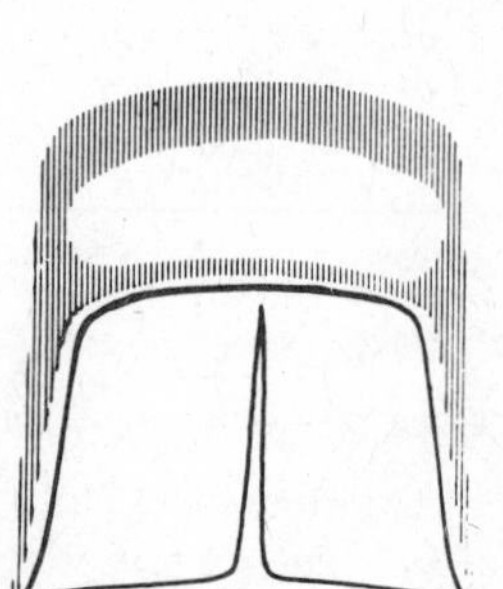

Design units:

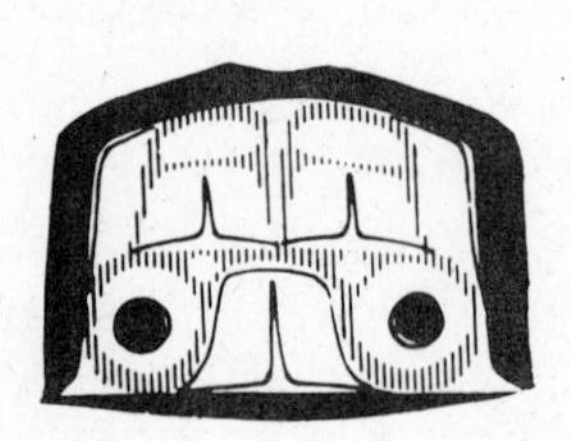

I.A. Shape of Whole

The terms *square, rectangular, round,* and *oval* should be self-explanatory, although it should be specified that they are not used in a mathematically exact sense. The term *irregular* is used to refer to a form delineated on an extended area with no edges of the design field indicated; for example, a figure painted on a rock wall in the manner of Paleolithic cave painting is considered to be unbounded and irregular.

Other is specified for each form. Shape is often defined by the object on which the decoration is applied. Some of these objects are not strictly two-dimensional, but are treated as such for comparative purposes. Shallow trays, plaques, bowls, and baskets, decorated on the inside, are treated as if flat and described as round, oval, or whatever. The outsides of deep pots, baskets, and other containers are not of the same order, as anyone who has tried to paint one, or draw a picture of one, can testify. Even a cylindrical shape cannot be flattened without to some degree altering the quality of the design. Thus, while by convention we may treat these surfaces as comparable to flat ones, the shape is specified as *outside of vessel,* and such designs should certainly be described separately. That is to say, the description of a sample of pottery, for example, is divided into at least two groups on this basis—inside of shallow bowl, outside of pot—and each is tallied and described separately.

I.B. Distribution of Forms

This category refers simply to where the elements are placed in the design field. In a mechanical sense, it is defined as the areas in which the forms are found. However, this is not a purely quantitative matter (where most forms are), as, compositionally speaking, the emphasis may be on an area which is not the "fullest," as when there is marked convergence on the center, which is a small blank area. Usually, however, it is simply a matter of which parts of the field have figures in them, and which are left as ground.

In the case of the surfaces of three-dimensional forms such as pots and baskets, the traditional designations such as rim, neck, shoulder, and so forth are more accurate if these designs are to be compared to others on vessels of the same form. However, where the objective is comparison with other media, it is necessary to use some such terms as are given here. For the purpose of describing surface designs on vessels, the *center* is considered in terms of the distance between rim and base, as perceived by the eye.

I.B. Distribution of Forms

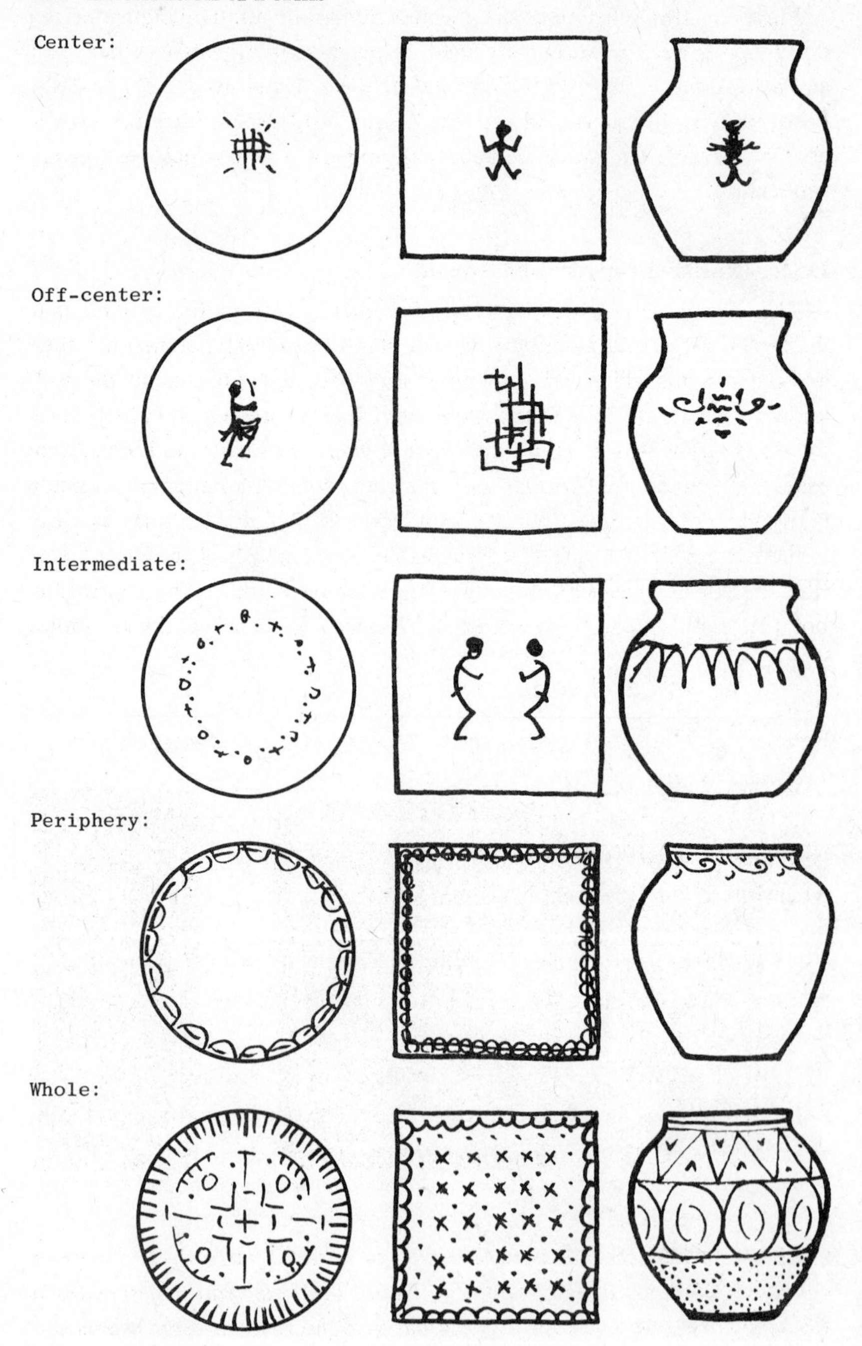

I.C. Relation of Figure to Ground

Figure in this sense does not mean a human or animate figure or the design unit, but the form perceived as the essential gestalt rather than as background. *Figure* and *Ground* are the terms used for this relationship in two-dimensional media; "form" and "space" are the broader terms used for three-dimensional and fully illusional perspective renderings.

I.C.1. Contrast of Figure and Ground

The clarity with which the figure stands out from the ground is a matter of degree. Sometimes figures stand out clearly, sometimes they are indistinguishable, and sometimes they are reversible, as in the well known vase-and-profile illustration often seen in introductory psychology texts. For the present purposes, *indistinguishable* and *reversible* cases are treated as forming a single category. A distinction is made between clearly *contrasted* figure and ground, where the form is clear without thought, and the distinguishable form, which is defined operationally as one that may require a brief examination. The contrast is not primarily a matter of contrast in value, as some of the examples show.

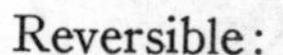

Reversible: Contrasted: Distinguishable:

As the terms are used here, a design is *positive* when the pigment or equivalent that is applied forms the figure or form, and *negative* when the applied pigment is used for the background, leaving the figures untouched. Where pigment is applied to both, or this cannot be determined, the category does not apply.

Negative:

STERNBERG 1958

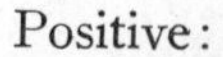

Positive:

STERNBERG 1958

Negative:

BOAS 1927

Positive:

ENCISO 1953

I.C.2. Ratio of Figure to Ground

This category refers to the emptiness or fullness of the design field. The middle category (3) is defined as an equal amount of area covered by figure as by ground. This, however, cannot be an exact determination, because if the areas of space are very small, the effect is one of fullness even though the forms may take up less area (as, for example, in an ornate drawing made up of fine lines), so in practice both the amount of the background area and the size of the isolated areas are considered.

I.C.2. Ratio of Figure to Ground

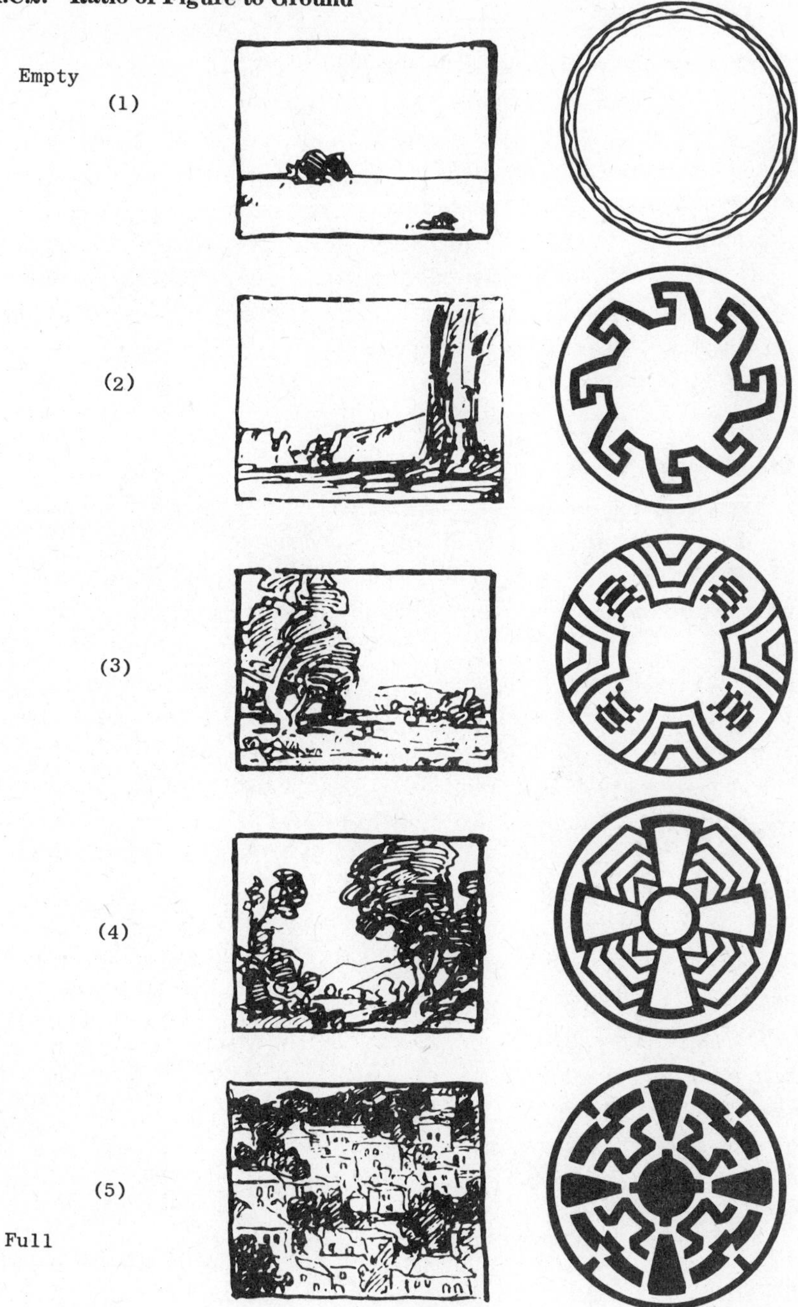

I.C.3. Spacing of Design Units

It is possible for a design field to be full even though the important design elements may be widely scattered. In this case the ground may be filled by small components. Thus the spacing of units is a separate category from that of ratio, above. The degrees in the scale used are defined as follows: (1) units overlap; (2) units are touching or immediately adjacent; (3) the space between units is less than the width of the unit; (4) the space between units is approximately equal to the unit; and (5) the space between the units is greater than the unit itself. It may be necessary to distinguish between primary and secondary design units, as in cases where human figures (secondary units) overlap to form a principle design unit.

I.D. Measure (size)

The two kinds of sizes described under this heading are the size of the design units and the size of the components with respect to the size of the whole design field. The design units, often referred to as "figures" in this connection, are considered in terms of the largest units in the design. In terms of area, a large design unit (5) is one larger than ¾ of the total area; a medium-sized unit (3) fills approximately ¼ to ½; and a very small unit (1) fills less than ⅛. In some cases, however, particularly when there is a long horizontal design field, the height becomes more important than the area and is the measure used; but where height alone is the measure of size, the proportion must be greater: a tall figure (5) must fill ⅞ of the vertical field distance, a medium-sized unit, ⅜ to ⅝; and a very small one (1), anything up to ¼. Since the impression of size is dependent on a variety of factors, these proportions cannot be regarded as precise measurements, but they do provide a scale that approximates the usage in this work.

The quality usually referred to as "amount of detail" is considered here under the heading of *size of components* and depends both on the size of the component or component lines and on the number of small or very small components used. A "very detailed" design is considered to have *very small components* (1), and a design "without detail" is regarded as having *very large components* (5).

While the sizes of units and components are recorded in relation to the size of the design field, the absolute size of the whole is of course significant and is noted.

I.D.1. Size of Design Units

Very Large (5):

ENCISO 1953

Large (4):

ENCISO 1953

Medium (3):

SIDES 1961

Very Small (1):

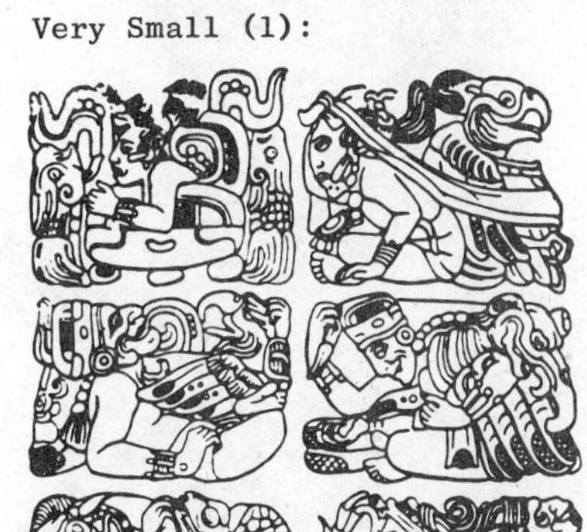

CHRISTENSEN 1955

Small (2):

CHRISTENSEN 1955

I.D.2. Size of Components

Very Small (1)

AFTER CODEX FEGERVARY

Medium (3):

DISSELHOFF & LINNE 1960

Small (2):

ENCISO 1953

Large (4):

ENCISO 1953

Very Large (5):

SIDES 1961

LAYOUT IN NAVAJO DRYPAINTINGS

The attempt to test the cross-cultural validity of the form-meaning hypothesis under the heading of layout brings out at once the great contrast between the requirements of this art form and those of painting in the European tradition. In the latter the shape of the whole has been treated as given, with only slight variation permitted the artist, so that Herbert Read assumed that all composition results from this constraint. Departure from a regular, usually rectangular shape is thought of as a revolutionary development. Yet, for the Navajo, the shape is not something one starts with, it is something one ends up with, and its form is almost a matter of indifference. On the other hand, drypainters do not choose what they are going to do with the background (or ground)—this is given, and it is always essentially the same color, which is never used for anything else in the painting, while in the European tradition

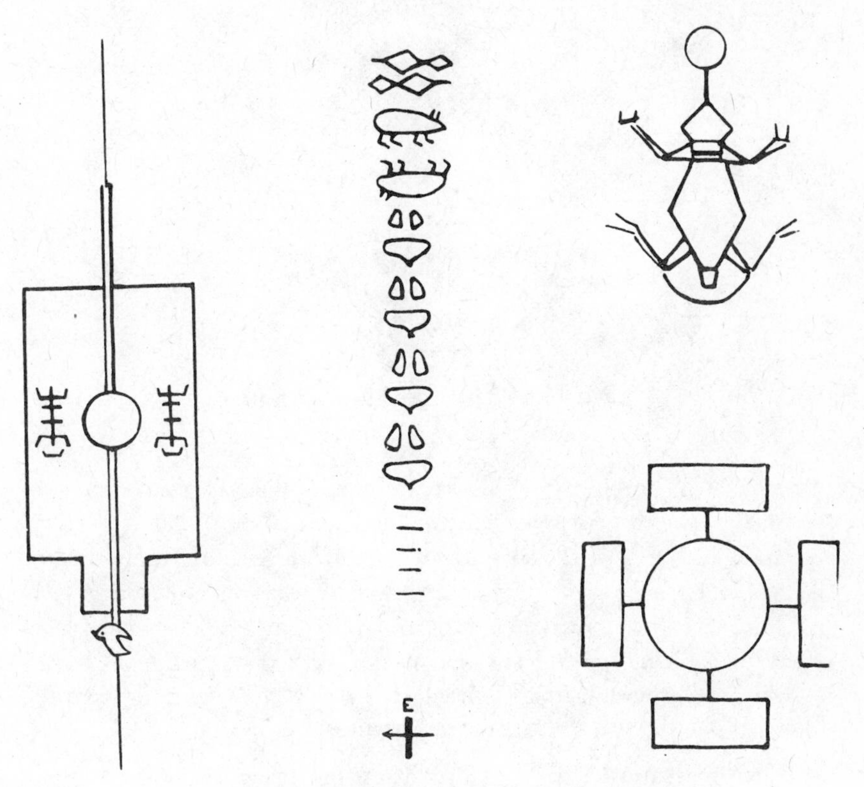

Layouts of Four Small Drypaintings

the artist has a good deal of choice within the conventions of his period. If investigation shows any degree of specific meaning for form-qualities, the range of distribution of the various form-qualities may be an important indicator of basic cultural orientations.

I.A. Shape of Whole

The Navajo drypainting is made from the center outward and is not so much fitted into a space as expanded onto a surface made to receive it. The result may be essentially round or square, oval or rectangular, regular or irregular. In part, the shape seems to be related to size, as

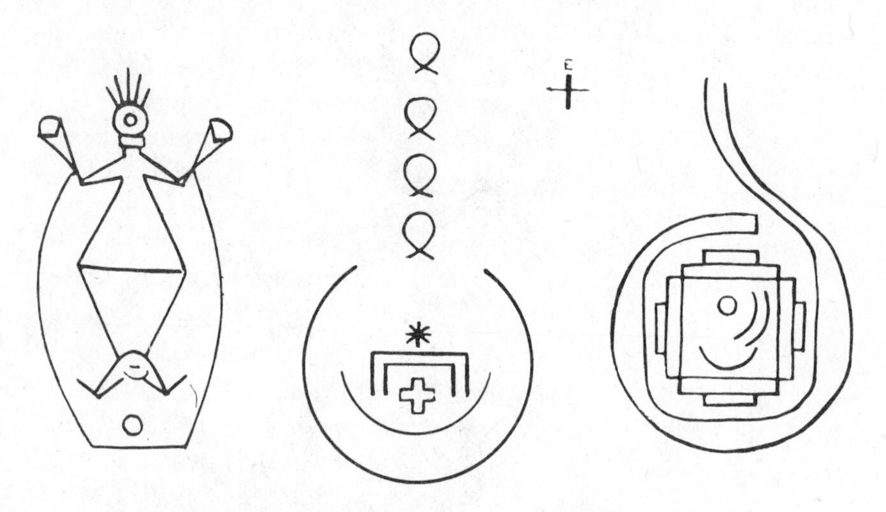

Layouts of Three Small Drypaintings

the smaller paintings are often irregular, while the larger ones are surrounded by the "encircling guardian" and tend to be round, square, or rectangular. In part, the shape grows out of the kind of repetition that is used. If the figures are laid out in the "linear" style the painting is usually rectangular; if the figures are laid out in a radial pattern, it is likely to be round or square, as can be seen in the sketches on pp. 29 and 58. Whichever format is used, it is the "same" painting from the Navajo point of view if it has the same symbolic elements.

When the basic idea is that of a path, the design is arranged along the path, usually without enclosure of the whole. All in all, the variety of shapes resulting from the two main structuring ideas—the cardinal directions and the pathway to (or from) the east—seems to make possible the inclusion of almost any shape except the triangle. If form-meaning hypotheses concerning these shapes are meaningful, they have to be studied in terms of the preferences of individual chanters, which seem to be marked. Insofar as the figures indicate a somewhat greater incidence of the round form than of any other, the interpretation seems to be one of wholeness or completeness, which is consistent with the values inherent in the functions of the art form, but not very specific.

I.B. Distribution of Forms

Forms in drypainting are never placed to one side of the area, or high or low, or with "large bottom margins" or other indications of unequal placement mentioned in the interpretations. The reason is, of course, that the field is not bounded like a piece of paper or canvas, and the painting is made from the center outward, creating its own boundaries; involved in this process is a step-by-step balanced repetition that insures a fairly even distribution of forms. Most of the paintings have the form distributed all over the design field, and where the emphasis is on the center, it is achieved by devices other than the concentration of forms. For example, the center may be emphasized by a design unit which contains a relatively large area of uniform color, making the unit bolder in effect than the more linear units which are in the rest of the field.

The description that most nearly applies is that of Aronson, who considers the quality of even distribution of forms over the field to be related to high "n-achievement." This quality may also be seen as related to the Rorschacher's concept of W, discussed under composition below.

I.C.1. Contrast of Figure and Ground

All layouts are contrasted and positive; there is no ambiguity regarding figure and ground in Navajo drypaintings. The forms are clearly distinguishable, and the background color is never used in the figures. If ambiguity of figure and ground is somehow related to a general tolerance of or preoccupation with ambiguity in social relationships, the lack of it in sandpainting is consistent with the message of the medium, where the aim seems to be to order and clarify the complexities of life and to remove confusion in any form. Oppositional tendencies are not appropriate to the ceremony. If the art form were a reflection or projection of psychological states, some indication of the ambiguities of the Navajo position and of oppositional tendencies might be expected.

I.C.2. Ratio of Figure to Ground

Drypaintings reproduced in the literature are certainly not empty, and they might be called full rather than crowded; hence the various hypotheses concerning emptiness and crowdedness do not apply. Closest is Kinget's (1952:90): "Ample covering is a sign of vitality and of a certain spontaneity. Combined with strong lines it may be regarded as a reliable indicator of actually operating driving force, or ardor and aggressiveness." The implication of the interpretations seems to be that this is the psychologically healthy alternative when compared to other possible distributions.

I.C.3. Spacing of Design Units

In terms of the hypotheses regarding interpersonal relations, it may be meaningful that the full but not crowded format is marked by a lack of contact between the various design units. They do not meet or overlap, and the elements do so only rarely. This characteristic is especially noticeable in the anthropomorphic figures, which are seldom in contact with each other, yet are not greatly separated by space distance or ground. There are usually at least two figures in each painting. These form-qualities are congruent with the value the Navajo place on social relationships, and their marked respect for individual autonomy.

Fischer's hypothesis that designs with little empty space should characterize hierarchical societies is not supported, since the Navajo are notably egalitarian.

If we consider "irrelevant space" as a matter of the ratio of figure to ground, the hypothesis of Kavolis is that fullness should be associated with a lineal relation value orientation and further suggests "total control in the sphere of action." These interpretations are not born out by the Navajo case. Romney and Kluckhohn (F. Kluckhohn 1961) place the collateral over the lineal value orientation, and accounts of the Navajo stress the fact that even children are not "totally controlled" in the sphere of action, but make decisions that are respected.

Newcomb and Reichard (n.d.) suggest the Navajo interpretation of this quality, "crowded with elements and therefore with power," that is, supernaturally compulsive power.

I.D. Measure (size)

In terms of absolute size, drypaintings may be from two to twenty feet in diameter, the average being about six feet. A component may be as small as a single grain of sand. The size of a painting depends on many factors, including the resources of the family giving the Sing, the number of experienced assistants, and the size of the hogan, as well as the ritual classification to which the required painting belongs. There seems to be little doubt that size is associated with power, that is, with the control of supernatural power for the benefit of the patient and those attending the Sing, although it would be only one part of the many means of attracting power in the whole ritual complex.

I.D.1. Size of Design Units

The size of design units, or figures, varies considerably, but they seldom tend to be either very small or very large, and where the units are recorded as large the effect is often a result of length only, rather than an expanse of area. Most interpretations refer to size in terms of power, self-esteem, will-to-power, and aggressiveness; the Navajo interpretation is consistent with these ideas:

> Bigness indicates an abstraction, a whole standing for its several parts—a large central cornstalk represents all corn, a huge Thunder (with small Thunders painted on it) all thunders. Length is a symbolic aspect of size. Sandpaintings gain power from the elongation of figures as well as by repetition. (Reichard 1950:179).

Long thin figures, which symbolize power to the Navajo, are seen by Machover as projections indicating concern over bodily health. This interpretation would certainly apply to most Navajo, and to the reason for the ceremony in which the sandpainting occurs. The two interpretations are not really incompatible, but are perhaps more comparable to the two sides of the coin. There may be a clue to culturally different concepts of power in the lack of massiveness, monumentality, or bulk in these figures; they are powerful by virtue of their mystic nature, not their overwhelming mass, and repetition is more important for building up power than is size.

Insofar as this quality may be related to social interactions, the important point may be that the design units are almost always of equal size. This is especially noticeable in the anthropomorphic figures. Even where, according to the myth and symbolism, one of the deities is more powerful than the others, he is portrayed as the same size in the layout. This fact offers considerable support to the idea that spatial relationships in this form have something to do with an egalitarian orientation.

I.D.2. Size of Components

Most of the paintings include a wealth of details, or very small components. This form-quality in the ritual context is in accord with the idea of trying to allay anxiety by meticulously executed detail which seem to underlie most hypotheses.

Layout of a large drypainting "The Water People" from the Shooting Chant by Miguelito

3

Repetition, Balance, and Symmetry

Symmetry is the "correspondence in size, shape, and relative position of parts that are on opposite sides of a dividing line or median plane or that are distributed about a center or axis" (Webster's New International Dictionary, 2nd ed.). The relation among symmetry, balance, and repetition may be seen differently from different viewpoints. From the point of view of the artist in the European tradition, composition is the balancing of all the elements or components that go into the whole field; all art is balanced in one way or another. Symmetry is one form of balance and is often thought of as the simplest and least subtle. Repetition ("sequence") is a device that may or may not be used to achieve balance. Symmetry and balance are of course aspects of layout, but are put in separate categories for ease in reference.

From the point of view of art and students of art, any work of art worthy of the name is balanced. Some maintain that the center of the design field is always the point around which the composition is balanced, and if we accept this dictum there is basically only a difference in degree between balance and symmetry. Other experts maintain that the "fulcrum" around which the balance takes place is determined by the design as well as by the field, and may be off-center. In this sketch, for example, the artist is illustrating "mass balanced by interest." The latter view, which seems to be the prevailing one, avoids certain difficulties and contradictions such as the necessity of giving "weight" to "space" and is useful in distinguishing balance from symmetry. My

PAYNE 1941

use of the terms *symmetry* and *balance* correspond, respectively, to the terms "obvious balance" and "occult balance" used by Beam (1958). His "axial" corresponds to my *bilateral*, and "central" to *biaxial, radial,* and *rotational.* In any schema there remains an element of judgment as to the degree of similarity that distinguishes symmetry from balance, or "obvious" from "occult."

As to types of balance, one can use the same categories as for symmetry. Balance, however, often depends on qualities other than those which, strictly speaking, are considered in the category of layout; it cannot be defined as solely a matter of spatial relationships, since it may depend on content and color.

If balance is not universal in art, it comes very close to being so. The remarkable tendency of apes to balance their "compositions" in the variety of drawing and painting experiments reported in the book by Desmond Morris (1962) suggests that this is indeed a very fundamental aspect of the activity. The weakness of his experimental methods do not affect his results with regard to this particular quality.

MEANINGS ATTRIBUTED TO SYMMETRY AND RHYTHM

Balance, symmetry, and rhythm are properly part of the category of spatial relationships, and thus they are often seen as mirroring social organization:

> Symmetrical design (a special case of repetition) should characterize the egalitarian societies; asymmetrical design should characterize the hierarchical societies. (Fischer 1961:81)

A similar hypothesis is to be found in the discussion of Caduveo face painting by Lévi-Strauss (1964:179): "asymmetry of class was balanced, in a sense, by symmetry of moieties." I suggest, however, that in some treatments of these qualities there is the implication that the relationships involved are not only the social ones, and that this aspect of spatial relationship implies attitudes toward nature and the supernatural to a greater degree than other aspects of layout.

Support for the idea that these qualities may be the ones most likely to present analogies to the world view of a people may be found, curiously enough, in the very rarity of specific hypotheses on this score. This is especially true of symmetry and repetition. Compared to the number of interpretive hypotheses to be found on the meaning of line, they are rare indeed. As all our hypotheses come from contemporary Euro-American culture, the fact that symmetry and repetition tend to be either ignored, dismissed as simple and inferior, or regarded as dire symptoms is suggestive. Seldom is there even recognition that there are other forms of symmetry beside the simple bilateral one; combined symmetry and multi-rhythmed repetition are either unrecognized or dismissed as curiosities of craftsmanship.

In the tradition of Western civilization, increasing artistic sophistication seems to bring with it greater subtlety in the matter of balance. In the language of art, various styles seem to develop from obvious balance to occult balance. But the emphasis is on balance in some form, repetition being a minor element which becomes increasingly free and less obvious as balance becomes increasingly occult. In other cultural settings increasing sophistication may bring about increasing complexity of repetitions rather than more occult balance. The subtlety is achieved by the interweaving of different kinds of symmetry and rhythms which combine different orders of repetition, rather than by decreasing the similarity of parts repeated. This is of course comparable to the multiple rhythms in African music. The best known examples in the visual arts are the Peruvian textiles (cf. Boas 1927).

Taylor offers a discussion of the nature and meaning of symmetry which shows some of the limitations of the culture-bound view, because he totally ignores the possibilities—and the existence—of rotational symmetry:

> A visual equilibrium will appear *static* exactly in the measure that a principle of symmetry governs it. That is a truth of the most fundamental importance, for it enables us to know of any field, irrespective of the particular forms which may be introduced into it, that an absolutely symmetrical distribution of those forms will give an absolutely static equilibrium, that a bilaterally symmetrical distribution of those forms will give a bilaterally static equilibrium, and where there is no symmetry, there can be no rest. (Taylor 1964:42)
>
> Symmetry produces within a visual field an effect of luminously intelligible order, uncomplicated and serene, in which the center of gravity is so lucidly apparent, and the balance about it so formally assured, that in all this measured world there is no detail whose importance to any other is not calculable, nor any detail whose counterpoint anticipation cannot predict. (ibid.:40)
>
> As a rule, an obvious balance or symmetry will excell in the expression of repose, and an occult, asymetrical balance in vitality. Similarly, an occult balance will suggest a high degree of energy. (Beam 1958:712)
>
> Individuals giving over-symmetrical drawings are usually compulsive, emotionally cold and distant, and precariously controlled personalities. (Machover 1949:87)

Barry (1957:381) finds that "asymmetry of design" correlates with "severity of socialization (.26)."

> In keeping with the previously reported psychological findings, I adopt the hypothesis that regular, symmetrical, geometric shape results when the tendency to simple structure is set free by a remoteness from the multiplicity of nature. The reasons for this remoteness vary greatly, and so correspondingly do the resultant patterns. (Arnheim 1954:127)

As symmetry has been considered only in its simpler forms, it is perhaps no wonder that it is usually equated with simplicity, or at least associated with it. Barron and Welsh (1952) have found that conservative and conventional persons tend to prefer simple, symmetrical figures, while artists and deviant personalities whose behavior tends toward the antisocial and psychopathic prefer complex, asymmetrical figures.

Repetition is ignored in psychological interpretations except in graphology, where regularity is said (Bell 1948:295) to be an "index of predominance of will. Irregularity is indicative of weak will, or of impulses of enormous strength relative to the strength of the feelings." Students of art have, however, quite definite ideas on the subject. Pearce (1947:89) says that different historical periods have characteristic line shapes which are repeated rhythmically in a great variety of forms, including architecture and clothing. Mundt says:

> Rhythm and symbol are the two elements of painting most closely woven into the cloth of society. The creative use of rhythm and symbol by the artist and the beholder, maintain the unitary character of their society and strengthen its vitality. (Mundt 1952:213)

And further:

> Strong rhythmic pattern reflects a period of communal existence . . . weakened patterns reflect a time when the communal pattern has begun to break up and critical individualism was taking its place. (ibid.:197)

Types of rhythm, like classes of symmetry, have been little examined in terms of interpretation, but Beam (1958:708) points out that:

> Extreme variety and alternation create an impression of marked vitality; extreme order and gradation suggest repose, stately order or some similiar condition. The principle is simple; great

> variety and rapid change will stand for vitality; uniformity or slow change will express repose.

Rhythmic repetition as an artistic device is seen as resulting from expert craftsmanship, as discussed by Boas, and partly also as a perceptual esthetic device:

> Rhythm in art gives a movement or condition of line that takes hold of all kinds of apparently irrelevant details and gives them coherence. As rhythm in verse helps the mind to hold on to ideas in a collected manner, so rhythm in form helps to grasp and relate many otherwise separate conceptions. (Pearce 1947:82)

PROPOSED DEFINITIONS FOR QUALITIES OF SYMMETRY AND RHYTHM

II.A. Symmetry (Finite Repetition) and Balance

From the geometric point of view, symmetry is a form of repetition; the type of symmetry is defined by the spatial motion or combination of such motions to produce from one original the repeated parts. *Symmetry* thus includes both *finite figures,* complete figures with a fixed number of motions (which are those the artist calls symmetrical); and *infinite figures* in which the repeated part can be repeated without limit, (which the artist is likely to think of as exhibiting "rhythmic sequence," not "symmetry" at all). Infinite figures are not symmetrical by the dictionary definition, and are considered here under the term *repetition.*

The two points of view are by no means incompatible, but the difference in viewpoint is significant for cross-cultural comparisons. Shepard has used the geometric point of view; her precise and careful analysis is used here in a very slightly modified form to provide consistent definitions of the different varieties of symmetry.

> The symmetric figure is classified by its motion, that is, by the manner of repeating the fundamental portion, and motions are described by reference to imaginary lines and points or axes. Only two motions, reflection and rotation, can be used in simple figures. Reflection produces corresponding right and left images and the symmetry is usually referred to as *bilateral* or mirror. Familiar examples are the isosceles triangle, regular trapezoid, oval, and semi-circle. These are described by reference to a line which separates the two halves and marks the position of the plane of reflection. Quite different is *rotational* symmetry, in which, as the

> name implies, the fundamental portion is turned about a point. We imagine an axis piercing the plane at right angles. If the figure repeats itself at regular intervals when swung about this axis it has rotational symmetry . . . . . A third class of symmetry of simple figures, *radial,* combines the motions of rotation and reflection, consequently it has more than one reflection axis . . . . .
>
> Varieties of each of the three classes of symmetric figures can be defined by reference to the position or number of axes or to the angle of rotation. Thus bilateral figures are distinguished as vertical, horizontal, or oblique, depending on the position of the axis. Rotational figures are differentiated by angle of rotation as twofold requiring a rotation of 180° to repeat their position, threefold having an angle of 120°, fourfold with an angle of 90°, and so on. Radial figures may be described either by the number of their axes or by the degree of rotation. (Shepard 1948:217)

In the following adaptation of Shepard's illustrations, the fundamental portions are black; the axes of reflection are indicated by dotted lines; the points of emergence of axes of rotation by dots at centers of figures; and the direction and degree of rotation by dashed arcs with arrows.

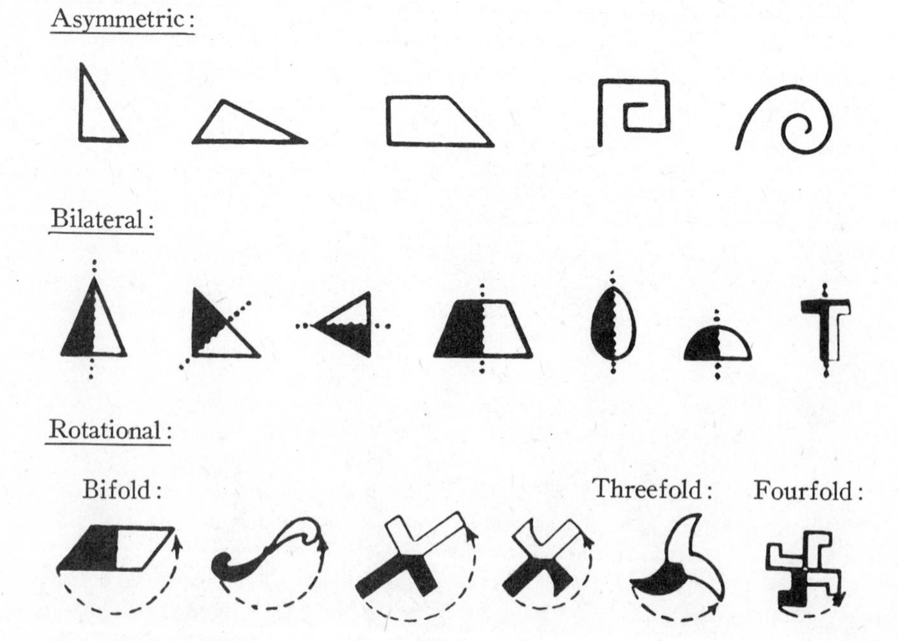

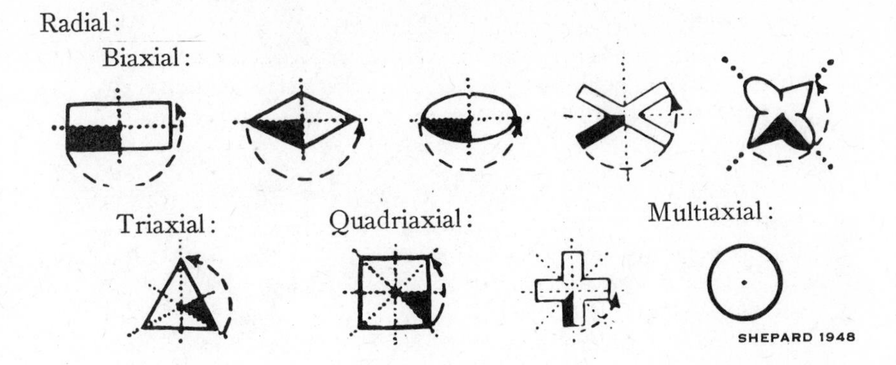

A minimum description of symmetry must include the principal classes, as described by Shepard. I have used the terms *asymmetrical, rotational, biaxial,* and *radial* and have added the term *circular,* which is properly a subhead of radial (infinite multiaxial radial), because of its distinct artistic quality.

For a complete description it would be necessary to designate the symmetry of parts as well as the whole. It is possible (and not at all improbable) for elements to be bilateral, design units radial, and the whole biaxial, or even for the elements and units to have several forms. To simplify this category, I have recorded symmetry in terms of a dominant and a minor type, regardless of whether the minor type is to be found in elements, in design units, or as a quality of the symmetry of the whole. In regard to the last case, it is always possible to make a decision as to how to classify the symmetry of the design in accordance with the principles discussed by Shepard, but the single classification that is technically correct is often less meaningful than a combined one. For example, the following designs are both "rotational," but the radial factor gives a very different quality to the second.

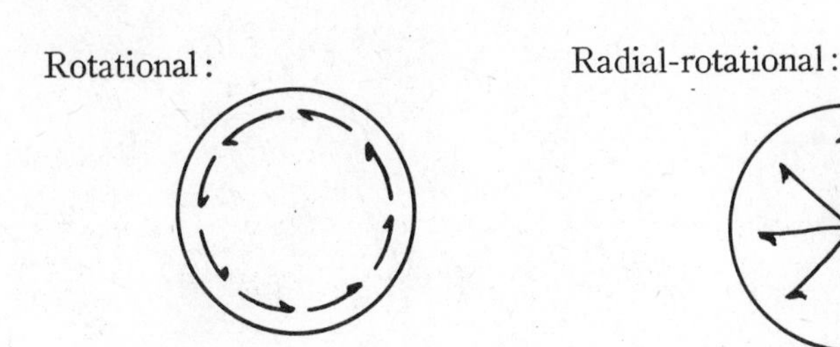

II.A.1. Type of Symmetry (Finite Repetition)

Radial

SIDES 1961

Bilateral

SIDES 1961

Biaxial

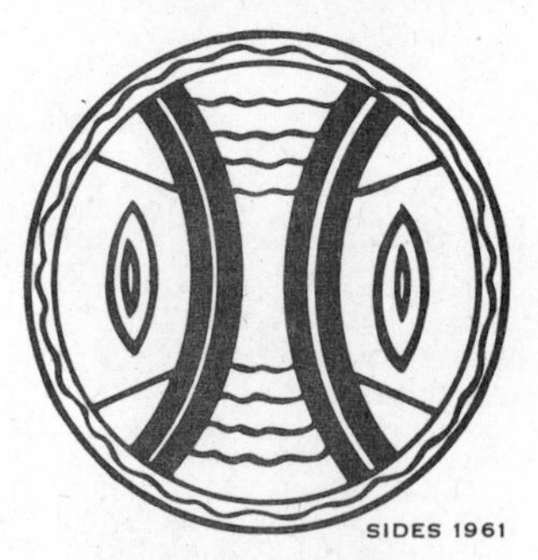

SIDES 1961

Rotational

SIDES 1961

Bifold-
Rotational

SIDES 1961

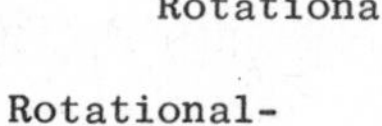

Rotational-
Bilateral

SIDES 1961

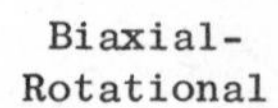

Biaxial-
Rotational

BOAS 1927

Radial-
Biaxial

SIDES 1961

II.A.2. Degree of Symmetry

When one considers symmetry, either as repetition or as balance, the question immediately arises as to how much latitude can be allowed in the similarity of the balanced or repeated elements. Some art styles, notably Navajo drypainting, have been characterized as symmetrical by some observers and as nonsymmetrical by others. Except insofar as the difficulty is the result of considering symmetry only in terms of bilateral or mirror symmetry, the problem arises because of different standards concerning how alike the different parts must be to qualify as symmetrical. This difficulty is eased by using a concept of degree of symmetry. While still requiring judgments concerning similarity, this concept greatly reduces the degree of difference possible among such judgments. Furthermore, the question is solved as to whether to consider the clear intention of the artist or only the actual execution. Should a design clearly intended to be symmetrical be so considered if mistakes mar the perfection of repetition? If degrees of symmetry are used, mistakes simply call for assigning the work to an appropriate degree of symmetry, and no assumptions concerning intention need be made.

The scale used in the tally sheets runs from 1 to 5, where (1) indicates balance but no symmetry, and (5) perfect finite repetition.

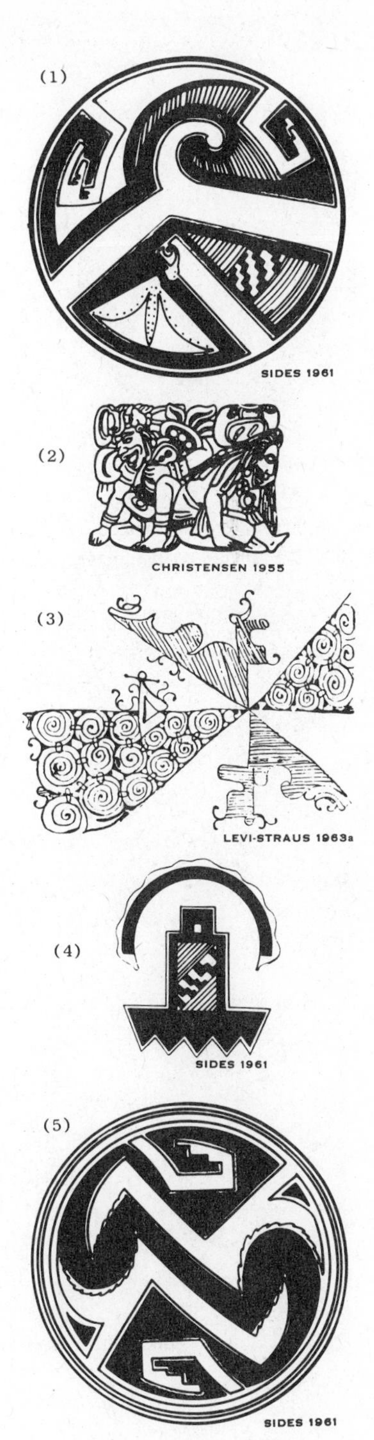

II.B. Infinite Repetition and Rhythm

Concerning the nature of repetition, Shepard (1948:218) says:

> The fundamental portion can also be repeated an indefinite number of times along a straight line to form a band or in two directions to form an allover pattern. Different motions can then be employed resulting in new pattern classes. It is of primary importance to recognize that each of these three major categories of design—the simple complete figure, the band, and the allover pattern—has its characteristic motions and pattern classes. To emphasize this distinction, I shall frequently use the terms finite and infinite introduced by Birkhoff. Simple complete figures such as polygons are *finite* because they have a fixed number of motions. When there is no limit to the possible number of motions of the fundamental portion, the design is *infinite*. The band which employs motion in only one direction is *one-dimensional* infinite; the allover patter, with repetition in two directions, *two-dimensional* infinite. There are seven classes of the former and seventeen of the latter.

Rather than employ the 24 classes of repetition, I find it more useful to distinguish several qualities and to use the idea of degree, that is, exactness of repetition, as in the case of symmetry. Rhythm is a term often used where the repetition is not exact.

II.B.1. Forms Repeated

The first item is the specification of what is repeated; a work may have, for example, single irregular design units and achieve a very rhythmic effect by the repetition of component lines of similar shapes.

Rhythmic variation of line and element

PAYNE 1941

Rhythmic repetition of units, component lines

Repetition of units

LEUZINGER 1960

THOMPSON 1954

Repetition of units with alternation of position and "color"

BOAS 1927

II.B.2. Type of Repetition

Repetition, exact or inexact, may be (a) one-dimensional or (b) two dimensional ("all over pattern") as illustrated below. It may also be (c) static or dynamic, corresponding to radial and rotational in finite repetition. I have tried to avoid such terms as "static" and "dynamic" because of the degree of interpretation implicit in them. They are in use, however, and since I cannot find any satisfactory alternatives, and the even more generally accepted term "rotational" is open to the same objection, it seems best to conform to usage and employ them. It must be remembered that the implied quality of perceived motion is not yet established as a universal human response. Examination of various works shows that this quality is a matter of degree, as shown in the scale illustrated below. The scale runs from (1) *static,* or least degree of "motion", to (5) *dynamic,* a high degree of "motion".

And finally, Taylor speaks of rhythm as being (d) either percussive or continuous, and these terms are applicable to all forms of repetition. Once the repetition involves more than very simple components, it is clear that this characteristic is better treated as a continuum than a dichotomy, with an appropriate scale. Scale II.B.2.d. utilizes (1) to indicate separate elements, "percussive", to (5) to indicate a high degree of continuity.

II.B.2.a. One-Dimensional

SIDES 1961

II.B.2.b. Two-Dimensional

LEWIS 1924

II.B.2.c. Static-Dynamic

Relation between finite and infinite classes of repetition:

Static-Infinite | Radial-Finite | Dynamic-Infinite | Rotational-Finite

SHEPARD 1948

Scale of static-dynamic:

(1)

SIDES 1961

(2)

ENCISO 1953

(3)

SIDES 1961

(4)

SIDES 1961

(5)

ENCISO 1953

II.B.2.d. Percussive-Continuous

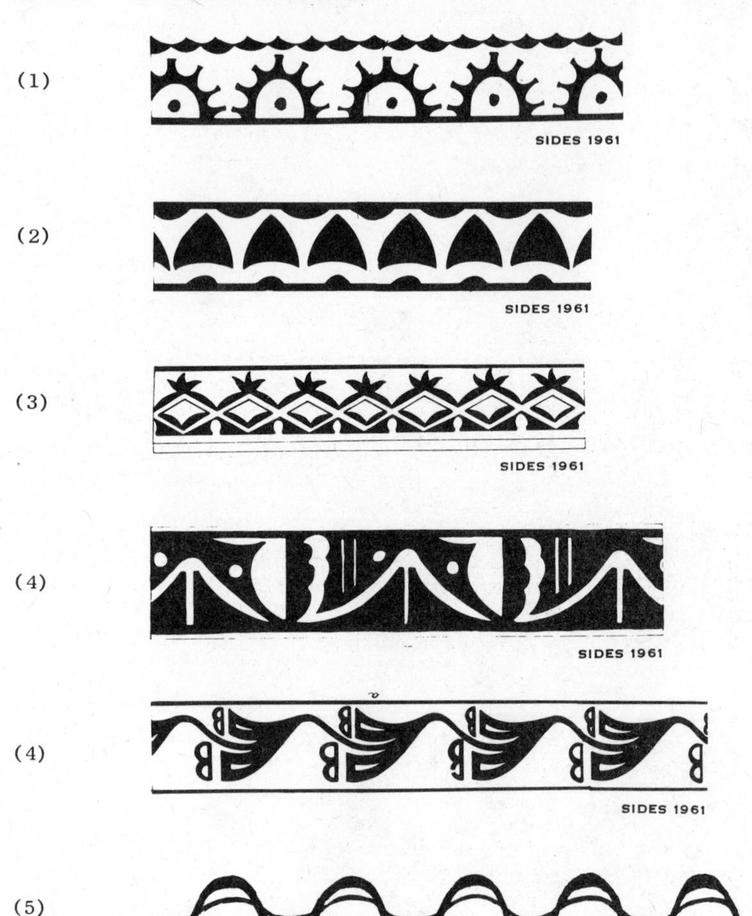

II.B.3. Variation of Repetition

The term "rhythm" as applied to the visual arts has been used in a number of ways as, for example, in the sense for which the term *movement* is utilized in this schema. *Rhythm* is defined here as repetition with variations, such as variation in size, shape, position ("interval"), or color. There is no precise way of defining the difference between rhythm and imperfect repetition, except insofar as rhythmic departures from exact repetition are patterned. Exactness of repetition is scaled in II.B.3.a. below as for symmetry; certain types of variation are noted in II.B.3.b.

II.B.3.a. Exactness of Repetition

This is scaled from (1) no repetition to (5) perfect exact repetition (compare II.A.2 above).

II.B.3.b. Types of Variation

1. Alternation

SIDES 1961

ENCISO 1953

2. Gradation.

3. Combination (multiple rhythms).

SYMMETRY AND RHYTHM IN DRYPAINTINGS

Lack of definition as to the nature of symmetry has led to contradictory interpretations concerning the use of symmetry in Navajo drypaintings. Mills says symmetry is used infrequently. Barry puts Navajo art high on the symmetry gradient. If the symmetry is defined as bilateral or mirror symmetry, in which the two halves are reversed and thus opposed to each other, then it is relatively rare in this art form. Reichard says:

> After remarking on the absence of mirror symmetry, especially in the circular sandpaintings, I became acquainted with the paintings of *Navajo Medicine Man* Plates I–X, laid out in mirror symmetry, requiring half the picture to be read sunwise, half anti-sunwise. The Bead Chant, to which these pictures belong, is concerned with eagles in a realm alien to the hero. The chant is associated with eagle trapping; hence the central theme is exorcistic—hunting is a dangerous and uncertain undertaking. The symmetrical arrangement, involving two opposite directions, may therefore be tolerated. (Reichard 1950:167)

This passage suggests such a different conception of symmetry that the hypotheses concerning its meaning must be re-examined. The European tradition places the emphasis on balance. The opposition that is implied in the reversed forms is overcome by the perfect balance between them; hence they are seen as static, serene, orderly. If this balance seems too precise, there is the suggestion of concern with control —of the "compulsive and emotionally cold" personality. In this view, the tension implied by the opposition is overcome by perfect balance. In the Navajo view it would seem that the tension and opposition in such an arrangement are stronger than the harmony. Perhaps this is because balance in most Navajo symmetry is not the operating principle, but repetition is.

The fact that for the Navajo it is repetition rather than balance that is the basic organizing principle is shown by the circumstance that the "same" painting may be laid out either in a rectangular format or in a circular one. In the first instance the arrangement is one of repetition, usually dynamic, and, while it is basically bilateral, the figures are not reversed, but "follow each other." The circular version of the painting consists of the same figure as in the rectangular one, with the field bent around to form a radial-rotational pattern. This latter form permits additional complexity by additions to both the radial and the rotational patterning. The possibilities of symmetry implicit in the idea of elements that can be repeated in a variety of relations to one another are far greater than the possibilities implied by opposition and balancing of two parts. The complexity and variation of repetition are perhaps the most characteristic feature of most Navajo drypaintings.

There are some bilateral designs in the paintings of Blessing Way, but these seem to be an incidental result of the emphasis on the central path rather than on balance between the two sides; the elements are often alternated rather than opposed. Considering the emphasis on duality in the mythological material, it is interesting that this does not seem to be often translated to bilateral symmetry in the paintings. A pair of supernaturals are often multiplied to four or more and usually travel in the same direction rather than being opposed. The quality of oppositional, reciprocal interaction suggested by Lévi-Strauss's interpretation of duality does not seem to apply—and, of course, the Navajo do not have moieties. Perhaps there are implications of meaning in terms of social structure in the very lack of bilateral opposition, in the fact that the figures, although similar in shape and size, "move" in the same direction. It is as though the whole was expected not to remain static but to be kept moving by equal and harmonious participation of each part. One is tempted to see a parallel in the emphasis on unanimity, or at least "going along with," rather than on the balanced opposition of moiety or two-party systems.

A comparison with European religious art shows a very fundamental difference in approach. In the early centuries of Christianity religious art is marked by bilateral symmetry and rather obvious repetition of forms; during the succeeding centuries the balance became increasingly occult and the rhythms more subtle. The main device for harmonizing opposing units is a kind of balanced opposition, and often a dominant figure enforces the balance. Raphael's *Theology* is a striking example of turbulence harmonized in this fashion.

Rhythm in drypainting takes the form of small variations in the repetition of the principal figures or design units. There is some alternation of units, especially in the more complex round paintings, where the anthropomorphic figures often alternate with plant figures of very different form. Variations in figures are never in size, since the same type of figure is always the same size in a particular work. A principle form of rhythmic variation is in color, with the main colors being varied or reversed in each figure. Other variations are in minor elements, such as in the shapes of objects and symbols accompanying each figure. There is rhythm, too, in the repetition of parallel lines and the intervals between them, which are varied in a repetitive way. In the more complex paintings, one could speak of multiple rhythms, since different patterns can be seen in the radial and rotational "movements."

Mundt's hypothesis that a strong rhythmic pattern reflects a period of communal existence is interesting. It is a little hard to apply in the case of the Navajo, since he does not define "communal existence." When one looks at art as a communication rather than as a reflection, however, it can be seen that the chanter is indeed calling for social solidarity and communal attitudes in order that the ceremony may achieve its objectives. As a value, communal existence is very relevant to the situation and accords with the stress on collaterality in the Florence Kluckhohn scheme.

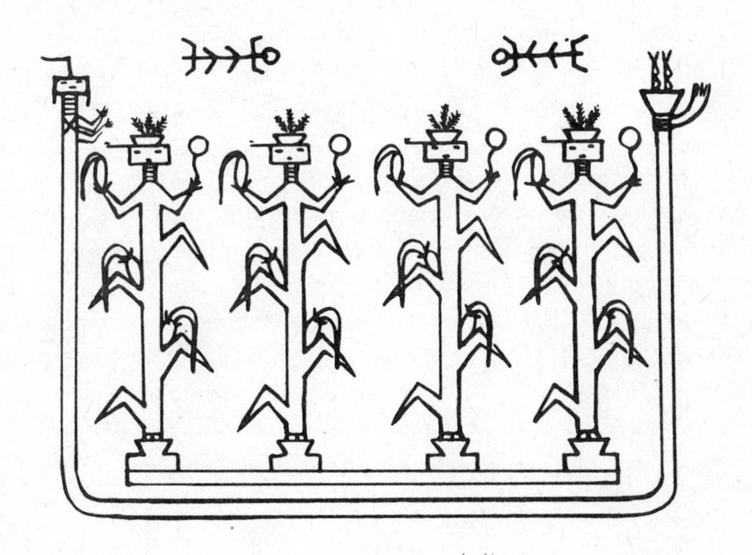

4

Lines and Linearity

MEANINGS ATTRIBUTED TO LINEAR QUALITIES

III. Treatment of Lines

There are more interpretations, and a greater variety of them, concerning line than any other category of form-qualities. This is owing in large part to the number of paper and pencil projective tests for which such interpretations have been formulated; where writing is part of the culture, writing tools are at hand and provide a ready medium. Some persons, however, see a deeper meaning in a general cultural emphasis on linearity. It has been suggested (Marshall McLuhan is the best known name associated with this idea) that literacy imposes a kind of thinking that is lineal and sequential and that this emphasis on line in art is one expression of it. But however "sequential" the linear mode may be to the artist, it is only partially so to the viewers, since the graphic production is perceived primarily as a two-dimensional gestalt.

The lineal aspect of art is sometimes considered the most intellectual, and the idea of line is often associated with control in one fashion or another. On the other hand, it is generally considered by students of art that there is no aspect of style more personally expressive than calligraphy, with the implication that this aspect of art is relatively free of the controls imposed by cultural style. This is particularly true of art in the European tradition where linear works are often sketches done freely and rapidly. One suspects that the greatest degree of self-expression in this case takes place when the artist (who in this culture has become technically so proficient with a drawing instrument as to be almost unaware of it) is preoccupied with planning a composition and not thinking about line at all.

These and many other qualities ascribed to line are highly varied for several reasons. There are many qualities called "linear;" most are related to perception, but some qualities of line result from direct motor expression. It is not possible to distinguish these in visual productions as a rule. The simple distinction, however, between component lines, which are at least in part motor expressions, and structural lines, which are almost purely perceptual helps to clarify some interpretations.

Component lines and structural lines are seldom distinguished in interpretations, partly because many of the form-meanings are drawn initially from the works of young children in which there is no distinction, or from very simple clinical material. Most of the artistic interpretations refer to particular cases, but the ones quoted often may be applied equally to both component and structural lines.

The degree to which line can serve as a medium for motor expression depends to a certain extent on technological factors. Chalk and charcoal, or ink and paint, if the applicator is effective, can make a record of a single free motion. If the line must be made very slowly or gone over repeatedly to become permanent, much of this quality is lost, as any forger can tell you. Such technological factors must be taken into account in deciding which interpretations are applicable in a particular case.

Many of the ideas that underlie the various interpretations center about the concepts of thought and control. Thought is seen in the delineation of form and many hypotheses concerning "line" have to do with shape; control involves the idea of the line as a boundary.

III.A.1. Degree of Linearity

The emphasis on linearity is seen as emphasis on the intellect, on control, especially in the control of energy. But there are other uses of the term "linearity." Linearity (or "draughtsmanly") as used by Wölfflin, refers to the treatment of an edge or surface so that the object is clearly shown and the separation of the object from the background is marked; this is a manner of seeing in terms of lines. The term is opposed to one that is translated as "painterly" in which the play of light and shade encompasses both the object and its environment. Wölfflin's usage is more closely related to concepts of figure and ground in the terminology used here. In this connection Wölfflin's "linearity" could be interpreted as a clear separateness of the individual from the environment, or as lack of ambiguity in social relations. This idea of linearity in Wölfflin's sense, however, is interpreted in a way similar to linearity in the literal sense in that such a rendering is considered more intellectual and less emotional than the painterly approach.

"Linearity" as used by Schuster, on the other hand, relates more to two-dimensionality:

> Linear-mindedness leads on the one hand to history and evolution, but on the other also to the pinpoint, to the atom, to the monads of Leibnitz, and to individualism. A mind given to three dimensionalism, by contrast, leads to a feeling of community with one's environment which is difficult to express adequately in words. It manifests itself as magic, as participation, as a form of socialism, as an art tending towards the abstract. (Schuster 1959:155)

Waehner (1946:66) says that a "preference for linear expression" suggests introversion. Her use of the word "linear" is consistent with the usage in the present work.

In another usage emphasis on linearity may be related to an emphasis on drawing as delineation of form.

> Language allows us to communicate and express; but before that, it clarifies, connects, and forms thought. Drawing does the same. The first function of both is precommunicative; to sharpen perception, to clarify it, and to give it an ordered form. Not until perception and thought are clear in our minds can we communicate anything but addlemindedness to others. Drawing as the fine instrument of vision centers its initial effort on the draftsman's own understanding of his experience. (Hill 1966:26)
>
> In order to apprehend the meaning in our experience it is essential for us to *see*, and drawing is the instrument of an inquiring eye that teaches us to see. (ibid.:39)

These illuminating statements clarify the concept of line as "intellectual" by defining drawing as a process of visual inquiry and analysis.

The implication is that, insofar as linearity is an emphasis on drawing, considerable use of this mode suggests an inquiring and analytical approach to the world.

III.A.2.a. Weight of Lines

The weight of line as found in a work as a whole is given a variety of interpretations. Kavolis (1965:7) puts forth the hypothesis that overlaid fuzzy lines suggest the quality of a "tendency to muddle along" and a Being value orientation, and that heavy, thick-set lines suggest a quality of "strong internal restraints" and a Being-in-Becoming value orientation. Longman (1949:9) says that "hard, dark, clearly defined" lines have the form-meanings of "strength, precision, and confidence," while lines which are "soft, blurred, and varied in emphasis" have form-meanings of "delicacy, sensitivity, timidity, and weakness." Other interpretations are those from projective drawing tests; some of the apparent contradictions may rest on the distiction between line as a motor expression and line that depends on perception:

> Strong lines are characterized by their darkness and deep imprint . . . they always reveal the presence of a strong vital drive or constitutional strength which the subject has available or which he discharges into action . . . they have different meanings depending on the configuration of elements (Kinget 1952:79)
>
> Another constant fact about strong pressure is its value as an indicator of deep emotionality. (ibid.:80)
>
> The stronger the intensity of the line, the stronger, generally, the subject's interest in tangible objects . . . especially with utility content. (ibid.)
>
> The acutely excited schizophrenic or the manic . . . give very heavy lines as graphic expression of their excess of motor aggression. (Machover 1949:95)
>
> A fuzzy, broken, or tremulous line with light pressure is often seen in the schizoid alcoholic as distinguished from the heavy line used by the paranoid alcoholic. (ibid.:96)
>
> Chronic schizoid alcoholics and those suffering from depersonalization fears, or from an acute conflict in regard to withdrawal trends, may give a thick heavy line as a barrier between themselves and the environment. (ibid.:97)
>
> The dim line occurs most frequently in the timid, self-effacing and uncertain individual. The dim line is also frequently fragmented or sketched. (ibid.)

> The fading in and out of line, with spotty reinforcements, is commonly seen in the drawings of individuals given to hysterical, often specifically amnestic reactions to their difficulties. (ibid.)
>
> The faint "ectoplasmic" line is relatively rare, appearing mainly in withdrawn schizophrenics. (ibid.)

III.A.3. Shape of Lines

This order of interpretation is based on the dichotomy between straight and curved lines, and the extent to which each is used. There is a certain feeling of consistency to all the various interpretations, but the specific meanings assigned are so diverse as to suggest that this quality by itself has so many possibilities as to call for considerable caution. Clearly, it is a quality which depends, even more than most, on where and how it is used. As to basic form-meaning Longman (1949:9) says that curved and rounded lines suggest ease, comfort, well-being, growth, while straight lines convey rigidity and stiffness. Psychological interpretations are quite varied:

> The children observed to work primarily in single straight-line strokes tended to stand out as a group for their relatively assertive, outgoing behavior. Typical of them were such traits as "realistic interests", "initiative for play," "aggressive" and "negativistic". By contrast, the children who worked with curved, continuous strokes tended to stand out as a group for their more dependent, more compliant, more emotionally toned reactions, viz., "affectionate", "lack of confidence", "seek adult attention", "random work habits", and "fanciful imagination".
>
> These differences became even more pronounced as comparison was made between specific forms. Children who emphasized circles tended as a group to be more withdrawn, more submissive, more subjectively oriented than children who predominately painted vertical, square, or rectangular forms. Among the characteristics illustrating the tendency to work in circles are "lack of confidence", "lack of ideas for play", "emotional interests", "imaginative interests", "follow", "imitate". (Alschuler and Hattwick 1947:55)
>
> Straight lines, representing the male form, as opposed to curved, should be associated with societies which strongly favor male solidarity in residence . . . We may assume that when an adult individual is psychologically secure he will be extroverted and look for pleasure by seeking out members of the opposite sex. In fantasy a man will be creating women, and vice versa. When, on the other hand, one sex is relatively insecure psychologically, members will be introverted and more concerned in fantasy with improving their own body image and seeking successful models of

> their own sex to imitate. Thus, to take polar extremes, in societies favoring male solidarity (and socio-psychological security) the men are looking for women as love objects and the women are looking for women as models for self-improvement, while in the societies favoring female solidarity in residence both sexes are looking for men. In visual art, I assume, this concern manifests itself as a relatively greater concern with curved and straight lines respectively. (Fischer 1961:84–5)
>
> Curved lines are one of the surest indicators of emotionality, of of flexibility, of capacity for adjustment and identification.
>
> Excessive use of the curved line, combined with nonrepresentational content, points to defective control, sensuous excitability and manic tendencies.
>
> Absence or very scant use of curves . . . is a sign of extreme rigidity, emotional as well as intellectual, and occurs generally with withdrawn, indifferent or hostile individuals.
>
> The straight line predominates in the drawings of subjects characterized by sharpness of attention and perception, general alertness and rational-volitional functioning.
>
> Excessive predominance of straight lines often reveals rigidity intransigence and even hardness, or at least, a limited capacity for establishing smooth and pleasant relationships. (Kinget 1952:86)

Waehner (1946:66) says that the use of many curved forms are "productive introversive" and may be an indication of "passivity" or "creativeness", while Barry (1957:381) finds that the presence of curved lines tends to be correlated with severity of socialization (.07). Students of art also provide a number of interpretations of this aspect of line:

> Most students who give a bias of straightness to their designs usually do so from conviction, for they like the severity such lines imply, but a number of other students give a bias of curvature because the graceful, and sometimes the sweet and cloying, appeals to them. (Pearce 1947:44)
>
> The relation of the straight to the curved and what we think to be a proper balance between them in a work of art depends largely on our attitude toward life and things generally. Both the age and the environment in which an artist lives help to determine such a balance. (ibid.)
>
> Straight lines and angular forms connote harshness, austerity, strength and masculinity. Since the straight line always implies a flat plane with sharp edges it is psychologically definite, and somewhat cold. (Beam 1958:695)

> We ordinarily connect curved forms with grace, flexibility, suppleness, femininity, and flowing movement. Only when combined with large scale and heavy proportions does the round form suggest massive strength or power. (ibid.)
>
> The arc of curvature and the type of angle employed with straight lines and planes are important in achieving any desired effect . . . long flat curves are ideally suited to the feeling of easy movement, whereas the same curves in tighter arcs endow [the work] with an air of turbulent activity. (ibid.)
>
> A curve is a rhythmic, moving line. A picture based on a curving line is apt to contain many other related curves, with angular forms subordinated. Gaiety, movement, and action are often expressed in related curving lines. (Bethers 1963:42)

Minetta's handbook on *Teacup Fortune Telling* provides some relevant interpretations:

> Serpentine lines indicate roads or ways. If they appear in the clear are sure tokens of some fortunate changes at hand; surrounded by many dots they signify the gain of money, also long life.
>
> Wavy lines show unsettlement.
>
> Straight lines signify a straight course.
>
> Dashes generally indicate enterprises afoot, but time must be given for maturity. (Minetta, n. d.)

III.A.4 & 5. Relation of Lines to Each Other and to Edges

> Every student of the fine arts knows that horizontal and vertical lines suggest the static, the stationary—give stillness, quietness and peace, whereas lines of a diagonal character give a general impression of movement. (Pearce 1947:37)

Other art scholars offer similar interpretations of the effect of line direction: "The *vertical* line, defying gravity, symbolizes uprightness and determination", (Mundt 1952:210) and "virility, rigidity, strength and static uprightness" (Longman 1949:9), while Bethers says:

> A line, a shape, or a direction is capable of making us feel an emotion. A very tall building, a tree, a Gothic cathedral, all have in common the quality of verticality, but none can be said to have a "subject". They just are.
>
> As Charles Lindstrom points out, there is a connection between "vertical and virtue". Church steeples have been reaching skyward for centuries. An "upright" man is another example. (Bethers 1963:38)

Horizontal lines suggest "passivity and relaxation" (Mundt 1952:210), "repose, peace and quiet" (Longman 1949:9).

> The actual horizon, seen far away, is always peaceful and elicits a quiet and restful feeling. A fallen object is horizontal; it has come to rest. In pictures, a dominant horizontal feeling may bring forth a similiar emotion, regardless of the picture's subject . . . The horizontal is not necessarily a quiet line but can be a "speed" line instead. (Bethers 1963:39)

As to the *diagonal,* "the slanting line, apparently falling suggests activity" (Mundt 1952:210), and "energy, dynamic activity, striving" (Longman 1949:9).

> The diagonal is off balance. Not many pictures are based on the diagonal alone, for that very reason. A strong diagonal is usually opposed by a similar diagonal, acting as a counterbalance to the picture. The diagonal is also a space line, and if it is not falling, it may then lie on the surface of a receding plane. It is very often used for the dual purpose of combining space with pattern. (Bethers 1963:40)

Aronson (1952:252) finds that the "drawings of the subjects with high n-achievement contained more diagonal configurations than those with low n-achievement". Barry (1957:381) tested for a correlation of "lines oblique to edges" and "presence of lines oblique to each other" with "severity of socialization", but the biserial correlation coefficients (.45 and .13) were below his level of statistical significance.

Altschuler and Hattwick found that in the paintings of pre-school children, those who emphasized horizontal lines showed different personality characteristics from those who emphasized vertical ones:

> Children who turned to straight-line strokes often tended to combine verticals and horizontals in easel painting. The two strokes are usually combined in what we have termed "structuralized or constructive" painting patterns. Some children, however, have shown such a preponderant use of horizontals, as compared with verticals, in their paintings that it has been possible to make a comparative study of the two. Results of these comparisons suggest that emphasis on either or both horizontals and verticals may be associated with assertive drives.
>
> Whereas verticals have frequently been used symbolically to indicate assertive or masculine drives, horizontals have not once been observed to be used in this way.

> Group comparisons between children with horizontal emphasis and those with vertical emphasis suggest that among children whose designs showed horizontal emphasis the pattern of behavior was likely to be more self-protective, more fearful, more overtly cooperative, and the children were more likely to come from homes where greater pressure was exerted.
>
> Individual cases have revealed strong negativistic streaks in children who emphasized horizontals, which leads us to believe that it is with negativistic rather than with the cooperative drives that horizontals are basically associated.
>
> A further differentiation in usage between verticals and horizontals has been suggested by Lowenfeld . . . he found a tendency for the horizontal to be identified with movement, and the vertical, which is relatively fixed in space in relation to a base line, to be identified with stationary objects. (Altschuler and Hattwick 1947:76)

Determination of the proportion of diagonal lines which is significant depends on the medium in which the lines occur. In a free medium, diagonal lines will be far more likely to occur by sheer chance than horizontal or vertical ones. If one considers anything within five degrees of true as horizontal or vertical, the probability of the occurrence of a diagonal line is $8/9$. This chance proportion is probably altered to some unknown degree by the structuring effect of rectangular format when this is used. In other media, such as basketry and weaving, the technique favors horizontal lines; vertical and diagonal lines represent various degrees of difficulty. It would seem important to assess the amount of effort which goes into line direction in order to judge the emphasis placed upon it, and to take these factors into account when considering how to interpret the importance of line direction in a work or style. Structural line direction must, of course, also be considered in this regard.

III.A.6. Line Endings

This is the only category to which I find no reference in the interpretative literature, although it seems a logical necessity. The following statement by Beam seems applicable to works characterized by free ends which result from a sketching technique, which seems to be rare in art outside the European tradition:

> Nervous vitality is expressed through a kind of vibrancy or suggestion of rapid, pulsating movements . . . extreme sketchi-

ness of technique plays an important part in objectifying this nervous energy. (Beam 1958:616)

Professor Hoebel, in a personal communication, has suggested several hypotheses: *Free ends* may indicate cultural openness, an adaptability, freedom from anxiety, emphasis on achievement, or a tendency to explore. *Terminal markers* set limits on these tendencies. *Endless lines* suggest introverted closure, "womb-oriented security" and anxiety toward external environment.

Hypotheses under the heading of outlining (III.C.) may also apply to the category of endless lines, especially the idea of control of whatever the endless line encloses. Where lines always meet other lines there is the obvious suggestion of tidiness, of a finished production with no "loose ends"!

III.A.7. Meeting of Lines

Bender (1938) and following him Waehner (1946) and Wallace (1950) all consider that the avoidance of sharp points is associated with repression of aggression. The implication is that sharp points have to do with aggression. This seems to be a form-quality which is so taken for granted that it does not need to be explicitly stated. Longman (1949:9) says that the form-meaning of angular and jagged lines is "harshness or brutality, dynamism, brittleness." Barry (1957:381) finds the correlation coefficient for "presence of sharp figures" and "severity of socialization" is .18, statistically not significant. Waehner (1946:66) regards the tendency to avoid sharp corners and to emphasize rounded corners indicates a personality which is "introversive, creative, restrained and preoccupied with self."

III.A.8. Simple Figures

If the basic assumption is valid, that is, if all peoples respond similarly to certain form-qualities, one would expect certain similarities in the meanings ascribed to simple figures, such as those interpretations of shapes listed under I.A. above. Although *simple figures* may be given a great variety of symbolic meanings, as was brought out by Boas many years ago, this does not invalidate the possibility of form-meaning which is in addition to, or underlies, the various symbolic meanings. As a matter of fact, the simpler the form, the more things it can be made to stand for. Nancy Munn (1966) has found the following usages within a single tribal group:

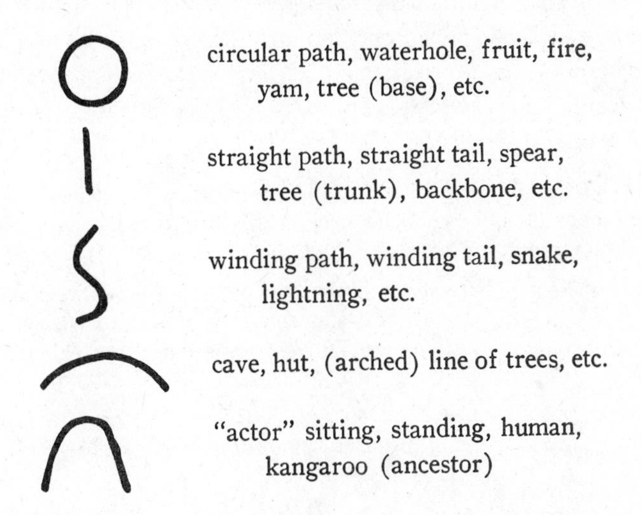

Regarding the circle, Arnheim says:

> . . . objects are often represented by dots, circles, or spheres when their actual shape is unknown or irrelevant to the purpose. (1954:170).

On the face of it, one would think that this would rule out any common meaning for the circle, but an examination of the various symbolic and form-meanings ascribed to it reveals an underlying feeling: the idea of "wholeness", "completeness", recurs again and again. Arnheim himself says:

> A circle is not a line of constant curvature, whose points are all equally distant from a center, but first of all a compact, hard, restful thing. (Arnheim 1954:432)
>
> Dr. M.-L. von Franz has explained the "circle" (or sphere) as a symbol of the Self. It expresses the totality of the psyche in all its aspects, including the relationship between man and the whole of nature. Whether the symbol of the circle appears in primitive sun worship or modern religion, in myths or dreams, in the mandala drawn by Tibetan monks, in the ground plan of cities, or in the spherical concepts of the early astronomers, it always points to the single most vital aspect of life—its ultimate wholeness. (Jung et al., 1964:240)

In seeking to determine the existence of underlying common meanings in simple figures, it is necessary to take into account that even the simplest figure has actually a considerable number of form-qualities. In purely symbolic usage one can abstract one such quality and ignore the others, but in the context of a work of art, all form-qualities are significant. For example, the multiwave line is assigned a number of meanings:

> Individuals with high n-Achievement drew more S-shaped (two directional, non-repetitive) lines than did those with low n-Achievement. (Aronson 1958:252)
>
> Lines: 7. Serpentine—lithe or languorous grace, feminine quality of suppleness, florescence, sensuousness, refined ambiguity, voluptuousness, feebleness, aimlessness, aspiration. (Longman 1949:9)
>
> The drawings of the "highs" [high n-Achievement] contained less multiwave lines (lines consisting of two or more crests in the same direction). (Aronson 1958:252)
>
> The wavy line suggests something lively, mobile, fluttering, growing or flowing. (Kinget 1952:36)

Each real multiwave line has weight, color, and can be the same or varying widths, be regular or irregular in wave pattern, have steep or shallow curves, have few or many crests, use either graduation or alternation in rhythmic pattern, and so on. Further investigation might reveal which variant is associated with each interpretation.

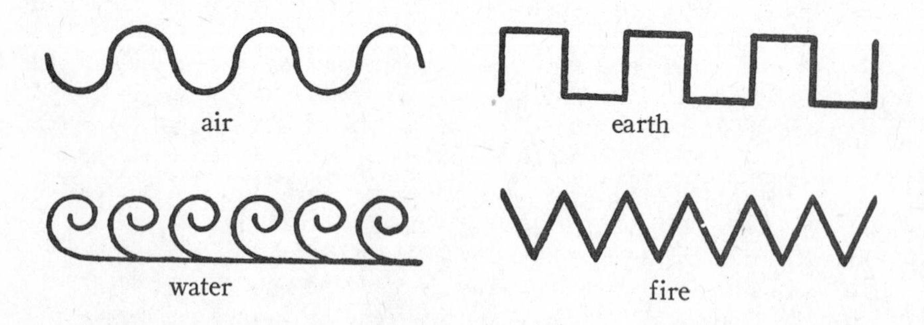

This suggests that the relationship between form-meaning and visual symbol rests, at least in part, on accepted conventions as to which form-meanings and combinations of form-meanings are selected as significant. Perhaps this clarifies what the artist is trying to say when he talks about art as a universal language and at the same time about cultural symbols.

> [The three shapes above are] fraught with symbolic content: there is violence in the first, serenity in the second, and finality in the third one. The fact that one cannot say whether this impression of finality in the cross derives from Christian memories, or from the canceling out of a vertical and active movement by a horizontal and passive one, illustrates the profundity of a symbol's power. In other words, the symbols [form-meanings] are there. The possibility of developing them into a socially coherent symbolism depends on the development of a participatory attitude by both artist and public. (Mundt 1952:211)

Comparative iconography is a field of considerable potential interest that is related to the study of form-meaning at several levels. The structural analysis of the symbolic meanings of representational elements, as has been done by Munn (1966) invites a testing of the form-meaning concept in specific cultural situations, where the "code comparison" between the semantic content and the stylistic form-qualities of individual works and works of a given class provides an opportunity for new insights. This kind of comparison is also open to cross cultural investigations. Meanings given by Munn for very simple linear symbolic elements are not really at odds with the form-meaning hypotheses, but are not very conclusive. The idea of motion in the multiwave line, however, seems to be present in all the meanings, and is consistent as well with Navajo usage.

III.B. Structural Lines

While the general meanings of line direction are similar for structural as well as for component lines, the artist naturally regards structural lines in terms of a deliberate means to achieve the desired communication, and leaves to component lines any implication of the unconscious or direct motor expression of personality that is implied by most psychological interpretations.

> The diagonals are *axes of dynamic stress;* the perpendicular axes are *axes of static stress.* (Taylor 1964:47)
>
> A balanced opposition of attitudes and directions is one of the artist's most useful methods of expressing vigorous physical activity, spiritual conflicts, and restless energy. (Beam 1958:714)
>
> Estheticians and psychologists agree on the emotional effects produced by different treatments of design. In applying harmony to the possibilities of attitude, an emphasis on the vertical creates an air of vitality; horizonal lines induce a feeling of repose; and diagonal line is an especially dynamic effect. (ibid.:683)
>
> We derive perhaps the greatest sense of vitality from diagonal attitudes, for these suggest the dynamic unstable movement of a falling tree, the momentum or forward drive of a warrior or a rapidly running man, the ascent or descent of a bird in flight, or a thrown spear. (ibid.:687)
>
> Oblique orientation is probably the most elementary and effective means of obtaining directed tension. Obliquity is perceived spontaneously as a deviation from the basic spatial framework of the vertical and the horizontal. This involves a tension between the norm position and that of the deviating object, the latter appearing as striving toward rest, being attracted by the framework, pulling away from the framework, or being pushed away by it. With the mastery of oblique orientation the child as well as the primitive artist acquire the main device for distinguishing action from rest, for example, a walking figure from a standing figure. (Arnheim 1954:407)

Kinget uses the term "orientation" for this quality, and says that, if marked:

> Orientation seems to be an expression of a particularly strong dynamism, of audacity and decisiveness, a positive attitude toward life and problems, and a healthy ambition . . . When combined with a high degree of carefulness, it is almost certain to be an expression of an immoderate striving toward excellence. (Kinget 1952:108)

In composition there can be no doubt that straight structural lines and squareness give the feeling of strength and security, but when their use is carried to extremes they convey sensations of harshness and crudity. Again, curvature may suggest vitality and grace, but when used to an excessive degree it gives a restlessness, insecurity and weakness. (Pearce 1947:45)

Harmonies of curved lines and forms are more likely to reflect the flexible, flowing, and plastic quality of nature. (Beam 1958:428)

Parallels between behavior and the use of circular and/or vertical patterns suggest the following tentative conclusions:

a) *A maturity difference.*—Whereas circular emphasis seems to reflect and be associated with relatively infantile (emotional, subjective, dependent) tendencies, vertical emphasis tends to reflect a relatively more mature (more rational, more objective, more self-reliant) pattern.

b) *A sex difference.*—Whereas circular emphasis reflects relatively feminine tendencies, vertical emphasis tends to reflect a more masculine pattern.

c) *A general personality difference.*—Whereas a circular emphasis seems to reflect and be associated with more self-centered, withdrawing, in-turned personality, vertical emphasis tends to reflect a more outgoing, assertive individual. (Alschuler and Hattwick 1947:59)

Dynamically the wedge shape represents a crescendo or decrescendo of breadth—a first illustration of the general rule that all perceptual gradients make for movement.

There is less ambiguity of direction in the wedge than in the square. Movement is preferably oriented toward the point. It produces the arrow effect. Presumably this is so because the broad end fulfills the function of a heavy base, from which movement issues towards the slim point. In steeples, pyramids or obelisks the effect is reinforced by the mass of the building or the ground on which they rest by the preference for upward movement in the vertical. (Arnheim 1954:404)

Radial structural lines have been given no attention in psychological interpretations. In the artistic sense they are discussed in terms of movement and tension. Radiating lines may emphasize movement outward expressing great vitality, and this may be contained by a border which increases the tension. "Radiating" lines may also be seen as converging, with the movement traveling inward to increase the dramatic impact of the center.

The discussion by Payne shows the tendency of artists of the European tradition to go in the direction of breaking an obvious pattern to achieve greater subtlety rather than complicating it to achieve greater complexity.

> The radiating or converging line organization generally presents a direct simple method of calling attention to the main area of interest . . . However, if converging lines are strong or well defined in the view, they may, in the picture, need some stiff interference such as secondary interest, opposition, or concealment. The glance must not travel too speedily, which it will if the general plan appears to be forced by an obvious spoke-like design. All lines should be irregular, broken, or intercepted. (Payne 1941:82)

III.C. Borders and Outlines

The attitude toward boundaries, outlines and borders is well expressed by Kinget (1952:107): "Closure seems to express a need to restrain, to concentrate, to protect, or to isolate." The interpretation of such forms clearly depends on what is enclosed. Knowledge of content is very important here, but purely formal characteristics may also be revealing. For example, in the area of content, are anthropomorphic figures separated from each other by boundaries? In the area of formal qualities, sharp points or strong colors may be outlined, suggesting control of aggression or of strong emotion.

Other interpretations seem to be extensions of this basic idea; thus Fischer (1961:81) says, "Figures without enclosures should characterize the egalitarian societies; enclosed figures should characterize the hierarchical societies." Barry (1957:381) finds that in samples of primitive art "presence of border" and "presence of enclosed figures" have biserial correlation coefficients of .20 and .32 with "severity of socialization", which are below the level of statistical significance. Machover (1949:97) considers that "the tendency to outline form elements carefully in black [indicates] repression of aggression."

PROPOSED DEFINITIONS OF LINEAR QUALITIES

III. Treatment of Lines

The descriptive terminology developed here rests upon three different ways of conceiving line. The first is in terms of lines as strokes, the moving point following the motor activity of the artist—line in a geometric sense. I call these *component lines.* Various aspects of line in this sense are noted in the subcategories of III.A. The second concept of line, under the heading III.B. *Structural Lines,* is not so literal; it is a way of perceiving layout in terms of linear relationships—the "lines" along which the composition is structured. The distinction between these two linear qualities is shown in simplified form in the sketches illustrating relations of lines (III.A.4 & 5.) below. The third way of looking at line considers the relation of lines to the spatial relationships in the layout, the use of linear forms to directly outline various parts of the design field, and under this heading I have included not only component lines, but also elements and spaces used in an elongated linear fashion as borders and outlines (III.C.).

III.A.1. Degree of Linearity

Some works consist entirely of lines, some of areas, some of a combination of the two in various proportions. The *degree of linearity* can be defined operationally: one can copy, or imagine copying, the design using lines of appropriate widths. If the design can be completely reproduced without filling in any areas, it is linear; if line exists only as an edge between tonal areas, it is non-linear. To be completely non-linear there should be no sharp "line" at the edge of form at all (as in Impressionist works), but the non-linear category (1) includes also all work without component lines.

The terms "linear" and "linearity" have been used in a variety of ways in the literature of art. In the famous work of Wölfflin (1915), for example, "linear" is related to "tactile values" as opposed to the "painterly" visual values. He refers especially to a "continuous, uniformly moving contour line" in the linear style, whereas in the painterly style contours are broken. Yet in a literal sense there may be many lines in "painterly" style. On the other hand Schuster (1959) includes both these modes in his idea of linear, which he considers characteristic of all European art. To him, linear involves a two-dimensional viewpoint as opposed to a three-dimensional one.

Thus the term as used here is much more simple, direct, and naíve than these conceptions, being simply a matter of the extent to which the work depends on lines rather than on areas of pigment or the equivalent.

III.A.1. Degree of Linearity

(1)

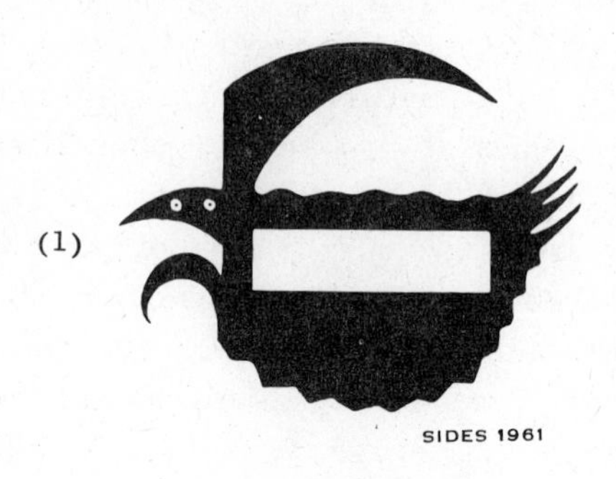

SIDES 1961

(2)

DISSELHOFF & LINNE 1960

(3)

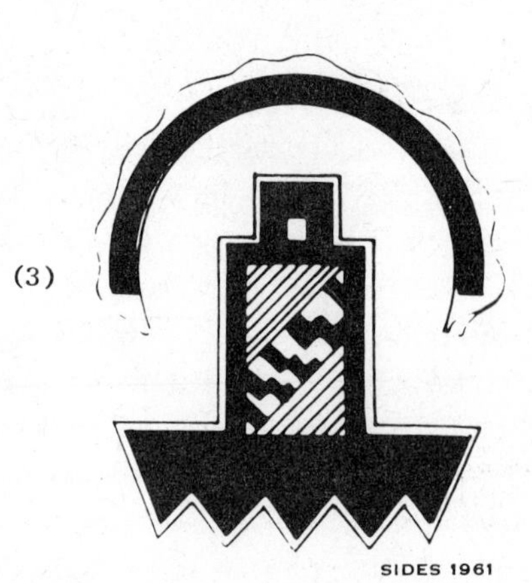

SIDES 1961

(5)

ENCISO 1953

(4)

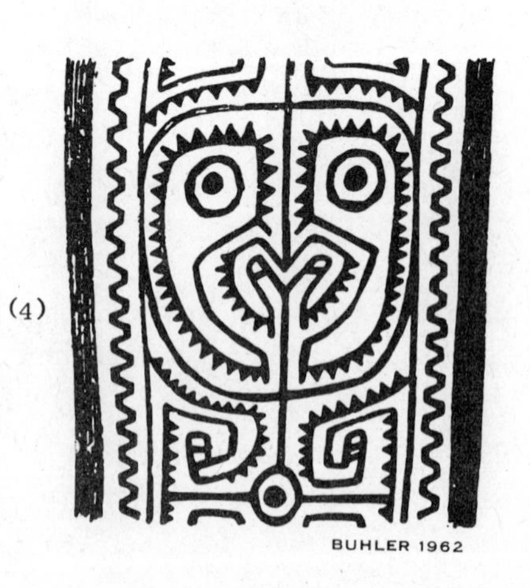

BUHLER 1962

III.A.2.a. Weight of Lines

This category refers to the width of line in relation to the work as a whole, but the contrast of line to figure and ground is taken into account to some extent. For some purposes these two aspects of weight may need to be separated, but for present purposes this seems too subtle, as these qualities are also considered under the headings of boundaries and color. The effect of "weight" varies with technique and materials, but insofar as it can be put in numerical terms, some such ratios as the following are used: a ratio between line and whole of less than 1:50 is considered a light line, one between 1:25 and 1:40 a medium line, and 1:15 a heavy line. An average of all the lines in the work is used, but of course range is to be noted in any fuller description. Value is taken into account as well as width, a darker line being considered heavier than a lighter one of the same width.

Heavy (5):

ENCISO 1953

Moderately heavy (4):

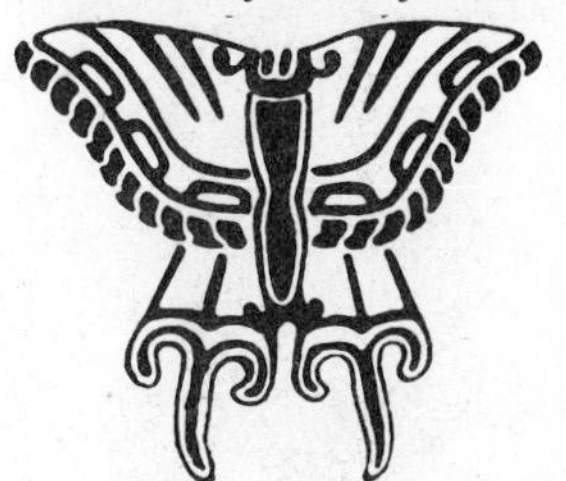

ENCISO 1953

Medium(3):

REICHARD 1933

Light (1):

SIDES 1961

Moderately light (2):

SIDES 1961

III.A.2.b. Length of Component Lines

Length of component line rests on the length of the actual lines in relation to the size of the whole field. As the quality is recorded in this study, the ratings refer to the length of line most frequently used; i. e., a mode rather than a median. The range here is from barely larger than a dot (1) to a line as long as or longer than the design field (5). A line of moderate length (3) is not longer than half the shortest dimension of the field.

III.A.3. Shape of Lines

In the interpretative hypotheses most statements concerning the meaning of shape of lines refer simply to the prevalence of curved or straight lines. This is subcategory a., Degree of Curvature. While it requires separate consideration of each work and a conscientious estimate, I have not considered it necessary to try each line with a ruler, or to make a line-by-line count. A work which is considered "non-linear," in the terminology used here, may still show a prevalence of either straight or curved lines, because of the contours of the edges of forms.

Although few interpretive hypotheses were collected, the inclusion of the subcategory b., indicating the types of curves seems a logical necessity.

Four types are distinguished: *arcs, exponential curves and spirals, multi-wave lines,* and *free and reverse curves.* By mathematical definition, an arc is a portion of a circle; its radius is constant. Other types of curves, as for example a spiral, have changing radii; the usual definition of a spiral is a curved path that goes around a point, receding or moving towards it with each revolution, and many such spirals are mathematically describable by equations.

I have used the term "exponential curve" because William Fagg in several of his well known works on African sculpture has considered this form important. As used by him, I believe the term refers to a line which increases in radius of curvature very rapidly, and does not make a full revolution around a central point; I use it with this meaning.

The arc and the spiral are quite clearly regular, mathematically exact types of curves; the reverse curve, and its extension, the multi-wave line, may or may not be regular. The exponential curve is regular when analyzed, but appears free. Free is by definition irregular.

III.A.3.a. Degree of Curvature

a. Overall

All straight (1):

SIDES 1961

Equally straight and curved (3):

ENCISO 1953

Predominantly straight (2):

SIDES 1961

Predominantly curved (4):

ENCISO 1953

All curved (5):

SIDES 1961

III.A.3.b. Type of Curve

Arcs:

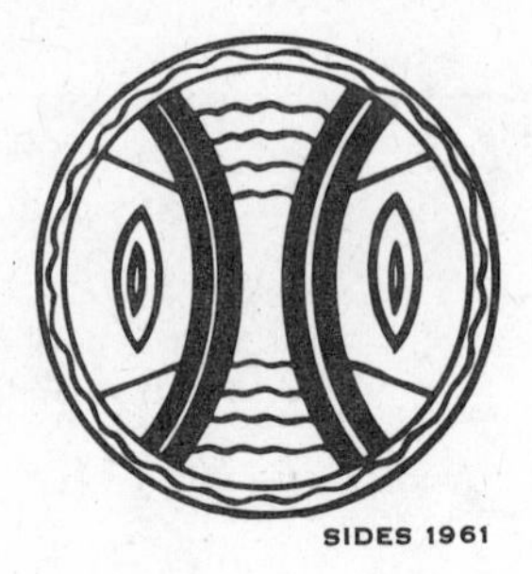

SIDES 1961

Free and Reverse:

CHRISTENSEN 1955

Multiwave:

SIDES 1961

PAYNE 1941

Exponential curves and Spirals:

SIDES 1961

ENCISO 1953

III.A.4 & 5. Relations of Lines

This aspect of line has two categories, one describing the relation of component lines to each other, and the other considering the direction of lines in relation to the edges of the design field. (In using this distinction I follow Barry (1952)).

All of the scales used here record the proportion of line relationships of each type, from (1) relatively few or none, to (5) predominate use. The effort is to estimate the number of lines in each category without regard to the effect produced by their relative weight, or by the way they are organized into structural lines.

III.A.4. Relation of Lines to Each Other

In the category of the relation of component lines to each other, the terms *oblique, parallel,* and *perpendicular* are used, but these are judgments which permit a certain amount of deviation from exact geometrical relationships. By this I mean that while in the geometric sense all lines which are not precisely parallel are at an angle to each other, or oblique, lines that deviate only by a few degrees give the effect of being parallel. Perpendicular also does not depend on a perfect 90° relationship. The category applies to curved as well as straight lines.

III.A.5. Relation of Lines to Edges

The relation of lines to edges of the design field is recorded in terms of *vertical, horizontal,* and *diagonal.* This category assumes a design field with a defined base. It may, however, be used to describe a circular design field by considering the circumference as horizontal and the radii as vertical. This practice is not entirely arbitrary, as it is a real relationship that can be observed by comparing the design of a round basket as seen looking at the side as compared to looking down into it. A painting on the ground that does not have defined edges cannot be rated as to this quality, although a wall painting obviously can be so rated.

In practice I find it unsatisfactory to depend mechanistically on the proportion of lines that fall under each heading. The matter of degree also enters into the judgment. What these categories really amount to is the effect of verticalness or horizontalness; this means that a design with all the lines (mathematically speaking) diagonal, but at very slight angles to the horizontal is recorded as both diagonal and horizontal because there is both a horizontal and diagonal effect.

III.A.4 & 5. Relations of Lines

Component lines all vertical (5);
Parallel to each other (5);
Structural lines opposed diagonals:

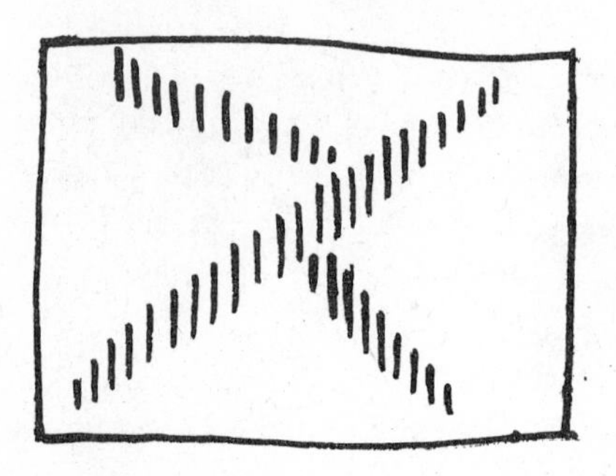

Component lines mostly perpendicular to each other (4);
Parallel to edge, that is, "horizontal" (4);
Structural line circular:

Component lines perpendicular (4); Diagonal to edge (5);
Structural lines parallel diagonals:

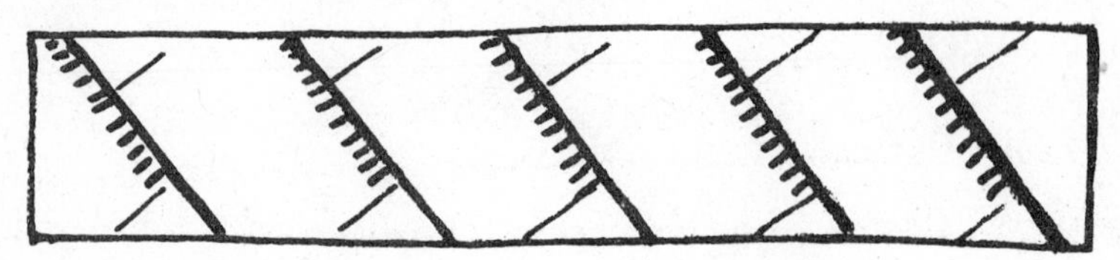

Component lines all oblique to each other (5);
Diagonal to edge (5);
Structural lines horizontal:

Component lines all oblique to each other (5);
Diagonal to edge (5);
Structural lines radial:

III.A.6. Line Endings

Common forms are:

(a) *endless lines,*

(b) lines which *meet others,*

(c) *terminal markers,* and

(d) *free ends.*

The scales indicate frequency of use of each type of line ending, from (1) occasional use to (5) most lines are ended in this manner.

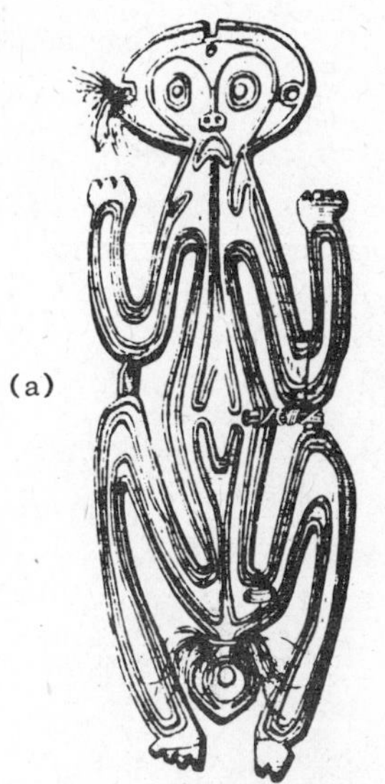

(a)

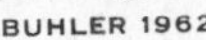

BUHLER 1962

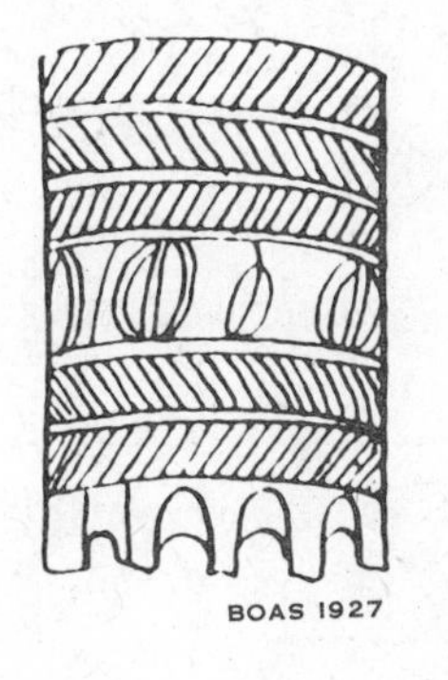

(b)

BOAS 1927

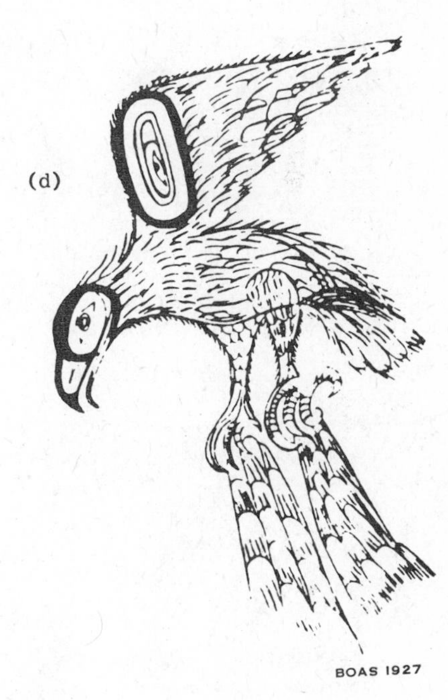

(d)

BOAS 1927

(c)

BASED ON LEVI-STRAUSS 1964

III.A. 7. Meeting of Lines (Angles)

The meeting of lines at corners can be described geometrically in terms of the size of the angle in degrees, and of the radius of the join.

III.A.7.a. Use of Points

The use of points refers to acute angles; however, the recording of acute angles alone does not conform to the quality designated in the interpretive literature as "use of points," so the less objectively definable term is retained. On the scale, (1) indicates that points are absent or rare, and (5) that points are a very prominent feature of the work, both in terms of sharpness and number.

(1):

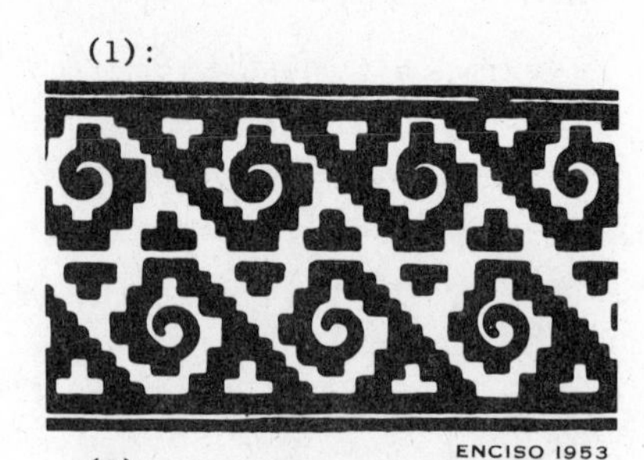

ENCISO 1953

(2):

HOLM 1965

(3):

ENCISO 1953

(4):

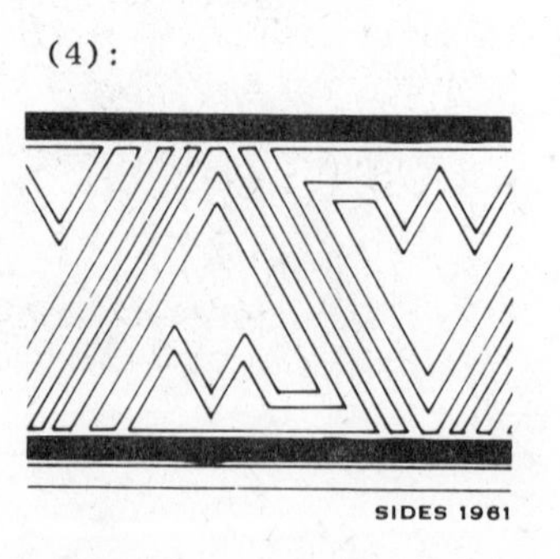

SIDES 1961

(5):

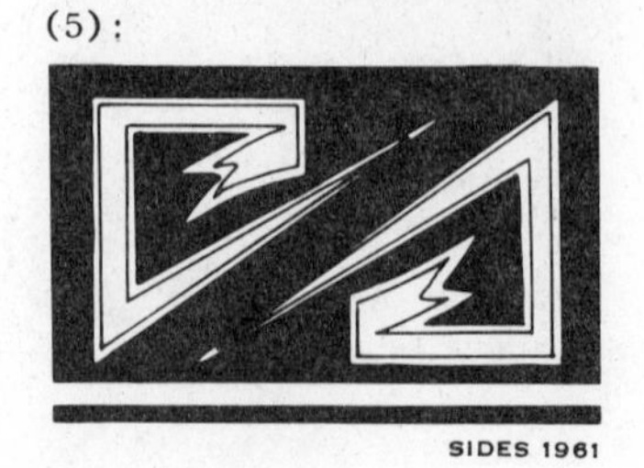

SIDES 1961

III.A.7.b. Corners

Corners are a matter of the radius of the angle at the terminal junction of two lines. A corner may be (1) *sharp* or "crisp" or it may be (5) *rounded.* A sharp corner is not necessarily a sharp point.

(1):

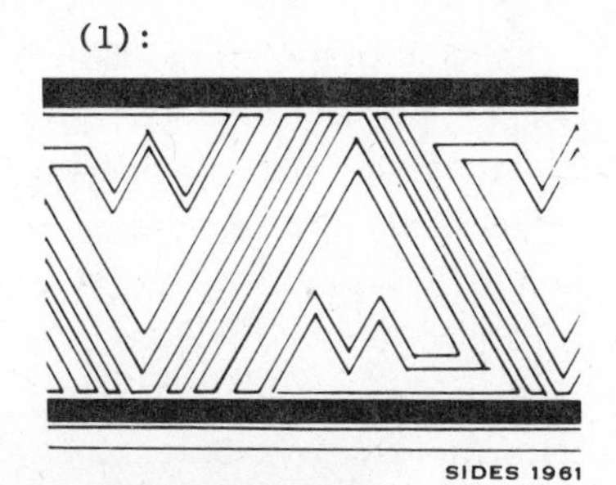

SIDES 1961

(2):

ENCISO 1953

(3):

ENCISO 1953

(4):

ENCISO 1953

(5):

HOLM 1965

III.A.8. Simple Figures

There is a great variety of simple abstract linear forms or shapes such as zigzags, spirals, multiwave lines, triangles, circles, and the like, to which form-meanings have been attributed. In describing an art style, the frequent occurrence of any such forms is a necessary part of the account, and *Notes and Queries* in Anthropology (1961: 313) gives a terminology for some of these figures. However, it is well to remember that a term such as "triangle" is an abstraction representing a number of possible figures, with a variety of form-qualities. The simplest figures are also form-qualities such as points, spirals, arcs and circles, multi-wave curves, and the like. Even these are abstractions which in use vary in form, by weight of line, color, and placement in the field. The objective here is to reduce all forms to the basic form-qualities.

This category is omitted on the tally sheets as the recording and analysis of such qualities lies in a different frame of reference, as do content and subject matter. Consideration of this category is included in the discussion because many of the interpretations of such figures can be applied to the appropriate form-qualities. A full description of an art style should include, on a separate scale, a record of the amount and kind of simple figures that are used, just as the representational content should be separately described. Such levels of descriptive analysis would clarify the interpretive distinctions between the symbolic meaning that is assigned to geometric and representational figures in a particular culture, and the form-meanings or metaphors which the form-qualities may convey.

III.B. Structural Lines

The arrangement of forms in a composition can usually be conceived in linear terms, resulting in what may be called *structural lines.* While there are a number of ways of analyzing compositional arrangement, the emphasis on structural lines permits categorization into a few basic types which are adequate for the majority of graphic art forms. Certain of these categories overlap with those of symmetry, but may be used where symmetry is lacking. The principle directions or forms of structural lines are: *Horizontal* (H), *Vertical* (V), *Diagonal* (D), *Simple curve* (⌒), *Reverse curve* (~), *Radial* (*), and *Circular* (o). The categories used consist of these types and combinations thereof.

III.B. Structural Lines

III.B. Structural Lines

Parallel Diagonals (D‖D):

Opposed Diagonals (D x D):

Radial (*):

DISSELHOFF & LINNE 1960

Simple Curves (⌒):

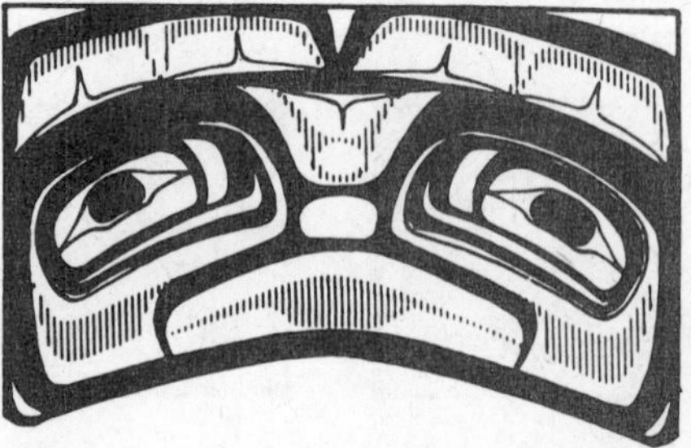

HOLM 1965

III.C. Borders and Outlines

III.C.1. Border: an external boundary around the work as a whole. Boundary in this sense is essentially linear, although the border may in fact consist of some kind of a frame, or band, containing design elements or units. A work bounded only by the shape of the object itself does not have a border in this sense. It should surround more than two-thirds of the periphery. An incomplete border is one with gaps of any size, continuous or discontinuous.

III.C.2. Divisions refers to the division of the whole into fields or arbitrary sections separated by lines, bands, or even by a linear strip in which design is conspicuously absent. In the case of boundaries surrounding design units, there is space between the bounded units, and between the boundaries and the figure.

Multiple border, section division:

III.C.3. Outlines follow the shape of a figure closely, and leave little or no space between the outline and the figure.

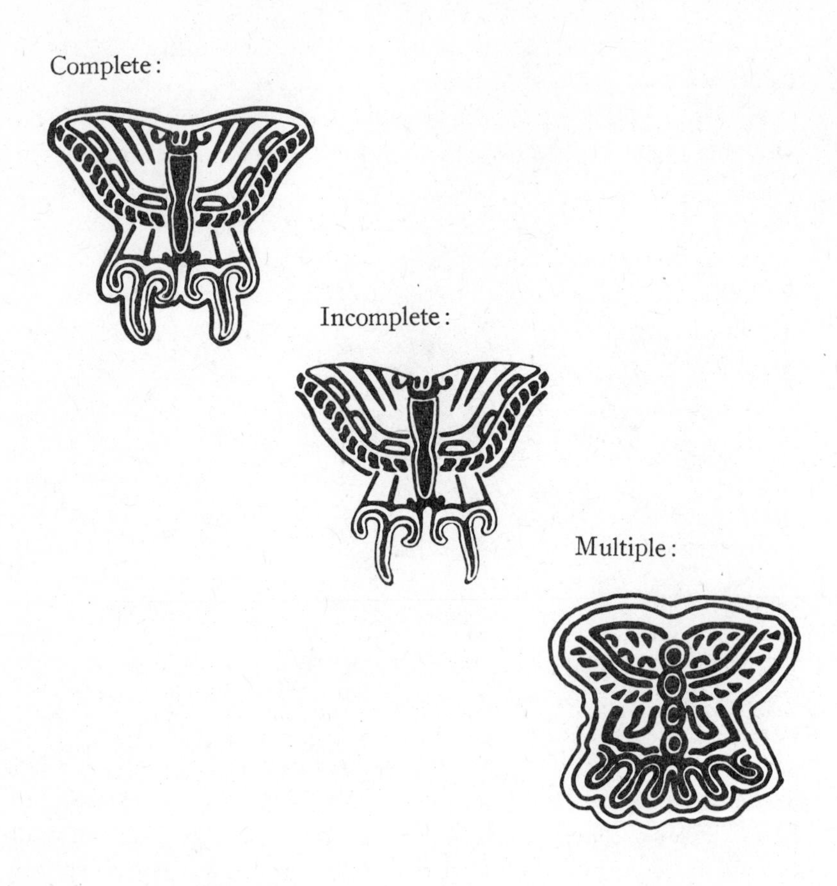

LINES AND LINEARITY OF DRYPAINTINGS

III. Treatment of Lines

Drypaintings employ the mode of line and local color, with somewhat of an emphasis on line which varies considerably from painting to painting. Some can be reproduced by line alone so as to convey a good deal of the effect; others depend to a far greater degree on contrasting areas of color. If an emphasis on line relates to an emphasis on the intellect and on control, then it is on these qualities that the drypaintings lay stress in general, an interpretation consistent with the function of the works and with the knowledge that goes with them.

III.A.1. Degree of Linearity

As to the relation of the linear to the sequential in the sense of the perception of time in historical and evolutionary terms, there seems to be little of relevance in the Navajo case, except possibly to note that the Navajo mythological concept of successive worlds has an element of evolutionary perspective which differs from the more cyclical view of pre-Columbian Mesoamerica. The emphasis on linearity cannot be said in this case to stem from the kind of thinking imposed by a literate tradition.

As to the individualism suggested by Schuster as being related to emphasis on two-dimensionality and on line, the Navajo case rather supports than contradicts this interpretation. The two-dimensionality is not complete, as sculptured effects are frequently used; linearity is not extreme, neither is the individualism in Navajo life. "Community of feeling with the environment" is considered a feature of Navajo religion, hence Schuster's hypothesis does not seem to fit in this regard.

On an absolute scale, or when compared to European drawings, the emphasis on line may not seem very striking. But when compared to the Pueblo drypaintings from which they are derived, Navajo work shows a considerable emphasis on, and development of, drawing. For all the elaborate symbolism and stylization, the forms are explored well beyond the necessities of symbolic representation. The elaboration of the Navajo drypainting as compared to the Pueblo altar assemblage can be attributed to the greater mobility of the Navajo, and this may well have been a factor in the transformation, but many of the objects used are not really so difficult to obtain or transport, and substitution in the form of objects would be as feasible as substitution in the form of pictures. In terms of human choice, what may have happened was that when a symbolic item was not available, the choice of substitution favored drawing because Navajo like to draw.

If we follow out the implications of Hill's insights into the drawing process, we can conclude that elements used in ritual which are carefully drawn are not only more thoroughly controlled but are more thoroughly analyzed and understood than are objects used symbolically. So the emphasis of the Navajo on drawing and on line may be related to an interest in examining and exploring experience in a way foreign to the Pueblo; a drawing is more analytic than an assemblage.

III.A.2. Weight of Lines

The lines in drypaintings are seldom strong or heavy. They are not thick and do not always present strong value contrast, although they are always contrasting in hue. On the other hand, they are never fuzzy, broken, faded, or dim, but are clear, discrete and definite.

Most of the interpretations of weight of line are based on the idea of unconscious motor expressiveness and have a clinical reference, and so refer to extremes. While drypainting is technically quite a free medium and could be very responsive to motor expression by the individual, this factor is probably minimal. The paintings are not individual productions, and the forms are so stylized that motor expressiveness is controlled. The kind of skill which is used demands a high degree of control of a rather mechanical nature; the skill is not combined with such qualities as flexible wrist movement or clever manipulation such as to be found in Japanese brush work, much less with the consciously achieved expressiveness of that medium. The lines have an evenness of width and a sureness of shape that requires care, patience, and concentration, although perfection is not required.

Longman's interpretation seems to be the most applicable. He contrasts hard, dark, and clearly defined lines which suggest strength, precision, and confidence, with soft, blurred, and varied lines which suggest delicacy, sensitivity, timidity, and weakness. Drypainting lines certainly suggest precision and confidence, but the strength, based on the sureness of the line, is balanced by a delicacy of width which enhances the feeling of precision and suggests that the strength lies in the realm of control rather than in force. This is certainly very much in keeping with the message of the art form.

III.A.3. Shape of Lines

In almost all of the paintings there is a balance between curved and straight lines, with somewhat more emphasis on straightness. Interpretations of these qualities hold that straight lines suggest: rigidity, stiffness, severity, and harshness; strength and masculinity; sharpness of attention and perception; general alertness and rational-volitional functioning; and that they are psychologically definite and somewhat cold. Curved lines, on the other hand suggest ease, growth, well-being, and grace; flexibility, suppleness, feminity, and flowing movement; emotionality and a capacity for adjustment and identification. Mills points out that in drypaintings "straight and angular lines are rarely separated from curves—each controls the other."

The interpretation of the "angular masculine assertiveness" of the art, as opposed to the "submissiveness" of the Navajo premises, is misleading. As I have said, the emphasis on the straight and angular is by no means overriding, and I find it very dubious to consider the premises of "do nothing" or "escape" as submissiveness. There is no suggestion of equality of submissiveness in the discussion of these premises by Kluckhohn and Leighton (1946) to which Mills refers. Emphasis on the bipolar alternatives of assertiveness and submission strike me as being ethnocentric, allowing no room for the Indian stress on endurance, for example. The use of the word "submissive" in characterizing the Navajo strikes a very false note, and "assertive" seems equally inappropriate.

As to the "obvious equation . . . with the duality of male and female" which is so often the principle interpretation of straight and curved lines, the tendency of paintings to combine both is certainly consistent with the Navajo view: "everything exists in two parts, male and female, which belong together and complete each other". (Kluckhohn and Leighton 1962:311). However, the usage of straight and curved lines for anthropomorphic figures does not suggest that the Navajo necessarily associate curved lines with the female and straight with the male. Anthropomorphic supernatural figures, with the exception of the rainbow, are drawn with straight lines except where they, in whole or in part, are portrayed by a full circle. Heads are sometimes round and sometimes rectangular. There is no consistent usage of these two forms in terms of male and female. Reichard (1950: 178) interprets the usage as a matter of relative power between the figures shown in the particular painting: The round headed forms represent the more powerful supernaturals. Where the painting shows both male and female figures, the female figures have rectangular heads. This runs counter to the association with strength as well as with the masculinity of the straight line. The potency of the circle in Navajo thought is clearly the operating symbol.

Curved lines are frequently used in the depiction of places, and are predominating in the drawings of plant and animal forms, and of the rainbow. The interpretation which may be relevant here is the association of the curved line with the idea of organic growth. However, preference for straight or curved lines is one of the choices often left to the individual, which suggests that whatever the form-meanings they are not very important in these contexts except as expressions of personality.

> It seems that the curvature or angularity of the Big Snake people depends on the taste of the painter, who often lays out a pattern in angles and fills in the spaces to make them arcs or curves. (Newcomb and Reichard n. d.:54)

According to the hypotheses of Barry, the tendency to straightness is associated with a lack of severity in socialization. This hypothesis is not supported insofar as straight lines predominate over curved ones, and if we accept the judgment of Whiting and Child (1953) concerning socialization among the Navajo. Fischer's revised hypothesis that a preponderance of straight lines over curved is connected with female solidarity in residence is supported.

A more refined analysis would probably place emphasis on the kind of curves used (i. e., the rarity of "free-flowing" and reverse curves), their relationship to the straight lines, and the use of shape in relation to the symbolic attributes of various classes of figures.

III.A.4. Relation of Lines to Each Other

In examining the use of component lines in their relationship to each other, one finds that there is actually more use of lines oblique to each other than parallel or perpendicular. This comes as rather a surprise, because the effect of the parallel lines is so much more noticeable. The figures recorded show, however, that oblique lines are far less usual than expected by chance, since nearly 80% of lines should be oblique (cf. p. 87). (The record is based on the *number* of lines rather than on total length of lines of one type or another). Oblique lines are characteristically short and used for detail, while parallel lines are most evident as long lines outlining the figures. Hence the ordering effect of parallel lines is more obvious than the tension and vitality of the oblique ones.

If one considers the number of oblique lines characteristic of sandpainting, Barry's hypothesis of the relationship of oblique lines to severity of socialization is not supported, as Whiting and Child rate the Navajo as above the median in socialization anxiety. However, a case might be made for the way oblique lines are used in relation to the figures, as they are humanized and controlled by the long parallel lines which are, furthermore, often in the "strong" vertical position. This could be seen as related to the overcoming of anxiety which is consistent with the function of the paintings.

A similar case might be made for the interpretation of need for achievement as correlated with oblique lines. If the oblique lines of the figures relate to need for achievement, then this is muted by the need for harmony.

III.A.5. Relation of Lines to Edges

The situation in regard to the relation of lines to the edges is similar to the relation of lines to each other. The long vertical (or radial) lines are more evident than the short diagonal ones which are numerically used about as frequently.

Horizontal lines are less frequent, but form an important element in the composition, as long or fairly long horizontals often form a base upon which the figures stand.

If the vertical means strength, then the emphasis on vertical lines suggests the power of the supernaturals which are portrayed. This strength, according to the interpretations, relates to uprightness, although in Navajo mythology the supernaturals are not conspicuously moral.

III.A.6. Line Endings

All varieties of line endings are found to some degree. The meeting of lines is most common, endless the least, for although the figures are often completely outlined, different parts of the figure are outlined in different colors, so that lines meet at the junctures, as of the head and neck. Free ends are far less common than terminal markers, but are by no means rare.

Free ends are usually found only in small figures composed of a group of parallel or radial lines. Most apparently free lines have a small terminal marker in the form of a contrasting color, suggesting, to follow Hoebel, a limit on the tendency to explore or adapt.

III.A.7.a. Use of Points

One of the most interesting things about the use of points is the fact that they are almost or even completely absent from some paintings and in others form almost the whole design. The paintings in which points are used so extensively are those in which arrows form a principle theme, and those in which the supernaturals appear in flint armor. The use of points is not confined to the areas depicting the arrows or the armor, but extends to the whole composition. Flint, according to Reichard, (1950: 557) is a symbol of protection.

In the Shooting Chant, for example, the Heroes are shown clad in flint armor in the "House of Points":

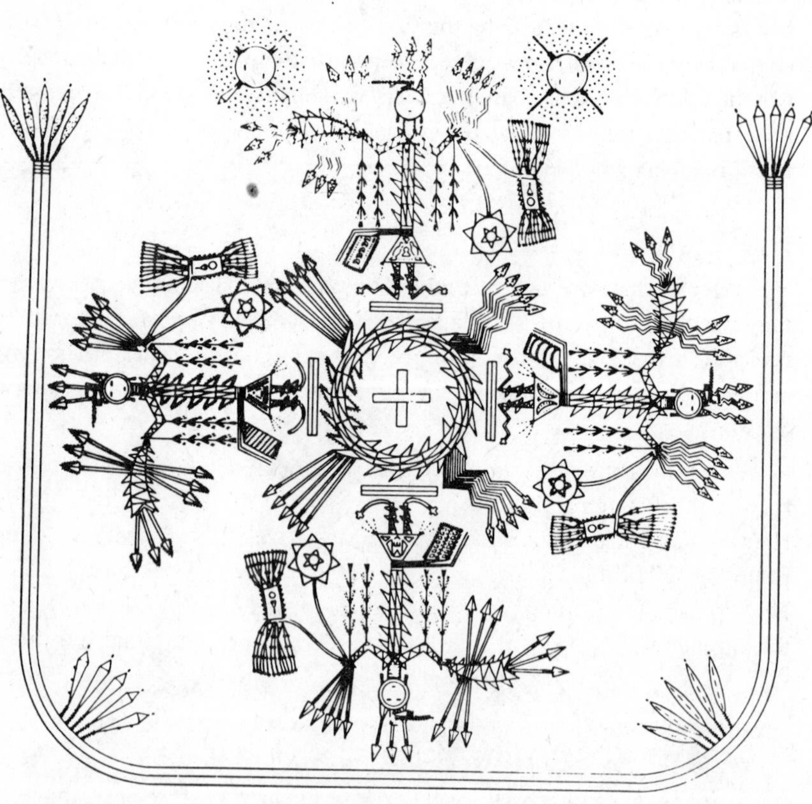

House of Points REICHARD 1939

Many of the paintings, especially those depicting plant and animal forms, have rather few really pointed forms. While acute angles are found quite often, the effect often differs from that of points because the converging lines meet a third line before meeting each other:

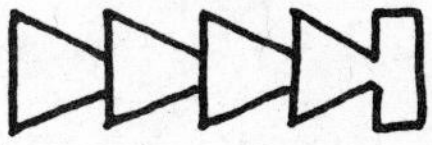

The rather specific use of points for certain definite situations suggests a controlled, vocabulary-like use rather than an unconscious expression of aggression, but the meaning is definitely related to aggressive feeling—seen as a necessity for protection.

III.A.7.b. Corners

Meetings of lines and angles of various kinds are characteristically crisp in all the paintings. That this is not solely a matter of the perfectionism found in the copies is attested to by the fact that the less exact samples in Wyman also exhibit this characteristic.

The only interpretation we have for this quality is that of Waehner who says that rounded corners indicate a personality which is "introversive, creative, restrained and preoccupied with self". She does not say whether the sharp corners indicate a personality which is extroverted, non-creative, unrestrained and unconcerned about self. If this is implied, it hardly fits the Navajo case.

III.B. Structural Lines

The most characteristic structural lines are vertical ones in the rectangular paintings, and radial ones in the circular paintings. It will be remembered that the two forms are corresponding in the Navajo view, as the base in one becomes the center in the other, often representing a base on which supernaturals are standing.

The various interpretations of vertical lines include "virility, rigidity, strength, static uprightness", "assertive and masculine drives", "uprightness and determination", "stationary—give stillness, quietness and peace". Verticality is also associated with religious sentiments. The Navajo ritual meanings are quite specific, and the esthetic device of the direction of structural lines effectively conveys the ritual meaning:

> The earliest witness of a Navajo ceremony noted direction as a symbolic device. Matthews discussed "the laws of butts and tips" at length and amply illustrated them in his later works. These laws are constantly observed and I need merely summarize their

> significance. Plants, like other living things, are ritualistically dealt with from base to tip, because growth, and therefore life, is upward. The earth may be the ultimate cause of all that is good —reproduction, vegetation, and power of attainment—but it holds within it the evils beaten into it at the War Ceremony. If the directional symbolism, which is relative, not fixed, is to represent growth, the ritualistic act must be upward, but since the sky also furnishes gifts, it must be included. Since rain falls, there must be downward motions. (Reichard 1950:161)

III.C. Borders and Outlines

The distinction between borders and outlines is significant in drypaintings. Most of the forms within the paintings are completely enclosed in outlines, but the whole painting is seldom completely enclosed by a border. Barry rates the Navajo as having relatively few enclosed figures, which is confusing, as this is true only of borders enclosing the whole, and not of figures in any of the usual senses.

III.C.1. Borders

The idea of line as a boundary which controls and which is a protection is very strong in Navajo symbolism. This idea of control makes clear the sometimes confusing meaning of open and closed figures, especially circles, in Navajo thought. The essence of the matter seems to lie in the size of the area (or what the area symbolizes). If the area is small enough so that a person can encompass it in some way it may be entirely enclosed by a boundary. If a person or the People are within the area that others might control, they must not be completely bounded lest they be enclosed and controlled.

III.C.3. Outlines

Many of the lines in drypaintings are in fact outlines, and the idea of control which is so commonly associated with outlining is consistent with the usage here. In the area of content, what is controlled is the supernatural in the form of the Holy People and other supernaturals portrayed. In the area of form-meaning, all or most shapes are controlled by line, as are areas of color. Color is said to be related to emotion, so the implication is that emotion is controlled by line. It is of interest here that the larger areas of color, and particularly the strong red and black areas, are often given multiple outlines with as many as four lines.

Although black is one of the hues of the sandpainting palette, the outlines are not usually in black, and are not heavy. This suggests not so much control by suppression as the moderating effect of the "opposite yet related" quality. Colors are usually paired symbolically, and the pairs, which are both associated and opposite, are the ones which outline each other.

If by "enclosed figures" Kavolis and Fischer mean the figures with line around them, then their hypotheses are not supported by the Navajo material. Outlining and even multiple outlining is highly characteristic of Navajo art, but the social organization is far from hierarchical, the value orientation rather collateral than lineal (Romney and Kluckhohn 1961:318). Barry's implied hypothesis that the predominance of "enclosed figures" is related to severity of socialization is supported, in the Navajo case, by the rating of Whiting and Child (1953:245).

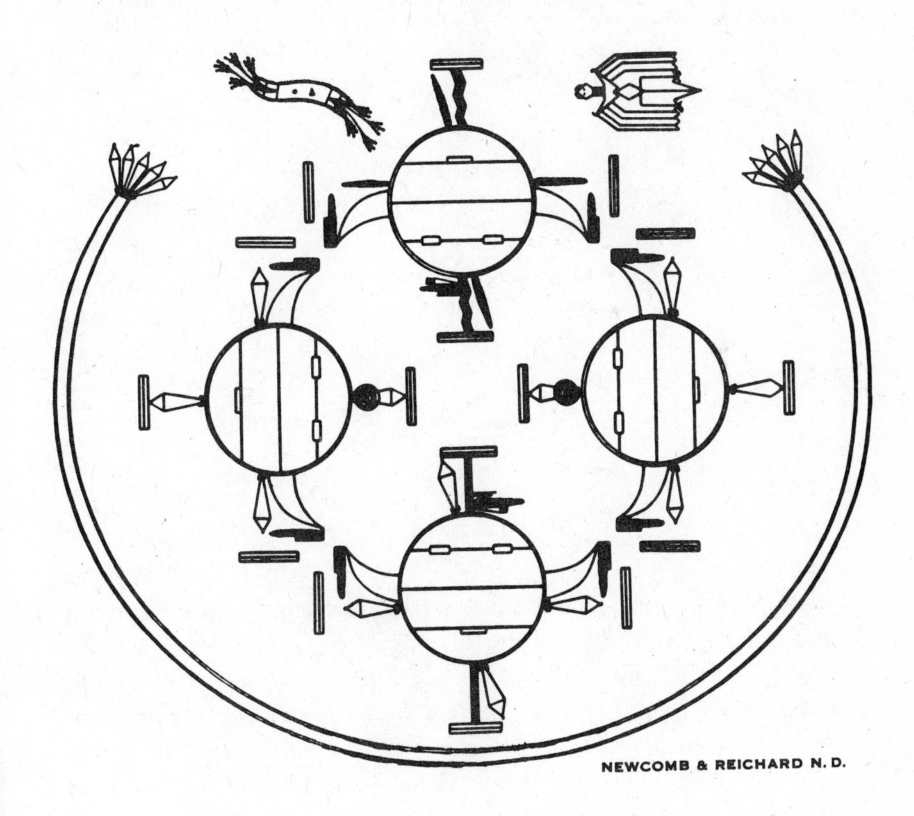

NEWCOMB & REICHARD N. D.

5

Color

Of all the aspects of graphic art, the one on which there is most agreement is color: color implies emotion. And yet color is the most difficult to consider cross-culturally, simply because the colors used by any people depend greatly on the environment and on the technology. In a developed technology the artist has a full range of pigments at his command and he uses certain ones by choice, according to the dictates of whatever psychological and cultural factors may be operating, and in accordance with what he wants to say in a particular work. In societies with simpler technologies, the artist's palette is less a matter of choice than of necessity, although his choice among the possibilities open to him may be significant. And here we come to another difficulty. We simply do not have much information on what peoples have used, and still less on the possibilities for choice. Many forms of art have not been preserved or recorded. Organic colors are often fugitive, and the art forms (or parts of them) are represented in museums by brown shadows of what must have been their former brilliance. Color photography did not appear until many art forms had disappeared or been affected by industrial technologies. Very few show art in context, and those of museum specimens are often affected by being placed against brilliantly colored, culturally irrelevant backgrounds. Verbal accounts are few.

Because color is not always true in photographs, nor are the values in black and white photographs, the very best color data we have is recorded by field copies or sketches of art works, in the few cases where such exist.

MEANINGS ATTRIBUTED TO QUALITIES OF COLOR

IV.A. Emphasis on Color

Several interpretations of the degree of emphasis on color come from the literature on the Rorschach test:

> CR color responses are very significant because they pertain to emotions as these are commonly differentiated from thoughts and actions. (Piotrowski 1957:217)
>
> The more color-dictated associations, the more the individual is capable of reacting with verve toward, and a warm feeling for, his fellow humans.
>
> "Color love" can form one factor in the cluster projecting too much warmth, which is really heat.
>
> . . . inability to react to color is the mark of the person insensitive to the world's exhilirating values. (Beck 1952:45)
>
> *The parallelism between color emphasis and strong emotions* is supported by the following findings:
>
> a) Children tend to express a primary interest in color (in contrast to line and form) during a stage of development when they are operating largely at an impulsive level. Their expressed interest in color decreases as their impulsive emotional drives become tempered and as controlled adaptive behavior comes to the fore.
>
> b) Color tends to be more intense and persistent among girls than among boys. Here, again, a parallelism with emotions is reflected, for girls have been found by many investigators to manifest emotion more than do boys.
>
> c) When a group of children who emphasized color was compared with a group of children who focused largely on line and form, the latter group stood out for their greater self-control, their greater concern with external stimuli, and their higher frequency of reasoned (in contrast to impulsive) behavior. (Alschuler and Hattwick 1947:15)
>
> The color scores on the [Rorschach] test reveal the subject's emotional relationships to his environment. To gain an accurate picture of the emotional life we must understand the interrelationships between form and color. Where color is used apart from form we expect to find impulsive emotionality. The more important form becomes in the concepts using color the more the emotion is brought under control. (Bell 1948:123)

IV.B. Hue

A great many of the interpretations of the meaning of color are symbolic associational interpretations of a particular hue. For example:

> . . . green, the color of vegetation and nature, and in folklore a symbol of hope . . . red, which is traditionally the symbolic color of feeling and passion . . . Blue often denotes the function of thinking . . . black, which is the color of darkness, depression and death. (Jung et al., 1964:282ff.)

However, Longman uses the terms "form-meaning" as well as "symbolic meaning" for interpretations of some hues:

Color	Form-meaning	Symbolic meaning
pale green	exquisite delicacy and lyric joy	sea foam
golden yellow	richness, well-being, radiant satisfaction	gold or sunflowers
red	warmth, excitement, buoyancy	flames
dark purple	aristocratic dignity, pride, affluence	a king's robes (Longman 1949:12)

These interpretations are analogous to the meanings given simple geometric forms, and could be investigated in the same way. That is to say, a cross-cultural compilation of such interpretations could be made and analyzed for underlying similarities and clusters of meanings.

Since the meanings of warm and cool color categories are described as being physiological or based on universal experiences they fall in a somewhat different class than the symbolic associations of particular colors and so are included as hypotheses here.

> In most contexts, the hues on the so-called "cool" side of the circle of hues will have a quieting, even depressing effect. Certainly the shadows of night are more restful and suitable for sleep than the light of day. If carried far enough, the emphasis on cool hues can express despondency. (Beam 1958:722)

> The warm colors are likely to excite, while the cold colors tend to calm . . .

> Rorschach noted that people who tried to control the intensity of their emotions preferred the blue and the green and avoided the red areas of his set of blots. (Piotrowski 1957:230)

The chief psychological difference between responsiveness to warm and responsiveness to cold colors seems to be one of degree of involvement with the environment. Those persons who prefer the cold colors and react more strongly to them than to the warm colors maintain in their emotional attitudes, be they positive or negative, a reserve, a detachment, or a natural avoidance of the extreme degree of attraction or repulsion. Those individuals who prefer the warm colors and who respond readily to them surrender themselves much more easily to the influence of their emotional impulses, regardless of their quality, and establish much more intimate and more intense contacts with the environment than do those who prefer cold colors. (ibid.:229)

Form Characteristic	Quality Suggested	Value Orientation
Green and blue colors (and somber tones)	Affective restraint	Doing
Red and yellow colors (and bright tones)	Affective spontaneity	Being
Brown and grey (black) colors	Alienation from "life"	Being-in-Becoming

(Kavolis 1965:7)

1. Warm colors such as red, orange, and yellow (particularly in full saturation or intensity and at appropriate value)—exciting, magnetic, buoyant, open, frank, sanguine, radiant, passionate.
2. Cool colors such as blue and green—soothing, quiet, reserved, inhibitory, depressing, aloof, repellent, haughty. (Longman 1949:9)

IV.C. Intensity

The terms *high* and *low intensity* signify an emphasis of either vitality or repose in the realm of direct visual stimulation. In addition, our mental associations give intensities much the same capacity to express gaiety, strength, and tragedy, repose, despondency, and moods as does the scale of values. (Beam 1958:726)

. . . intense colors can express gaiety or love of life, even the highest spiritual exaltation. But since vitality and optomism can turn to frustrated bitterness, a harmony of high intensitites may sometimes express tension, anger, or violence. (ibid.:729)

On the whole, . . . brilliant hues have signified a general youthfulness of outlook. Children and primitive artists have always loved them, as have those simple or prosperous societies which retained a confident outlook toward life. (ibid.)

> If a society grows older and wiser without becoming cynical, its color preferences are likely to show a trend toward harmonies of lower intensity. (ibid.:728)

> Bright colors are cheerful, optomistic, spirited, jovial. (Longman 1949:9)

IV.D. Value

> Generally speaking, a predominance of high values will signify a high degree of vitality. (Beam 1958:724)

> Dark values, or absence of light, connote lesser energy which is soothing and reposeful in proportion to its lesser stimulation. Ideologically, however, it may have a number of depressing, morbid or tragic meanings, notably the suggestion of death. Evil and the so-called "powers of darkness" have been associated for centuries. (ibid.)

> A harmonious emphasis of the darker values has been the stock in trade of all artists who wished to express an air of repose or a mood of mystery, sadness, infinity or tragedy. (ibid. :725)

> Shading evidences a predominately emotional personality make-up, tending towards passionateless when it is dark, toward great sensitivity when it is light. (Kinget 1952:95)

> The basic, most important and unqualified definition of the meaning of all shading responses . . . states that the ShR control the outward manifestations of strength and energy, determining the release or inhibition of action tendencies. (Piotrowski 1957:261)

He goes on to say that dark or black color responses show a tendency to decrease fear and anxiety by doing something, while responses prompted by the light shades of grey show the tendency to relieve anxiety by doing less. (Note that this is essentially a contradiction to Beam's interpretation.)

> All perceptanalysis writers agree that the shading responses are indicators of fear and anxiety. (ibid.:253)

> In Rorschach's definitions of all types of ShR which he distinguished occur the concepts of depression, caution, timidity associated with emotional excitation, sense of personal inadequacy—all of which boils down to inhibition. The definitions differ in the emphasis placed on depression. The light ShR, prompted by the grey hues, were less intimately connected with depression by

Rorschach than the dark ShR and reactions to white as a color. (ibid.:244)

Dark colors are reserved, serious, somber, gloomy, inaccessible, pessimistic, depressing, melancholy, morbid. (Longman 1949:9)

Shading. The shading responses as described by Bender were of two varieties: those which were characterized by diffusion (*hd*), found to be prompted by the general inner mood of the subject as distinguished from the emotional contact with the environment (*color*); and those which were characterized by the use of shading as a surface aspect (*Fb*) which reflect the sensitivity of the individual—the capacity to use sense experiences as an aid in adjustment. An excess of these (*Fb*) responses would indicate an oversensitivity approaching sensuality, an absence of them, a lack of refinement in contact with the objective world. Bender noted especially the lightness or darkness of shading responses, finding that, in the case of *hd,* the dark diffuse responses were associated with unpleasantly toned, and the light with pleasantly toned moods. Likewise the light (*Fb*) responses stand out from the dark in showing the delicacy of the sensitivity as contrasted with morbidity, depression, and anxiety. In the dark (*Fb*) responses the individual is manifesting a restrained, overconscientious type of adaptiveness. (Bell 1948:127)

IV.E. Combinations of Color

In the interpretive literature derived from clinical psychology, little attention is paid to color combinations, as the combined response analysis in the Rorschach follows a different line of organization, and drawing analysis, such as that of Machover, do not deal with color.

Most of such interpretations in the literature of art are imbedded in discussions of particular works, but Beam makes a few general statements which give an idea of the nature of this kind of interpretation:

Two characteristics stand out when sequences of color are considered in relation to expression. One is the power of gradation to suggest subtlety, sophistication, control, and the sense of repose that attends these qualities. The other is the contrasting vitality of alternation, a method of design which bombards the eye with a series of abruptly repeated changes. (Beam 1958:730)

The exciting qualities of alternation carry with them, however, one disadvantage. Their power to stimulate is inevitably attended by a certain obviousness. It is one of the most vital of an artist's resources, but by no means his most refined or mature. (ibid.:732)

In regard to specific works some quotations such as Beam (ibid.:724) show the kind of interpretations used: "The use of low intensities in conjunction with bluish hues . . . add to the reposeful effect," and "Warm hues in low intensities add to the over-all effect of warm-hearted social grace."

> Alternations may vary in their implications of energy content according to a simple rule. Color vibrations, as they are called, can be intensified up to a certain point by increasing the number of contrasting factors—that is, by striking the eye with an accelerated variation of hues, values, and intensities, and a larger number of units . . . But if this subdividing process is carried too far, a turning point in effectiveness is passed. A surface dotted with minute colors misses the maximum visual impact. (Beam 1958:730)

5. Paintings in monotones or close harmonies are the most calm and unexciting, because emphatic responses to the colors do not clash.
6. Paintings in complementary colors are more stimulating, but the complementation is a quieting factor, like symmetrical balance.
7. Paintings which are in colors which are not analagous and not complementary are the most exciting, turbulent, or discordant and irritable, e. g. red and blue, or red and yellow.
8. By combining colors appropriately, one may express the delicate, diaphanous, and hazy; the spacious, sympathetic, contemplative, reflective, and dignified; the restless, kaleidoscopic, and spontaneous or the stolid and prosaic; the harmonious or the discordant and treacherous, etc.
9. Yellow added to green tends to make it sickly or bilious, irritable, peevish, unreliable. Blue added to green tends to check its good nature, and increase its reflectiveness and strength of purpose. Every combination has some character. There is no inherently bad combination. (Longman 1949:9)

PROPOSED DEFINITIONS OF VARIOUS ASPECTS OF COLOR

IV.A. Emphasis on Color

By this is meant principally how "colorful" a work is, in the sense of the variety of hues and their intensity. The scale goes from (1) no emphasis on color to (5) very colorful.

IV.B. Hue

Hue is what is usually thought of as "color"; the blueness or redness or greenness of a color. Hue may be thought of as the position of a color in a color ring or color circle, sometimes called a scale of hues. Below is a color ring based on the primary hues of pigments:

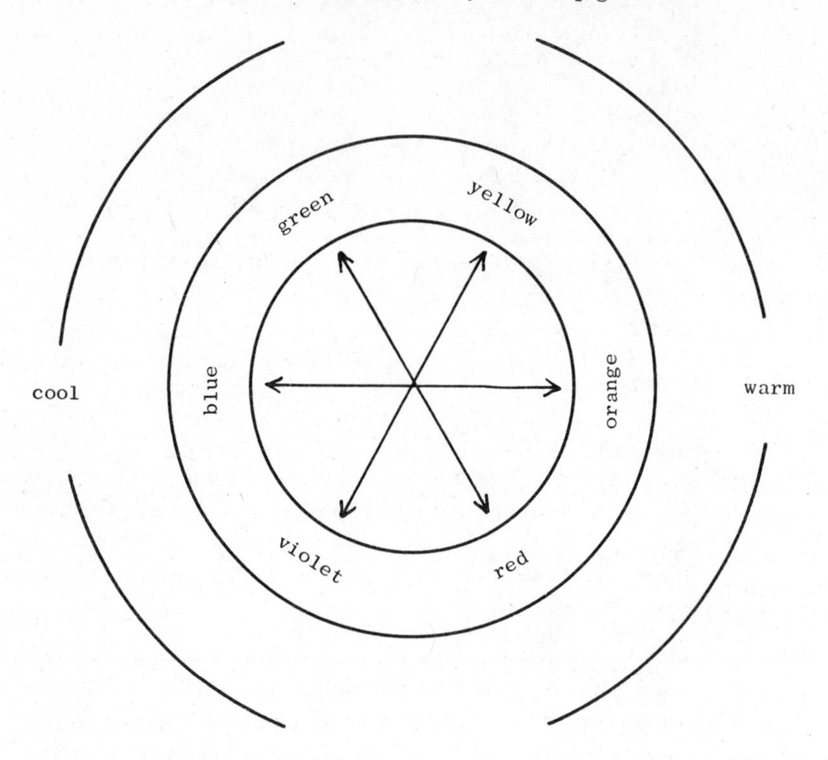

The number of hues available to an artist, like their intensity, is largely a matter of the environment and the technology of the culture to which the artist belongs. Studies of the perception of color cross-culturally have centered on hue and on the naming of segments of the scale of hues. For example, the Navajo word for "blue" is said to represent a hue on the green side of our spectrum blue, while "green" is on the yellow side of our green.

About 150 hues can be distinguished by many persons in our culture, but the artist usually limits his "palette" to a much smaller number. He often consciously constructs for himself a very specific limited scale. With less self-conscious artists the scale of hues may be similarly limited by the symbolic meaning of hues as well as by technological limitations. It is very possible that many such limited palettes are also chosen for esthetic reasons, or for unconscious expressive ones. The scale indicates the actual number of readily distinguishable hues used.

IV.C. Intensity

Intensity is sometimes called "purity" or "saturation". It refers to the brilliance or strength of a color. A color with a low degree of intensity is weak or dull. The intensity of color available in materials the artist uses depends on technology and environment. The scale runs from lowest to highest for the work as a whole.

IV.D. Value

Value, which is sometimes called "tone", refers to the lightness or darkness of a color. Any color can be light or dark without changing hue or intensity.

In Rorschach interpretations the term "shading" refers to response to variation in value. This can be readily seen not only from the nature of the responses so classified, but also from the fact that such value gradations in the blots themselves originally resulted from uneven printing. Similarly, the word "shading" in the Machover and Kinget drawing interpretations refers to the giving of dark or light tones to certain areas with the pencil. However, in both Rorschach and drawing analyses, some types of value gradation are primarily a matter of the expression of space depth. Gradation of value used to express space depth is sometimes known as tonal perspective, and where the interpretation seems to be chiefly a matter of this quality, it is treated under the heading of perspective. On the tally sheets, it is the degree of contrast in values which is to be recorded.

IV.E. Combinations of Color

It can readily be seen that even when the possibilities of hue, value, and intensity are limited (either by availability or choice) to a far smaller number than the eye is capable of perceiving, the possible number of combinations is very great.

By the organization of these possibilities under more general categories, the artists (consciously or unconsciously) and the analyst of art (quite consciously) make the relationships more manageable. The usual approach is to consider the ways in which the various aspects of color are in harmony with each other, and the ways in which they are contrasted. Hues can be harmonious or contrasting, as can values and even intensities. So one can talk in terms of harmonious values used in conjunction with contrasting hues and harmonious intensities.

The aspect of this complex situation which is included on the tally sheets is the contrast of hues, from very low contrast, harmony (1), to very great contrast (5).

COLOR IN NAVAJO DRYPAINTINGS

IV.A. Emphasis on Color

Color is very important in drypaintings. The symbolism of hue is elaborate, and all color use shows great awareness of the importance of hue and value. This awareness and interest in color suggests, according to the psychoanalytic interpretations, verve and a warm feeling for fellow humans, and sensitivity to the "world's exhilarating values."

The colors are, however, of only moderate intensity and are always harmonized and controlled by one device or another.

IV.B. Hue

The drypainting palette consists of seven hues which are never mixed, in addition to the tan or "pinkish tan" of the background. All the hues are not necessarily used in each painting, and although each hue tends to be balanced by another, as in outlining, one hue or another may predominate in a particular work in accordance with its symbolic significance.

> The discussion of colors has shown that each color [hue] has an abstract meaning. White is the color of day, of hope, of newness, of change and commencement. The symbol of divinity, white expresses perfect ceremonial control.
>
> Blue is the color of celestial and earthly attainment, of peace, happiness, and success, of vegetable sustenance. Yellow is the symbol of blessing, of generation, of safety, of promise. Black, sinister but protective, is the color of darkness, night, confusion, smoke, omnipresence, of threat, doubt, indefiniteness, wonder, and origin, of finality. Red is the color of danger, warning, and threat, and of protection from these very things; it also represents flesh and blood. Pink is the color of "deep sky" or a deep water emotion. Grey is the color of the unpersuadable deities, those known to be against man, of the indefinite and fearsome, and protection against them as well. (Reichard 1950:206)
>
> Brown is considered the natural color of persons and of the earth. (ibid.:194)

Grey is not used in drypainting, and as a matter of fact "blue" is actually a neutral grey which appears blue in contrast to the background.

Although there is a ritual requirement of balancing hues, the warm background color gives a prevalently warm tone to drypaintings which may be even more marked than is indicated in the ratings because no paper quite captures the warm tone of the preferred hue of sand.

The interpretive hypotheses are in accord in regarding the warm hues as being related to warm emotions: spontaneity, excitement, response to emotional impulses, emotional relationship to the environment. There are, however, several possible ways in which these rather general meanings can be used to interpret the sandpainting message. Because the warm hues are of moderate intensity, i. e., are soft rather than brilliant, the effect is not one of high excitement, and these warm impulsive emotions can be seen as being controlled by well-delineated form, by pattern, and by balancing and pairing with the colder colors. This could be interpreted to mean: (a) everything is in order so enjoy the warm spontaneous emotions, or (b) the warm spontaneous emotions have to be kept under control because they are dangerous, or (c) the warm spontaneous emotions have to be kept under control so they can be enjoyed. Subjectively, the effect of the color usage (with the exception of those paintings which have large black areas) brings to mind the phrase the Navajo use concerning Blessing Way: "for good hope".

The interpretations of Kavolis are difficult to apply because they are so general—the warm reds and yellows of drypainting are not bright—brown and grey and black cannot be lumped together in this usage as they have very different qualities. If one takes this interpretation as equivalent to saying that warm hues suggest a "being" value orientation, this is consistent with the various other interpretations of this aspect of hue. However, Romney and Kluckhohn (1961:334) found in their study of Navajo values that "there is almost no question as to the almost unanimous choice of the Doing alternative of the *activity* orientation".

I find nothing in the literature nor in the elaborate color symbolism to indicate that the Navajo use the terms "warm" and "cool" in connection with hue.

IV.C. Intensity

Insofar as can be determined from reproductions and such few examples as I have seen, the colors in all drypaintings are of moderate intensity. No hue varies in intensity within a painting.

IV.D. Value

While the value contrasts due to the colors used are very much the same for all the paintings except Blessing Way, the overall effect of value contrast as recorded above varies because of variation in the size of areas of solid color, particularly black. Some paintings have very few large areas and are quite harmonious or even delicate in effect, while others have quite large areas giving the effect of strong value contrast. Outlines tend to be contrasted as to value as well as hue.

Values tend to be on the high side except for the strong contrasting note provided by the use of black. It is to be noted, however, that the black in most drypaintings is probably not as dark as is shown in reproductions (because the charcoal is mixed with sand to give it body), with the result that the harmonies of value are greater than the latter convey. Both the use of high values and of strong contrast are said to signify "a high degree of vitality".

There is no gradation of value in any hue used in a drypainting. Everywhere that a color is used in a particular work it is of the same value, hue, and intensity.

The complete absence of value gradation or shading is to be noted in regard to the consistent psychological interpretation of anxiety or sensitivity. This interpretation is puzzling if the art form is regarded as a projection, because a "high anxiety level" (Kluckhohn and Leighton 1962:242) is attested to by all students of Navajo personality. Viewed as a communication within the context of a ceremony the function of which is to allay anxiety, the relation of shading to anxiety becomes more plausible.

IV.E. Combinations of Color

The contrasts in hue and to some degree in value which are continually stressed by the ritual requirements are harmonized by several devices: 1) The tendency to limit the size of an area of color which contrasts strongly to adjacent ones, especially in the use of contrasting colors as outlines, 2) the softening color effect of the background color of the sand which often comes between areas of contrast, and 3) the lack of intensity of most pigments.

If color represents emotions, it represents here not only emotions harmonized with each other, but brought under careful control. Color is controlled in drypaintings chiefly by 1) the intricate formality of the design, 2) the use of precise lines to outline all color areas, 3) the limitation of the number of hues, and 4) the fact that hues are never mixed and only occasionally intermingled.

The treatment of color pairs as both associated and opposite is, of course, characteristic of the complementary and inclusive character of the Navajo concept of duality to be found in all forms of categorization, including language, emphasized by C. Kluckhohn (1960) and Reichard (1950).

Color and color symbolism in drypaintings seem to provide another example of the Navajo tendency to achieve desired effects by intricate combination rather than by subtle variation. It is, in fact, in the area of color that this tendency can be most clearly understood, although evident also in the treatment of rhythm and repetition.

6

Perspective

"Perspective" is not a formal quality in the sense of being purely abstract. The term is used for the variety of devices by which representation of three-dimensional reality is portrayed on a flat surface. It is, however, a formal quality in the sense that it would not be included in a content analysis, that is, a classification of what is represented. Therefore it seems practical to include these qualities or devices in the schema of form qualities lest it fall between two stools and be ignored.

MEANINGS ATTRIBUTED TO VARIOUS TYPES OF PERSPECTIVE

V. Perspective

It seems quite amazing to find the frequency with which the various interpreters regard perspective (the projection of three-dimensional form into two-dimensional space) as related to concepts and attitudes about time as well as space. There is really nothing mystical about this; the rationale is contained in Boas's discussion of realism, which brings out the special temporal quality of linear perspective:

> In a graphic representation of objects one of two points of view may be taken: it may be considered as essential that all the characteristic features be shown, or the object may be drawn as it appears at any given moment. In the former case our attention is directed primarily towards those permanent traits that are the most striking and by which we recognize the object, while others that are not characteristic or at least less characteristic, are considered as irrelevant. In the latter case we are interested solely

in the visual picture that we receive at any given moment, and the salient features of which attract our attention.

This method is more realistic than the other only if we claim that the essence of realism is the reproduction of a single momentary visual image and if the selection of what appears a salient feature to us is given a paramount value. (Boas 1927:72)

One cannot reproduce total three-dimensional reality in a two-dimensional form, therefore any two-dimensional reproduction is a selection of characteristics which are considered the most important in conveying the reality of the object to the beholder.

Geometric projection is based on the fact that our minds tell us that men do not actually become smaller; their diminution in scale is only an illusion and a temporary one at that. If the oriental artist elects to depict what his mind knows to be permanently true, he has a reasonable right to ignore the apparent reduction of measure in distant objects and make them as large as any in the foreground. The main fault that we might find within this system is that it does not conform to our point of view. Yet we must admit that it is both consistent and logical . . . Artists who hold to that conception of perception usually place more importance upon the symbolic values of objects than upon appearance. (Beam 1958:212)

Here then lies the implication of time in the depiction of space: the momentary quality of illusionistic projection as against the permanent or essential qualities that are known from observation of the object at various times or from various points of view. It would seem reasonable that a tradition which places great emphasis on illusionistic perspective is trying to capture the fleeting moment. Such an emphasis, of course, can be achieved by the ubiquitous camera. The hypotheses of Kavolis in regard to space depth are based on this idea.

Form Characteristic	Quality Suggested	Value Orientation
Location in clearly depicted depth	Distant events still relevant	Past
Location in front of vaguely recognizable space	Superior importance of present over past	Present
Perspectiveless space	Only extended present real	Present
Abandonment of recognizable space	Time irrelevant or future unknown	Future

(Kavolis 1965:14)

There is a second aspect of illusional perspective emphasized by several observers, and often seen in combination with the attitude toward time; such a projection represents not only a momentary viewpoint, but also a unique spatial one, and hence is related to a specific individual observer.

> Perspective space, existing only for the individual point of view, singles out both painting and beholder and emphasizes a chasm existing between the self and his environment—a chasm that can . . . be bridged only by observation. It seems to connect with the alienation between individual and society. (Mundt 1952:184)
>
> Rorschach explained the meaning of the three-dimensional perspective or vista response:
>
> "There chiaro-oscuro responses emphasize the depth of the picture as a dimension more than any of the other interpretations. Our subject also stresses perspective and in his other interpretations of this kind notes a three-dimensional quality. According to my experience, this indicates a peculiar type of psychological correlation is functioning here. There is a special talent for the appreciation of spatial relationships, of depth and distance, which appears to be correlated with the cautious and measured affectivity with depressed nuances. This talent frequently, perhaps always, is correlated with a feeling of insufficiency, the content of which is feelings of loss of solidity, or instability, of being 'out of joint with the times' ". (Piotrowski 1957:247)

Concerning a society that would use all the devices of illusionistic perspective to achieve a photographic kind of realism, Arnheim has said:

> . . . the eye has been reduced to registering the presence of subject matter—a type of reaction suitable only to a civilization in which ideas have been separated from their concrete manifestations so that the material object is valued only for its own sake as the target of man's social, economic and instinctual strivings. According to H. Kühn, illusionism in the arts is found in civilizations based on exploitation and consumption. Only in such a climate did it become possible seriously to describe art as springing from the desire for reputation, power, fame, wealth, and the love of women, as Freud did in his lectures on psychoanalysis. (Arnheim 1954:114)

Sometimes it seems as if there exists nothing but scorn for those who use illusional perspective, and condescension for those who have not developed it.

But such perspective is not a simple all or none proposition. As Boas pointed out, artists usually modify the momentary appearance with aspects of the more permanent qualities. It can, in fact, be said that it is this quality of transcending the transitory that gives meaning to representational art forms beyond that to be found in the color photograph.

Illusional perspective is actually achieved by a variety of means which are not inseparable; linear projection, overlapping planes, decreasing sharpness of outline, value and hue gradation. While the complete use of illusionistic perspective rules out other types, the various individual means are not necessarily incompatible with other forms. Various combinations are possible. These various devices and modes are seen as having interpretive possibilities aside from, or in addition to, the effect of the whole. The possibilities are by no means simple. The devices of perspective are also relationships of figures in the plane or space of the picture, and the interpretations of social relationships are also involved. The devices of size and overlapping are considered to express social dominance as well as physical distance. The two are not mutually incompatible.

> The intimate union achieved by overlapping is of a peculiar nature. It impairs the completeness of at least one—and mostly all—of the parties concerned. The result is not simply a "relationship", that is, the exchange of energy between independent, serenely intact beings. It is togetherness as interference through mutual modification. By renouncing the clarity of juxtaposition, the artist accomplishes a more subtle and more dramatic interpretation of communion. He shows the tension between the conflicting tendencies involved in social intercourse and the need for safeguarding the integrity of the individual.
>
> . . . overlapping establishes a hierarchy by creating a distinction between dominating and submissive units. A scale of importance leads, through any number of intervening steps, from foreground to background. (Arnheim 1954:105)

Regarding transparency or mutual overlapping, he says, referring to modern art:

> One and the same area was made paradoxically to belong to more than one object, thus destroying the cherished value of well defined property. The same twilight of ambiguity also blotted out the traditional hierarchy of dominance and submission; no longer was one unit whole and in front, the other curtailed and in back. Both were whole and curtailed, in front and in back at the same time, and no decision in favor of either solution was suggested.

> The price to be paid by the intercourse of one individual with another was no longer clear. There was an insistence on completeness, and yet no denying that this integrity was being invaded; and the question as to who was invading whom remained unsolved. Interpenetration undermined also the solidity of the object; . . . thus the pictorial object acquired the transparency of an apparition, which could be suspected of being a product of the mind rather than a thing of matter. (ibid.:122)

The most virtuoso use of perspective devices for expressive effect is considered to be *The Last Supper* of Leonardo da Vinci. Here linear perspective, rather than mere size, is used as a form of "social perspective" to enhance the importance of the figure of Christ and at the same time serves to give great significance to a certain moment in time.

The use of size to indicate importance rather than position in space depth carries its own interpretation in the phrase *social perspective* because it is such a well-known device. The method of indicating three-dimensional form in solid objects by value gradations, usually called shading, is considered by the students of projective drawing to indicate anxiety.

> Any degree or type of shading is considered an expression of anxiety. As with other types of conflict projection, the particular area of the figure that is shaded is considered in the light of its functional significance. (Machover 1957:98)

ISHIKAWA MORONOBU 1625-1694

Use of perspective devices to capture the fleeting moment

PROPOSED DEFINITIONS FOR QUALITIES INVOLVED IN PERSPECTIVE

V. Perspective (Space Projection)

V.A. Illusional Perspective (Space Depth)

Devices used in illusional perspective include *linear perspective, overlapping planes,* and *color perspective,* but each of these devices may be used separately.

Linear perspective—a system of spatial projection conceived as a system of imaginary lines converging on a vanishing point. An inexact linear perspective can be achieved by decreasing the *size* of distant figures without the exactness of proportion used in complete linear perspective. A feeling of space depth may also be conveyed by hiding part of one form by another, which then appears to be in front of it. This use of *overlapping planes* is frequently used where other aspects of illusory perspective are lacking.

Linear:

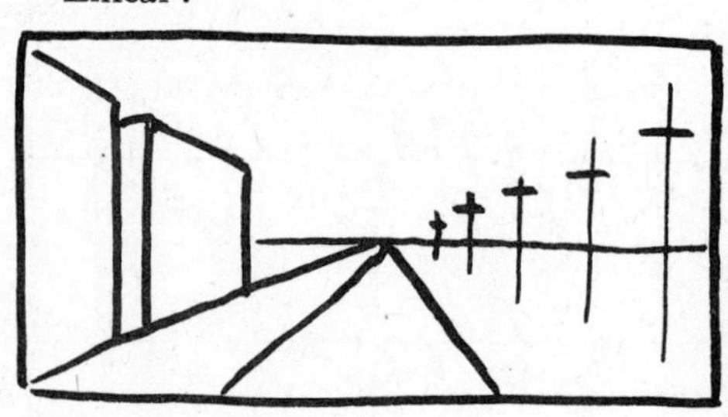

Overlapping planes:

Color perspective, which is often combined with linear perspective, portrays near objects in warm hues, distant ones in cool hues; near ones

Tonal:

Shading:

with high contrast of values, distant ones in neutral values. The latter is sometimes called *tonal* perspective. *Shading* is a form of tonal perspective in which a three-dimensional quality is given to an object or figure by gradations in value on the form itself.

V.B. Geometrical Perspective

Positional perspective uses a convention in which near figures are shown in the lower part of the picture plane, and far objects above them, without difference in size, and often without overlapping. The Maya murals of Bonampak are the best known works of art employing positional perspective.

Diagonal is a similiar convention in which near and far are shown along a diagonal scale from one corner of the picture plane to another. It is sometimes referred to as parallel recession.

Positional:

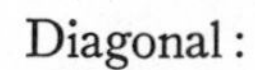

V.C. Conceptual Perspective

Multiview perspective refers to the portrayal of qualities seen as most characteristic of an object, whether or not they can be seen in nature at the same time. Boas called this "symbolic realism". "X-ray art" or *transparency* is an example. The split figure, double profile device so well known from the art of the Northwest Coast of North America falls into this category.

Social perspective is the term widely used in cases where persons of greater importance are shown larger than those of lesser importance.

Topographic perspective is a map-like projection which is oriented to the cardinal directions.

V.C. Conceptual Perspective

Multiview:

Social:

Transparency:

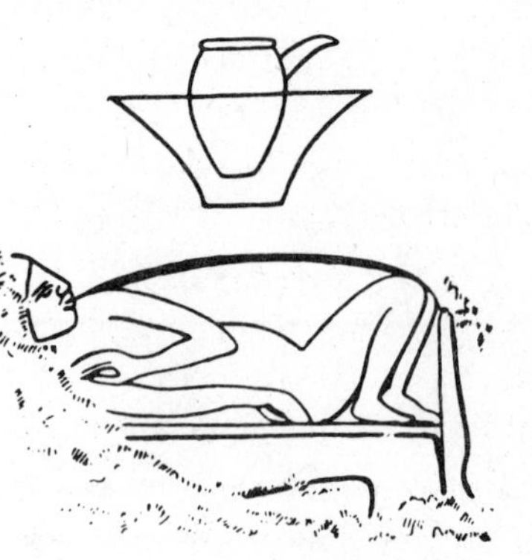

BOAS 1927

Transparency:

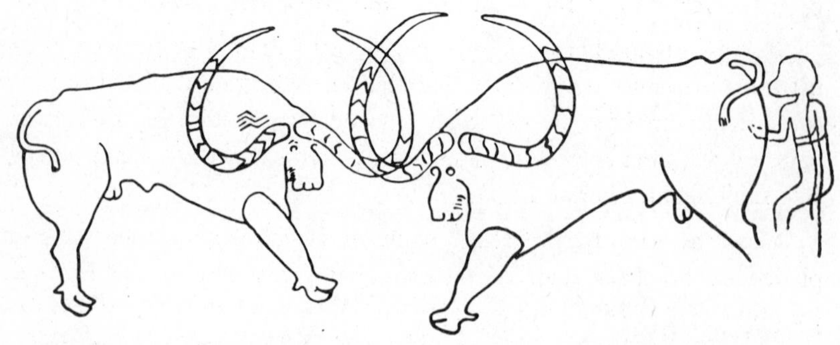

BASED ON CHRISTENSEN 1955

PERSPECTIVE QUALITIES IN NAVAJO DRYPAINTINGS

V. Perspective

In the usual sense of the term, drypaintings may be said to "lack perspective", that is to say, they do not present an illusion of space depth. To say that they do not show awareness of three-dimensional space or project it onto the almost two-dimensional form of the paintings would be inaccurate.

Some indication of space depth is actually given in the form of overlapping, which occurs in about one quarter of the paintings. Such overlapping is found in parts of the same figure, as when a snake's head is seen on top of the coils, and, very rarely, when a personage is seen over an object, as Scavenger overlaps the Eagle's nest (Reichard 1939: Plate I) or conversely when Crooked Snakes are hidden behind their home (Newcomb and Reichard n.d.: Plate IX). Plant, animal, and anthropomorphic figures very seldom overlap each other and then only in a minor way. Arnheim's interpretation regarding dominance and submission in this form of space representation is of considerable interest here.

The fact that the device of overlapping is known and used, yet seldom for animate figures, suggests an analogy to the Navajo premise of "respect for the integrity of the individual" (Kluckhohn and Leighton 1962:309). As with all the other qualities presenting such rather striking analogies, much comparative work needs to be done before the significance of such uses is thoroughly accepted. Offhand one would say that overlapping figures are rare outside of the traditions of Europe and the Orient; but it is notable that some overlapping occurs in the art of the Maori and of the Indians of the Northwest Coast.

Absence of another form of "perspective" may also be seen as significant. In spite of the fact that the supernaturals depicted are indicated in the mythology to vary in power, anthropomorphic figures in a painting are always of the same size. This absence of social perspective suggests an egalitarian outlook.

It can be said that Navajo painting is more concerned with the projection of space than is the illusional projection of the European tradition, but it is not space depth which is emphasized, but space expanse. Geographic orientation in terms of the cardinal directions is very important in the Navajo conception. Geographical features are often symbolized and kept in directional relationship to each other. All the paintings are oriented to the cardinal directions. Many have a center which represents a place of mythological importance, and sacred locations may be indicated on the four sides. Spatial projection takes the form of a map-like layout in which the spatial relationships are formalized by ritual requirements.

A view from above, combined with figures as viewed from ground level, would be simply a kind of multi-view perspective comparable to ancient Egyptian usage if it were not for the directional requirement. While at first blush this emphasis on the cardinal directions would seem to be a ritual requirement and not part of the art form, further thought will show that it is as much of a conceptual part of the whole as the requirement that a picture be hung right side up. The illustrations of drypaintings in this work demonstrate the importance of this quality, because in consistently placing "east" towards the top of the page, the paintings come out "wrong" for the reader a part of the time. Hence the coinage of the term topographic perspective to describe this projection. There are no hypotheses in the literature interpreting this form of projection, but comparison with the interpretations given for illusional perspective brings out some interesting possibilities.

Reference to the myths which the paintings illustrate suggest that the relationship of space to time implied in this "topographical perspective" is rather that of an identification of past and present, a pulling together of mythological time and present time by means of spatial identification. That space is more potent than time is shown by the importance of proximity in ritual efficacy, and by incidents such as the following:

> When BWW was affected by "weakness all over", her illness was ascribed to the fact that unwittingly she had camped on an ancient trail that led to a deer impound. Deer were confused when driven into it to their death; it is reasonable to assume that BWW would become confused in such a place. (Reichard 1950:81)

Space enfolds time, rather than capturing a fleeting moment of it.

The emphasis on place which is brought out in the paintings has been noted as an emphasis in other aspects of Navajo life. The location of sacred geographical places seems to be part of a sense of security in spatial orientation which has been mentioned in connection with the concept of life space and the protection offered by boundaries. Geographical location plays an important part in Navajo myths, and position plays an important part in Navajo language. In the language, position is not only important in the morphological sense, but by the variety of directional distinctions which the language makes. In this language "the Navajo divides space into zones and circles or into lines and directions, or indicates many other refinements of these ideas." (Kluckhohn and Leighton 1963:262) The drypaintings could be described in much the same terms. Spatial orientation for the Navajo seems to be part of the whole system of security through order. Lewis Mumford's ideas (1934) of the emphasis on mastery through the ordering of time in the tradition of European civilization is in contrast to this.

Shading is discussed above in terms of value gradation.

RAVENNA MOSAIC ABOUT 520 A. D.

7

Organization of All Form Qualities: Composition

Composition is the combination of all the qualities in a particular work, and especially the *way* in which they are combined. In the interpretation of composition, the simplest approach is to note the emphasis which is placed on different aspects of the work. In the introductory paragraphs to the principle sections above, I have discussed the kinds of interpretations which are applied to these larger categories. Alschuler and Hattwick have summarized the interpretations of these main aspects of graphic projection as they have found them to be valid in the paintings of young children:

> Our findings lead us to the following conclusions:
> a) Color tends to give the clearest clues as to the nature and degree of intensity of the child's emotional life.
> b) Line and form tend to give the most intelligible clues as to
> (1) the amount of engery the child is expending
> (2) the degree of control the child is exercising
> (3) the direction in which that control is operating.
> Color and line form considered together are likely to indicate the balance which exists between the child's impulsive drives, on the one hand, and his overt, controlled behavior, on the other hand.
> c) Space usage and spatial pattern tend to give less a picture of the child's inner life than a picture of the child as he relates, and is reacting, to his environment. (Alschuler and Hattwick 1947:14)

MEANINGS ATTRIBUTED TO VARIOUS ASPECTS OF COMPOSITION

In the discussions of compositions by the students of art, interpretations of formal qualities are more likely to rest on a different order of combination which cuts across this categorization, using some such terms as are defined below under this heading, i. e., complexity-simplicity, repose-vitality, etc. Sir Herbert Read views this basic polarity in terms of beauty and vitality:

> Composition is born out of containment, out of imposed discipline. The vital surrenders to the abstract—the image to the concept . . . Composition, with its laws of harmony and proportion, its unity and serenity—what is it but the paradigm of that intellectual ideal which the Greeks were to call *to kalon,* and which we call beauty. What in the course of the Neolithic period had been born was therefore the first consciousness of beauty. It is the second great principle of art, the first being vitality, established in the Paleolithic period. (Read 1965:49)

Beam (1958:144), under the heading "The Interrelations of the Universal Values" discusses the universal qualities of vitality and repose, finiteness and infinity, order and variety. He points out that while these are alternatives, they are polar alternatives, one or the other in each pair may be favored in a work, but that each must be present and balanced with its "opposite". "The esthetic quality of a work of art is thus a dynamic equilibrium of characteristics lying within these extremes." This is shown in tabular form:

Uncontrolled	Controlled		Controlled	Uncontrolled
deadness	Repose	versus	Vitality	wildness
obviousness	Finiteness	versus	Infinity	nebulousness
monotony	Order	versus	Variety	chaos

The qualities used in my schema differ somewhat from these used by Beam, but they partake of this polar quality, and I suggest that the quality of control stressed by him applies to all such qualities in productions which can be designated as art. To the extent that such control is lacking, we may perhaps consider that they are projective expressions rather than artistic ones.

The analysis of Fang esthetics and social structure by Fernandez, which is based on direct investigation in the field, shows that the Fang have very similar ideas to those of Beam. The conclusions are worth quoting at length, because they show that more is involved in duality than the simple matter of bilateral symmetry. They also show a relation of esthetics not simply to social structure, but to the whole culture conceptualization of the dynamics of social life.

> In both aesthetics and the social structure the aim of the Fang is not to resolve opposition and create identity but to preserve a balanced opposition. This is accomplished either through alternation as in the case with complementary filiation or in the behavior of a full man; or it is done by skillful aesthetic composition in the same time and space as is the case with the ancestor statutes or cult ritual. This objective is reflected in interclan relations. The Fang, like many non-literate people, lived in a state of constant enmity with other clans. However, their object was not that of exterminating each other or otherwise terminating the hostility in favor of one clan or another. The hostility was regarded as a natural condition of social life, and their concern was to keep this enmity in permanent and balanced opposition. So in their aesthetic life, they aimed at a permanent and balanced opposition. In this permanent tension between opposites lay the source of vitality in Fang life. (Fernandez in Jopling 1971:373)

Under the heading of composition, then, I consider various qualities, usually conceived as polar, which are conveyed by the work as a whole.

VI.A. Simplicity-Complexity

> The correlation between severity of socialization and complexity of design (.71) in art works indicate the presence of a connecting link between these two variables, to which both are related. (Barry 1957:382)
>
> Design repetitive of a number of rather simple elements should characterize egalitarian societies; design integrating a number of unlike elements should be characteristic of the hierarchical societies. (Fischer 1961:81)
>
> Complex, non-repetitive design, representing a hierarchical society, should be associated with societies which strongly favor male solidarity in residence. (ibid.:84)

In regard to the Rorshach Piotrowski says:

> The larger the number and the greater the structural differentiation of the W (the more diverse and numerous the details combined into wholes), the stronger the tendency to leave nothing to chance, but to exert oneself in order to plan and organize everything so that all thoughts and actions contribute directly to the achievement of a paramount and all-embracing goal of life, complex and difficult of attainment but likely to be recognized as outstanding, constructive and praiseworthy by those whose approval and support are sought. (Piotrowski 1957:58)

> Since W is an important indication of the ability to organize, synthesize, plan, and carry out plans, it is one of the most important measures of potential energy output and of optimism. People who have few W do not entertain pleasant hopes for the future. (ibid.:79)

> In cases such as these [the Maori, the Northwest Coast Indians, and Victorian England], value seems to be attached to size and complexity and elaboration for its own sake; also there is a tendency to produce decorated versions of everyday objects which are not only flamboyant but technically useless. The adjective "ostentatious" sums up the whole complex. From this point of view these primitive art styles from the Pacific area have much that was characteristic of the artistic taste of mid-nineteenth-century England.
>
> I believe that such correspondences are not altogether accidental. The resemblences in artistic taste reflect common moral values, in this case the moral values of the socially ambitious. For as in Victorian England, the primitive societies of British Columbia and New Zealand were characterized by notions of a class hierarchy coupled with much social competition. (Leach 1961:37)

> The prevalence of elaborate decorative art among the primitive peoples, whether to wear or to possess for particular reasons, illustrates the importance of personal prestige as a force behind many examples of their art. (Wingert 1962:61)

Concerning the possibilities of environmental influences of perception and esthetic preferences, there is a suggestive correlation in the work of Barry, which is not explored by him or by Fischer, who says:

> One of the statistically significant results he [Barry] obtained by this wholesale testing, and association of complex art with root rather than grain crops, seems on the face of it implausible to me and I assume it is a sampling accident. The other result, an association of complex art with sedentary rather than nomadic residence, fits in with the social stratification hypothesis in an obvious way. (Fischer 1961:89)

While, as I have said, Barry's work may be open to criticism in the matter of sampling, it would seem rather arbitrary to dismiss the possibility of any significance to one set of results and attach significance to more congenial ones. Root crops are often associated with areas of lush vegetation, and the possibilities of environmental esthetic conditioning cannot be dismissed without exploration.

VI.B. Delicacy-Boldness

These terms are in themselves a form of interpretation. I have not seen extensions of these meanings into other kinds of interpretation, but this quality joined the schema somewhat late, and such interpretations may have been overlooked. The quality I have called *boldness* is often referred to as "strength" and is associated with the concept of power.

VI.C. Repose-Tension

These broad terms have at various times been used as basic categories to encompass all art styles, and one or another have been seen as the basic ones. Read, for example, sees vitality as a basic quality, and opposes it to beauty rather than repose. Or perhaps, one should say he equates beauty with repose and serenity.

> It should already be clear that the term "Aesthetic" covers two very different psychological processes, just those processes whose first tentative differentiation takes place in paleolithic art, the one tending to an emphasis on *vitality,* the other discovering the still center, the balance and harmony of *beauty.* The contemplation of beauty lifts the sensibility out of the stress of life, out of the intentional purposiveness of the symbol, into a state of suspended animation, into a condition of serenity. (Read 1965:32)

> Tension is a term used to describe the attraction and repulsion of elements in a composition. This spatial sensation of activity can be used not only to create a dynamically alive picture, but also to intensify the communicativeness of a picture.
>
> The student exercises illustrate optical communication of

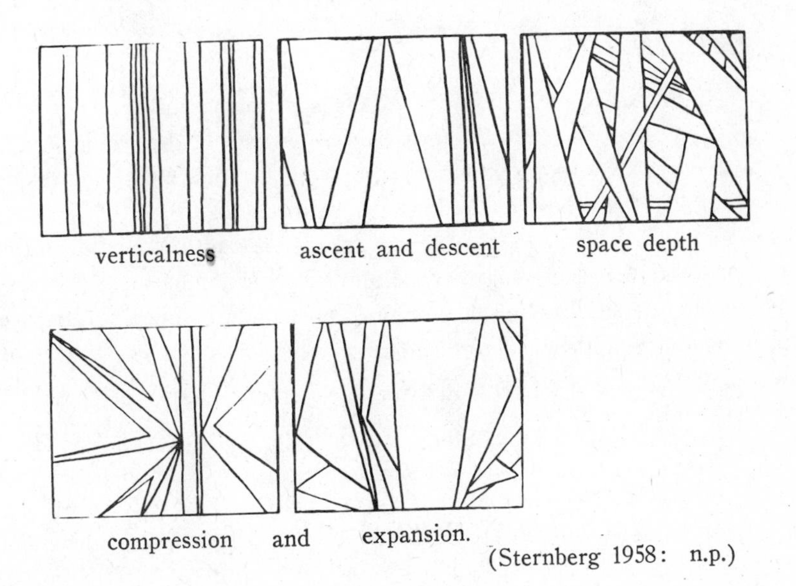

(Sternberg 1958: n.p.)

The term "tension" has been popular in recent usage for any form of contrast or for competing foci of interest.

VI.D. Stillness-Movement

The interpretation of movement in graphic art is difficult because the perception of movement is so particularly subjective. As Beam says,

> Compared to the temporal arts, the visual arts are static. Movement in them can never be more than implied and thus quite dependent on appreciative cooperation. (Beam 1958:165)

Piotrowski says:

> Rorschach warned that the scoring of the M is the thorniest problem in the entire perceptanalysis . . . Rorschach placed great emphasis on the condition that the movement be felt as a change in muscular tension. According to him, it is felt movement, not the movement rationally inferred, which changes the form response into movement responses . . .
>
> Rorschach rightly sensed that the animal- and inanimate-movement responses do not have the same significance as the human-movement responses, but he did not explain the difference . . . In discussing the scoring, he stressed the condition that a kinesthetic sensation accompany the response and the content of the response be an object imagined in actual movement. However, even objects that are not in motion may be perceived with accompanying kinesthetic sensations, . . . [and] he admitted the existence of subjects who can feel genuine movement "in all kinds of animals, plants, geometric figures, and even single lines." (Piotrowski 1957:122)

Furthermore, Rorschach's idea of the significance of the M rested largely on the type of movement—extensor and flexor—which seem to call for actual representations of the human figure. If, however, movement as perceived in the formal qualities (regardless of the representation) is "felt" movement for the artist and for the observer, Rorschach's interpretations may be applicable, with the content (i. e., M, Fm or m) a form of context in which cultural meaning plays a part in modifying the basic form-meaning.

Regarding human movement, Piotrowski says:

> Rorschach asserted that subjects who see predominantly extensor movements, stretching or rising figures, are basically different from subjects who see mostly figures which are bent and bowed, burdened and twisted, kneeling and reclining; those with expansive movements are active individuals, people with a strong urge to

> be somebody and to keep occupied, although they often suffer from neurotic inhibitions, while subjects with flexor movements are passive, resigned to their fate, and frequently troubled with neurasthenia. (ibid.:131)

From the point of view of the interpretation of art as communication, it is largely immaterial whether we consider the perception of movement as related to the fantasy life as stated by Rorschach, or to overt behavior, as conceived by Piotrowski. There is some question in my mind as to whether an attempt to equate formal qualities with Rorschach's types can achieve any insight which is not already available from the direct use of such terms as "vitality and repose", "contained movement", and the like.

However the degree of *emphasis* on movement may possibly be meaningfully interpreted in terms of Piotrowski's analysis of the "strong M person":

> The strong M person shares one essential trait with Jung's introvert. Like the introvert, he begins any new and fundamental adaption to the environment by means of thought, preceded by an attempt at an intellectual understanding of the new or difficult situation. The emotions most prominent in the strong M person cluster around his scale of values, his goals and methods of handling people and objects, his pride in a personal style of life, his desire to maintain his individuality, to strengthen his personal qualities so as to become as independent of others as possible, and his effort to endure, unhurriedly and unchangingly, in the face of external influence and threats. (Piotrowski 1957:144)
>
> People without M are intellectually dependent on others and their ability to appreciate cultural and human values is extremely limited. Their motivation is limited chiefly to gratification of the basic needs for food, shelter, and security. (ibid.:146)
>
> The formal criteria [of movement], although called *secondary movement elements* [may indicate, when high], . . . superior emotional balance [and] originality. (Waehner 1946:65)
>
> These . . . elements are elements of introversion, contributing to the liveliness and originality of visual experience and affording imagination. (ibid.:41)

Machover says that action or movement is most commonly portrayed in the drawings of pre-adolescent boys, but

> When highly developed action is intended, action which does not bear relevantly upon the subject's age, I.Q., or vocation, or appropriate interests, fantasy preoccupation may be assumed. (Machover 1957:85)

The M person in the Rorschach test is therefore, and the point bears repetition, one moved by strong feelings. They are feelings which the person holds in. In clinical pictures, and in healthy living, the mental stuff of M emerges as achievement of the new. The individual is converting his emotions. It is "inspired" work. In neurotics, it is daydreaming. In the psychotic the daydreaming degenerates into autistic, dereistic living. In the strong, healthy adult it is sublimation. (Beck 1952:50)

Movement. The M scores were explained by Rorschach as reflections of the associative life of the subject. The higher the productivity of M's, the greater the richness of associative life. Movement responses, then, are indicative of the deep forces in the personality which produce imaginative life. The significance of the M was interpreted by Beck to vary with different personality structures. In healthy adults and some neurotics, especially those of superior intelligence, it has the significance of inner creative activity; in schizophrenia, a more personal creative experience; in adults with conduct disorder, but without psychosis, the character of fantasy living; in the feeble-minded, a rudimentary fantasy experience; in the depressed, the residue of such capacity escaping intra-psychic constriction; and in the manic, egocentric wishfulfillment. (Bell 1948:123)

The urge to represent objects in motion or in action seems, in this kind of projective material [drawings], to be an indication of a vividly imaginative and vitally strong, often creative personality. (Kinget 1952:111)

VI.E. Freedom-Formality

The great variety of polar qualities which are related to this formulation, and the even greater number of interpretations that have been attributed to them, are covered rather fully and succinctly by Longman:

Classicism. Like romanticism, classicism may be viewed from the points of view of (a) form, (b) content, and (c) social attitude.

a. The rational, controlled, ordered, general, clear, intellectual, perfect, universal, Taoistic, commensurate, formal, finite, static, architectonic, tangible.

b. The serene, restrained, reposeful, poised, decorous, congruous, sanguine, peaceful, Apollonian, tasteful, ceremonious, categorically dignified.

c. The conservative, traditional, disciplined, conformist, dependable, constant, normative, communicable, teachable, scholastic, conventional, calculated, endowed with categorical expectancy, public, endowed with integrity, responsible.

Romanticism.

a. The irrational, uncontrolled, disordered, obscure, unique, uncommunicable, emotional, imperfect, accentual, amorphous, fragmentary, chaotic, infinite, boundless (*Sehnsucht nach dem Unendlichen*), dynamic, intangible, individualistic.

b. The unrestrained, inspirational, mystical, Dionysiac [sic], intoxicated, fermentational, experimental, excessive, spontaneous, expressive, expressionistic, incongruous, fantastic, voluptuous, colorful, frustrated, exuberant, diffuse, melancholy, preference for the remote in time and space, escapist.

c. The rebellious, progressive, innovational, undisciplined, nonconformist, undependable, irresponsible, private, unconventional, bohemian (*épater le bourgeois*), subversive, corrosive, fluctuant, unattached, culturally anarchistic, socially without obligations. (Longman 1949:25)

Recognizing art as an expression of societal form, and recognizing the individual as being suspended between allegiance and revolt in relation to this form, the beholder should discover in the strength of a painter's patterns an indication of the strength of his participatory involvement; in the freedom of his subject matter, an indication of his freedom as a critical bystander. In other words, periods of strongly integrated form should have created strong patterns and made the subject matter fit; periods of weak or distintegrated form should reveal the corresponding independence of the individual by producing weak patterns subordinated to the "naturalistic" freedom of the subject depicted. (Mundt 1952:196)

In order we find a reassuring sense of mastery, a symbol of control over nature and life; this may be the reason why "primitive" artists often lay a particular stress on regularity and repetition. (Eitner 1961:28)

Summary

It will be noted that the polar qualities in the composition category seem to be related to each other, which is perhaps why one or another of them has been used as the basic polarity in art. Recent work by psychologists supports and clarifies the nature of these basic properties. A summary of this work by Berlyne provides some relevant passages:

These are the properties for which I have suggested the term *collative,* since they depend on comparison or collation of stimulus elements, whether they be elements appearing simultaneously in different sectors of a stimulus field or elements that have been perceived at different times. They comprise the properties that

> we designate by words like ***novelty, surprisingness, incongruity, complexity, variability,*** and ***puzzlingness.*** Just as the psychophysical properties are derived from distributions of energy and the ecological properties connect stimuli with the factors that govern natural selection, thus making contact with the two great unifying concepts of 19th-century science, the collative properties have close connections with information, the unifying concept responsible for some revolutionary developments in 20th-century science.
>
> The technical language of information theory does not suffice for an adequate description of the collative variables, but its concepts can help a great deal in specifying and measuring them. Providing that certain assumptions are fulfilled, how "novel", "surprising", "regular", or "orderly" a structure is, how numerous its elements are, and how interdependent, determine its information content, uncertainty (from an external observer's point of view) regarding an organism's reaction to it, and the organism's degree of subjective uncertainty regarding what will happen next or regarding the nature of elements that have not yet been inspected . . .
>
> The motivational effects of collative stimulus properties are by no means confined to occasioning and directing exploratory responses. They include the factors making for "good" or "bad" form, which were shown by the Gestalt psychologists to govern many perceptual phenomena. They include the factors constituting "form", "composition", or "structure" in the visual and performing arts, in literature, in music, and in humor. (Berlyne 1966:30)

Some experiments show that the more exciting and puzzling properties are not always the most pleasing:

> When a subject is shown a pair of patterns . . . and then asked to choose one of the two patterns for further viewing, which he is likely to choose depends on the duration of the initial exposure. If he has seen the two patterns briefly (for 1 second or less) before making his choice, he is more likely to want to see the *more* complex pattern again. Preliminary exposures of such brevity are presumably not long enough to allow him to see what the patterns are like and thus to relieve his curiosity. He chooses the more complex pattern, presumably because that is the one about which he has more residual curiosity. If, on the other hand, the preliminary exposures are long enough (3 seconds or more) to allow him to become adequately acquainted with the patterns, he is more likely to want another look at the *less* complex pattern. In this case, curiosity, having been largely eliminated by the initial exposure, must play a minor role. Factors akin to esthetic taste will presumably have more influence. (ibid.:32)

The qualities Berlyne classifies as *complex* include irregularity, asymmetry, incongruity, amount and heterogeneity of elements, and random distribution, as opposed to regularity and symmetry, congruity of content, fewer and more similiar elements, and patterned distribution. In my schema these would not all be placed under complexity, but they would fall at the same end of the scale in the various polar qualities of composition. Berlyne and his colleagues place their emphasis on the active pole, and the concepts of arousal and conflict in relation to curiosity and exploration. There are, however, hints at the kinds of situations which make the opposite pole, the familiar and comprehensible, satisfying:

> A number of experiments have indicated that conditions conducive to abnormally high levels of arousal (for example, hunger, pain, fear, noise, exposure to an incomprehensible tape-recorded message) make rats and human beings less eager than usual to seek out novel or complex stimulation. (ibid.:33)

Thus these experimental findings tend to bear out the students of art when they see beauty, order, and repose as providing surcease, security, and renewal.

> Harmony comes about through the conciliation of contrast. Every work of art involves the pitting of contrasting forms against one another. Where contrast is lacking, there is monotony; where contrast is too strong there is danger of disorder and restlessness. The artist attempts to distill harmonious unity of effect from the conflict of hostile and discordant forms. He achieves this through balance and symmetry, through the interweaving, counterpoint-like, of the rhythmic repetition of contrasting forms, and through other manipulations. The pleasure which harmony holds seems to result from the dissolution of anxieties and tensions inherent in the conflict. (Eitner 1951:29)
>
> A work of art is no more to be described sufficiently by its inherent harmony, balance, and order than an organism by its tendency to simplicity and minimum tension. The reason why art is so often discussed in this one-sided manner may be partly a surviving preference of classicist aesthetics for simplicity and stillness, partly the fact that simplicity of shape can be analyzed purely as a matter of formal relationship without any reference to content and meaning, whereas the dynamic theme makes little sense without such a reference. Thus a formalistic analysis talks about balance or unity but avoids the question without which the existence of the work remains incomprehensible: What is being balanced and unified? (Arnheim 1954:423)

The combination of this aspect of composition with the categories of formal qualities discussed in the rest of the outline, provides a broad conceptual framework within which to examine the meaning of form in relation to content and context.

PROPOSED DEFINITIONS OF QUALITIES OF COMPOSITION

VI. Composition

Composition is a term which refers to all the relationships in a design. Any description of a composition is a selection of what the viewer regards as the most important organizing principle in an art form. One way of describing the composition of an art work or style would be to summarize in terms of the descriptive categories defined above, indicating which ones were given the most emphasis as organizing qualities.

In describing art works as wholes, however, certain terms which cut across these categories are used very frequently and are considered of great significance in indicating the meaning of the visual forms. These terms are for the most part somewhat metaphorical and interpretative in themselves, although they are treated as descriptive by students of art. The compositional qualities used here are all polar qualities: simplicity-complexity, delicacy-boldness, repose-tension, stillness-movement, freedom-formality. I have approached these qualities subjectively, and have defined them by analyzing my judgments after I had rated a considerable number of works as well as by reference to the literature. As a result of this process, I have come to believe that their basis lies entirely in a combination of the more objective qualities described above. The question as to whether a formula can be devised in which such combinations could be used instead of the broader more subjective judgments can only be answered by extensive investigation.

VI.A. Simplicity-Complexity

This quality depends on the number of elements, the variety of elements, and to a lesser extent the quality of subtlety which makes some designs more difficult to understand than others. For example, in a layout which is symmetrical except for color reversal, the symmetry is not always apparent; this adds to the quality of *complexity*. A *simple* design is one with few elements and little variety in the form of those elements.

VI.A. Simplicity-Complexity

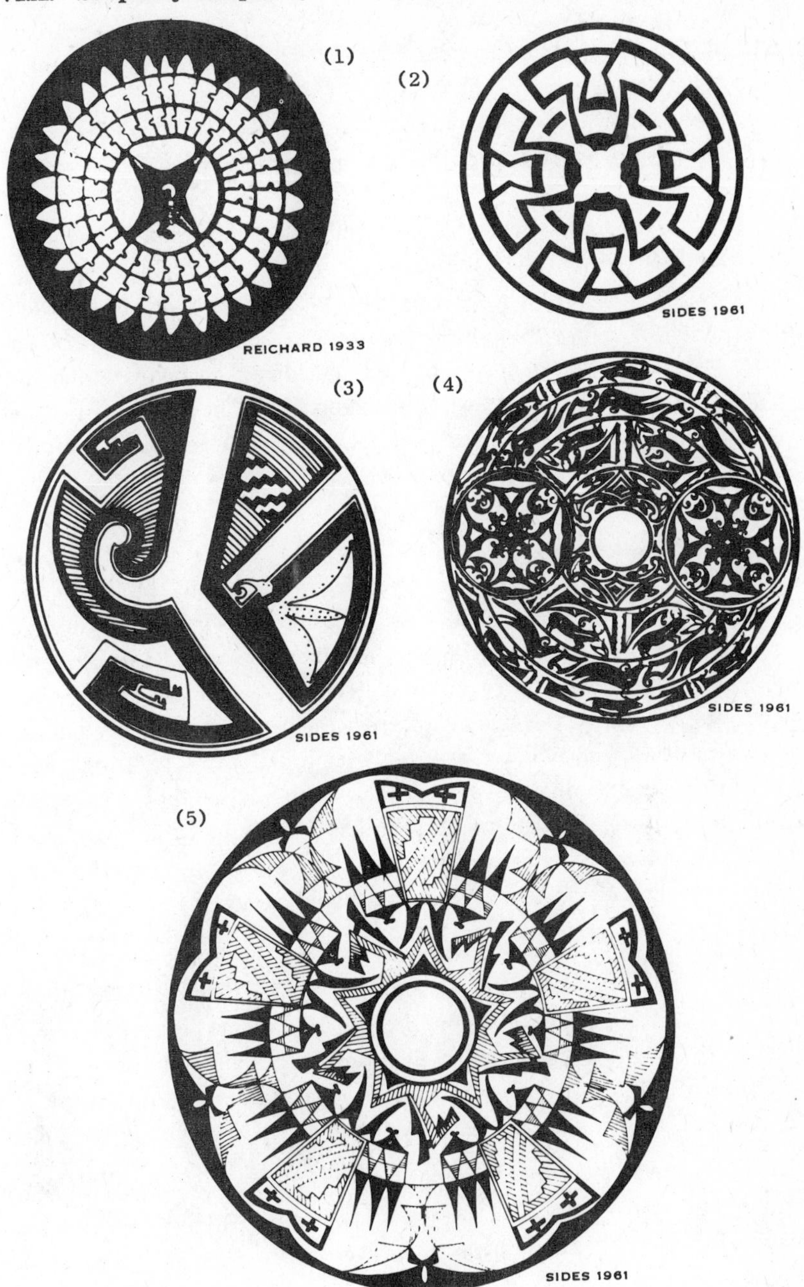

As I have said above, subtlety and ambiguity enter into the perception of complexity. For a more objective category, it would be better if these were separately considered. This would mean that complexity can be defined simply as more parts (components, elements, etc.), more kinds of parts, and more ways of interrelating the parts. Subtlety and ambiguity depend in part on the familiarity of the viewer with the style.

A descriptive word which is often used is "ornate," and I have considered how it is related to the various form-qualities. In some interpretations complexity would be a near equivalent, but I am not satisfied with this usage. I view the term ornate as a useful one for describing either three-dimensional forms or the collective impact of a number of design fields. A single, two-dimensional field may not in itself be complex, but a number of design fields which are moderately complex and have a high ratio of figure to ground would contribute to this effect when included in some kind of larger whole.

VI.B. Delicacy-Boldness

While the term most frequently used in referring to this quality is "strength", this word implies a polar opposite of "weakness", and has broader and more evaluative connotations than *boldness* and its opposite *delicacy,* which seem more purely descriptive. Qualities which are taken into account in this judgment are measure, contrast and intensity of color, and weight of line. This has been a difficult category to illustrate in the format of this volume, because of the limitations of scale. Furthermore, use of color and gradations of tone are important, and these are not available in line drawings. However, the common meanings of the terms are such that the intent should be clear.

This is a quality in which absolute size, i. e., size in relation to the beholder as well as proportions within the design field, affects perception of the quality. That the oppositeness of these qualities is not complete is indicated by the fact that in rating on a scale from one to five, I find that an in-between rating of three sometimes means to me a combination of boldness and delicacy rather than a mere halfway point.

This category is one that has possibilities for use as a quality defined with relative objectivity if it is divided into two separate qualities, so that we have degrees of boldness, and degrees of delicacy.

Monumentality, as the term seems to be used, would refer to a work which showed qualities of both boldness and simplicity.

VI.B. Delicacy-Boldness

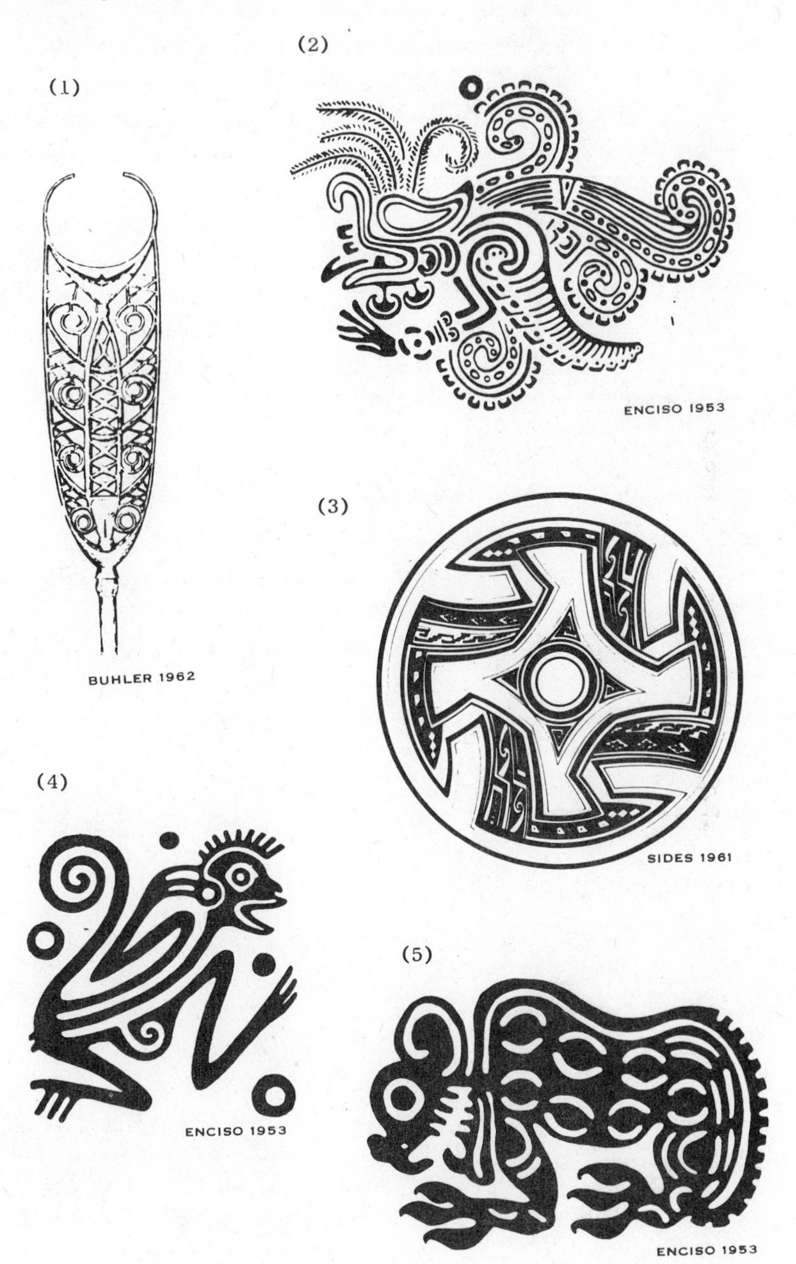

VI.C. Repose-Tension

The dichotomy between *repose* and *tension* is often discussed in terms of "vitality" rather than tension, but, perhaps because the tendency of the times is to place such a high value on "vitality", the term is sometimes equated with excellence, and to rate a work as low on a scale of vitality has a pejorative connotation. "Movement" and "vitality" are sometimes considered under the same heading, and are often confusing in application, but there is a real distinction which often appears in usage, because "slow" movement can be restful, and tension does not always imply overt movement.

Repose is conveyed by harmony rather than contrast, low color intensities and values, long lines, parallel rather than opposed lines, curves of large radius, rounded corners and few angles, considerable use of static repetition and symmetry, especially bilateral and biaxial symmetry, horizontal or circular structural lines. Read's use of the word "beautiful," which seems related to what I have called repose, is an interesting one, and useful in terms of the problem of explaining how a work can be considered of high esthetic quality without being beautiful.

The qualities which contribute to tension are intense colors, short component lines, a variety of line direction and width, free ends, sharp and acute angles or many curves of small radius; asymmetry, dynamic repetition of small elements, opposed structural lines, and contrasts of all kinds. Qualities making for movement are controlled by opposition or contrast; some rotational and radial symmetrical designs can be seen as high in tension partly as a result of this control of movement.

The quality that I am calling tension is more closely related to the "collative" or stimulus elements of Berlyne than are any other of the qualities I am listing under composition. However, it does not involve the ideas of complexity or cognitive ambiguity that are important in his more inclusive view, as can be seen in some works which are bold and simple, but high in tension in this formal sense.

It is very difficult to describe this as a purely formal quality in an objective way. The history of art in the Euro-American tradition shows repeated instances of a reaction in terms of tension to new works and an increasing perception of harmony and repose as stylistic devices become familiar. That this is not simply the effect produced by novelty is shown in the case of the Fang, who apparently perceive more tension in works familiar to them than is perceived by persons in other cultures to whom the works are not so familiar.

VI.C. Repose-Tension

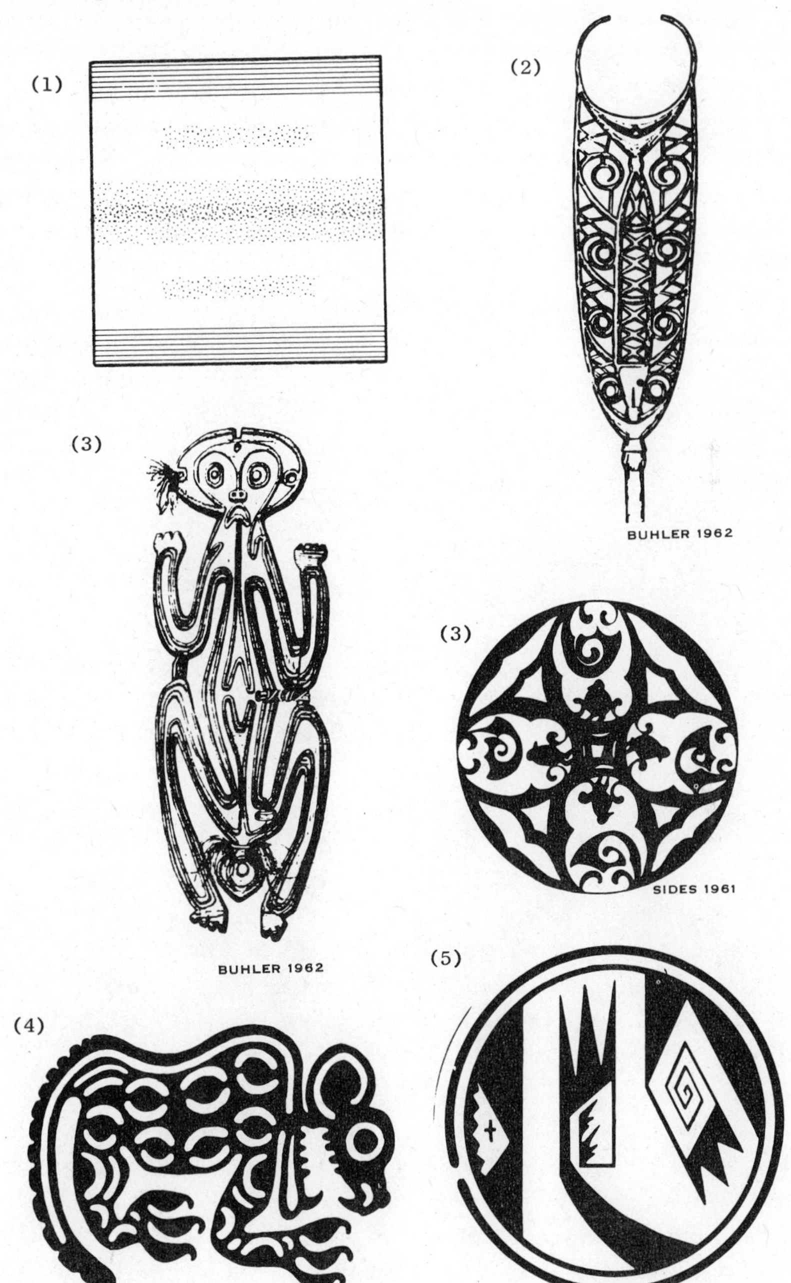

VI.D. Stillness-Movement

In a sense *movement* is like tension, but in a different scale. The effect of movement results from long lines, "slow" "flowing" curves, or curves with large radii, and structural lines based on long diagonals and reverse curves. If the work is symmetrical, the rotational quality is marked; rhythm and repetition, especially in dynamic, continuous forms, contribute to the quality. Colors in all aspects tend to combine harmony and contrast in such a way as to lead the eye from one part of the design to another.

Lack of movement, or stillness, is conveyed by exact symmetry, especially in bilateral form, and in vertical lines. Repetition is static; there is little emphasis on rhythm. Colors tend to be harmonious rather than contrasting in all aspects.

In some usage, all art has "movement," based on the movements of the eye as it follows the forms of the design, but even this usage admits of relative lack of movement. There have been a number of studies of the eye movements of a person examining a painting or drawing, and such results as I have seen show an eye movement back and forth to the areas of representational interest or ambiguity rather than following the lines of movement as they appear to the art analyst. Perhaps studies done with non-representational works might be useful to clarify the relationship between eye movement and movement perceived subjectively.

There are various qualities of movement that may be perceived, although in the present descriptive schema they have not been considered. For example, some qualities seem to convey slow movement, and others a rapid one. Varieties of intermittent, or pulsating movement, as distinguished from continuous movement, are also discernible. In developing a formal description, however, one ought to be able to include the devices by which these effects are achieved, rather than to develop a more refined classification of the effects themselves.

The quality of movement is an interesting one, because in still pictures motion must of necessity be conveyed by some kind of analogy. Yet it seems to be a more "objective" quality than tension, in the sense that motion and the degree of motion are perceived in a similar fashion by different persons and different peoples, insofar as I can tell from the present evidence. As I have remarked regarding forms of repetition, the idea that motion is conveyed by motionless forms is so taken for granted that it is hard to find purely descriptive terms which do not involve concepts related to motion.

VI.D. Stillness-Movement

(1):

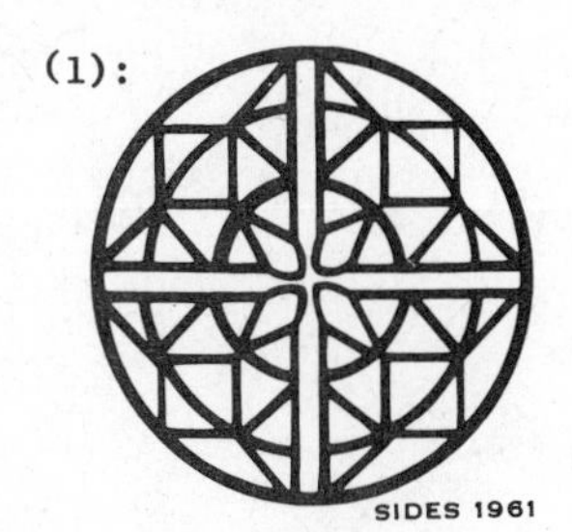

SIDES 1961

(1):

BUHLER 1962

(5):

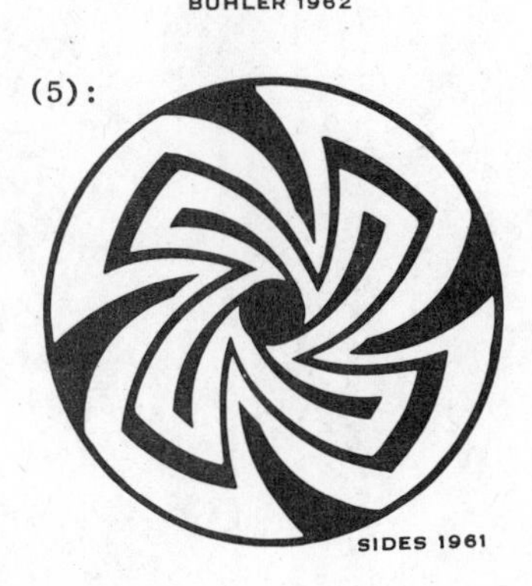

SIDES 1961

(1):

SIDES 1961

(2):

ENCISO 1953

(3):

ENCISO 1953

(3):

SIDES 1961

(4):

ENCISO 1953

(5):

SIDES 1961

VI.E. Freedom-Formality

The distinction between *formal* and *free* is one which has been discussed in a great variety of guises in studies of art. Many of the enormous variety of terms and concepts related to this quality have been compiled by Longman (1949) and are quoted above.

Insofar as the distinction rests on objective criteria which can be related to form qualities, rather than on the basis of adherence to or departure from a given tradition, it seems to be a matter of order and regularity. A formal style is a controlled style which is marked by regularity of shape, for instance curves which are arcs of circle rather than being free form, and repetition of all kinds. In some usages the term "pattern" describes this quality.

A free work on the other hand is marked by apparent spontaneity, variety and irregularity in shape of line, in the width and weight of line, and in color, without exact repetitions of any kind.

Free (1):

Formal (4):

VI.E. Freedom-Formality

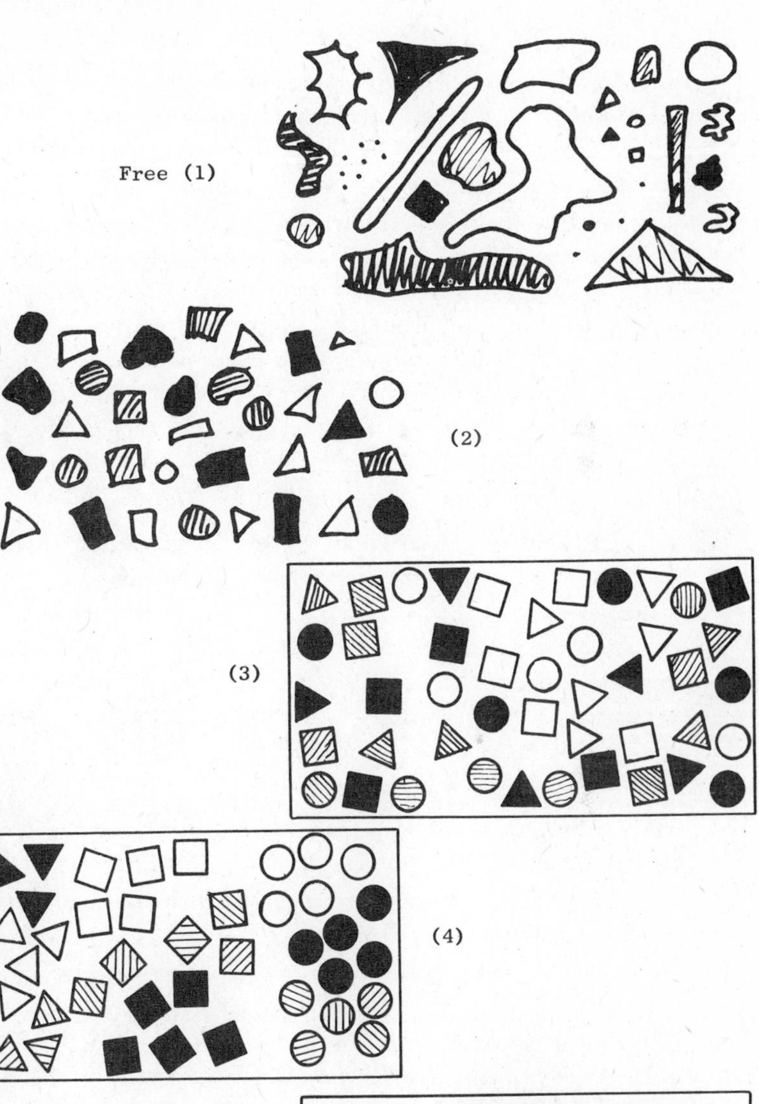

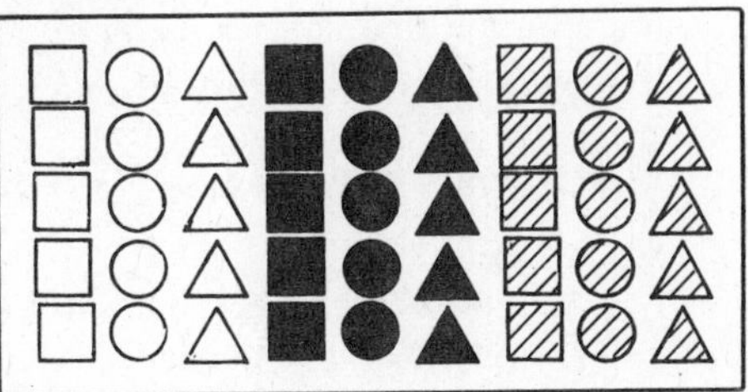

COMPOSITION OF NAVAJO DRYPAINTINGS

VI.A. Simplicity-Complexity

With the exception of the paintings from Blessing Way, drypaintings are rated as relatively complex in terms of my definition. By avoiding the ethnocentric tendency to equate symmetry with simplicity and clarity, we can see this art form in terms of the ordering of complexity, which tends to both resolve the descriptive problem and clarify possible interpretations. Barry's hypothesis concerning "socialization anxiety" seen in terms of what art does rather than what it reflects might then be stated as follows: if complexity is related to socialization anxiety, then drypainting may serve to allay the anxiety by communicating the ordering and control of the complexity. While my scaling is probably too high, due to the fact that more complex paintings are on record, it seems clear that a chanter tended to direct that paintings be made as complex as resources permitted.

Kavolis suggests that complexity implies a high degree of social differentiation, associated in different forms with individualistic and lineal value orientations. The study of Romney and Kluckhohn (F. Kluckhohn 1961) concludes that the Navajo relational value orientation is primarily collateral. A high degree of social differentiation is not characteristic of Navajo society. Fischer's hypothesis of hierarchical society is not supported, nor is his hypothesis that complexity is found strongly favoring male solidarity in residence.

That there is some kind of a direct relation of complexity in art style to wealth and possibly to status, and the "moral values of the socially ambitious" is suggested by some remarks found in the writings of Reichard and those of C. Kluckhohn:

> One painting representing more figures, or another depicting fewer, will be used according to the sum paid the chanter. The paintings involving a large amount of work are used when the payment is large, the simpler ones when it is small. There is no indication that simpler and therefore cheaper ones are less effective. (Newcomb and Reichard n.d.:75)

Kluckhohn differs in the matter of effectiveness when he says:

> It appears to be generally accepted as part of Navajo theory that the more that is paid for a ceremonial, the more effective it is likely to be. (C. Kluckhohn 1962:114)

Other statements by Reichard, such as that more repetition means greater power, are consistent with the view of Kluckhohn.

In any case, the dependence of complexity in style on material good is not only a matter of the fee paid the chanter directly. Because a painting must be finished in a day, a more complex painting requires a greater number of painters with some degree of skill, and the number of persons available depends on the extent the patient's family is able to provide food for a large gathering.

Whatever else may go into the production of complex art forms, the first requirement would seem to be enough goods to support the time and effort necessary to produce them. The wealthy person may indeed enhance his status by such expenditures, but it would not necessarily follow that the society is structured into a permanent hierarchy.

In the Navajo case, there is the possibility that the personality of the chanter is a factor, because a family which can afford a large and elaborate ceremonial is more likely to employ a famous and successful chanter. Such a chanter will be the one who knows the most complex ceremonies and paintings. The nature of the painting in regard to this characteristic is in large measure the choice of the chanter who knows the possible combinations of the traditional elements. The Piotrowski interpretation of the Rorschach W would apply very aptly to the character of such a chanter.

Concerning Piotrowski's interpretation of the W in regard to optimism, it would follow that to the extent that the drypaintings are executed in complex and elaborate form, the Navajo could be said to maintain hope and confidence in the Navajo way and Navajo values. The facts seem to be that in the period under consideration ceremonial activity increased, but the ceremonies tended to be simpler than in former times, which would tend to support this interpretation.

VI.B. Delicacy-Boldness

The handling of contrast and harmony in a number of formal aspects results in a balance of delicacy and boldness which seem subjectively to be more of a combination of the two than a halfway point between them. This may indicate something of the concept of "power", which is so much a part of the meaning of the paintings, and of the power of the supernaturals portrayed, who are by no means powerful in the sense of overpowering majesty.

VI.C. Repose-Tension

As with some other qualities, the variation is great enough to suggest that an average rating may be less significant than an examination of the relationships in the context of usage and in various types or sub-styles. However, certain of the relationships between qualities creating tension and those which quiet the tensions can be seen for the style as a whole.

In my opinion, and this is, as Mills points out, a particularly subjective category, the qualities making for repose not only control those making for tension, but tend to harmonize them; the movement which is opposed is the radial one—other movements, as the circular ones, are notably lacking in opposition (see VI.D., below). Colors are more harmonized than contrasted in hue and intensity, and the harmonizing effect of repetition is very marked.

There is tension in the lines of individual figures, but the devices which make for tension between figures are minimized. The overall impression of tension lies to a great extent in the quality of expansion, especially in the radial format, whether or not this expansion is controlled by the encircling guardian. The tension of the figure is for the most part directed outward, rather than toward the other figures in the composition with which they are harmonized by various devices, especially in the similarity of shape and line. Other tensions seem contained by the individual design units, separated from the others by space and sometimes by boundaries.

VI.D. Stillness-Movement

Movement as perceived by the Navajo in drypainting seems to rest largely on dynamic repetition or rotational symmetry, and on assigned sequences of color. The kind of movement which is dependent on the movement of the eye in following structural lines, which is vertical or radial, is not perceived in terms of movement. I view the movement in drypaintings, especially the circular ones, in terms of rotational motion, and consider the outward "movement" of structural lines in terms of tension or vitality. To me the radiating lines definitely move outward rather than converge, and are often opposed and contained by the border. Perhaps I have been influenced by the Navajo conception, or by the reduced scale in reproductions.

Just as symmetry does not employ the opposition of the bilateral form, so the movement which is conveyed by the figures is not that of opposed or conflicting actions. The anthropomorphic figures are not in violent action. The movement is a collective one. All move in the same direction at the same rate like celestial bodies. This is very striking when one comes to consider the myths which the paintings illustrate. Illustrations in the European tradition would center on the battles of Monster Slayer with much use of conflicting movement in the form of opposed diagonals and active lines full of wiggly curves, such as can be seen in the numerous representations of St. George and the Dragon. But the drypaintings, both in content and in form, glorify not the conflict but the order achieved as a result of it.

As to evidence that the Navajo perceive motion as conveyed by the same artistic devices which are said to do so by students of art, there are several bits of useful evidence, in addition to the statements that the paintings move "sunwise". The Navajo term for a series of small pointed figures (dynamic repetition) is translated by Fr. Berard as "pointed ones following one another" (James 1937:128). Certain motion symbols involve appropriate form qualities; Reichard mentions the following: Lightning, snakes, and arrows are closely identified in the Shooting chants as "things which move in a swift, squirming fashion" (Reichard 1950:485) often represented by zig-zag lines or forms.

> Spiral shape or motion stands for escape from the circle of frustration or prevention from entering it; it is a form of the danger line. Crow and Turkey Buzzard could not get near the Twins because of flints arranged in a spiral; coiled snakes are one of its forms. (ibid.:599)

Circles, if provided with a rotational component or components, also suggest movement:

> Provided with a life feather, hoops symbolize a swift, easy, magical means of travel; they are closely identified with Winds, Stars, Hail . . . Buffalo, and Snakes. (ibid.:564)

Diagonal lines are probably also seen as contributing to the feeling of motion, at least as part of dynamic repetition, and the effect of motion is consciously sought in some drypaintings as is shown by the following account by Reichard of a painting, a portion of which is shown below, rotated 180° so that west is at the top:

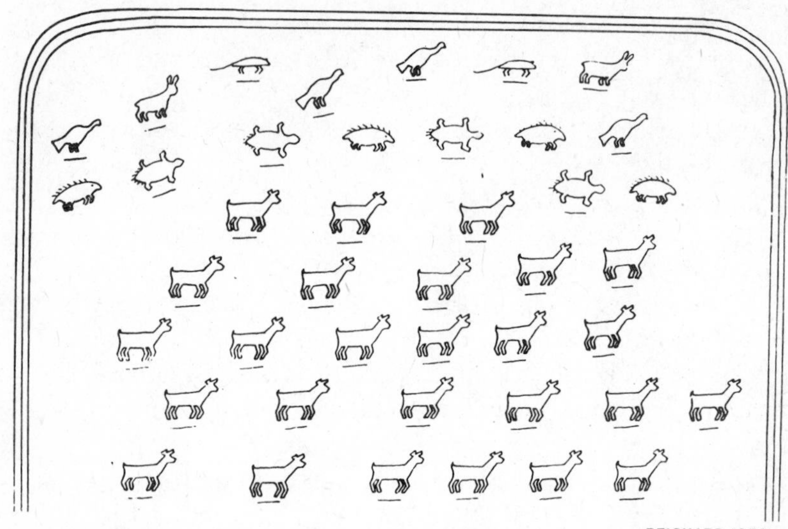

REICHARD 1950

> The painting of day 7 (Fig. 21) has six deities in line east of the center bar; the entire field at the west [which is reproduced above] is filled with animals, so arranged that they seem to be running fast from southwest to northwest. The effect of motion was very well carried out and when the painting, about twenty feet in diameter, was finished, the chanter complimented the workers on their success in getting the effect. (ibid.:701)

It would seem apparent from such clues that movement is regarded as an important quality in the drypaintings. It is tempting to think of the chanter as the "strong M person" described by Piotrowski, but one could translate his interpretation to mean that the chanter seeks to communicate the stated values in social terms; i. e., pride in a style of life, the desire to maintain separateness and independence, and the "effort to endure, unhurriedly and unchangingly in the face of external influence and threats." (Cf. p. 153 above.)

VI.E. Freedom-Formality

The technique of drypainting would appear to be one which permits considerable freedom in the range of possible effects, and hence the great emphasis on patterning, and the formal effect of repetition are especially significant.

The emphasis on order and control which this quality of formality indicates have been repeatedly discussed in terms of many aspects of Navajo art and thought, and do not need to be repeated here, except to remark that the ordered and precise and often complex effects achieved may be especially satisfying because the materials are so simple and unstructured. By knowledge, control, and cooperative effort, an elaborate, ordered, beautiful thing is produced from simple materials, mostly from the earth itself.

REICHARD 1939

8

Navajo Secular Arts and the Navajo Style

The aim in this chapter is to discover to what extent we can speak of a Navajo style in the visual arts, and to explore in a general way the possibility that differences in style in the various forms are related not only to their technological differences but also their uses and functions. Do the form-meanings which can be applied to these styles seem sufficiently appropriate to justify the use of the term "communication" in forms of art not deliberately symbolic?

The arts considered here are weaving, pottery, silverwork (jewelry), watercolor paintings, and basketry, all of which contribute to the Navajo reputation as an artistically productive people. These are primarily secular arts, and to a very large extent are made for use by peoples other than the Navajo themselves. The baskets are an exception, as the Navajo actually use more than they produce. Although the use nowadays is chiefly ceremonial, baskets are included with the secular arts for convenience.

The treatment of each medium is less detailed than is the case with the drypaintings because the data is not sufficient to place these forms firmly in contexts where the situation gives clues as to the kinds of communication to expect. In the case of the drypaintings there is a known symbolism, a stated purpose, and the functions of the ceremonies of which the drypaintings are a part have been studied and analyzed, so there is a limiting of possibilities, a framework which serves as a kind of test of the form-meaning interpretations. In the other arts, the information as to use and function is scanty. In the case of the crafts there is no symbolism with which to compare meaning, and in the watercolors only the symbolism provided by a representational content. In such circumstances an examination of form-meanings is frankly speculative, providing a variety of questions and hypotheses the significance of which can only be determined by intensive study of the social history of each of the art forms.

Navajo crafts are produced and used in a situation of many cross-cultural contacts and influences. As all of these are American, in one way or another, I have used certain specific terms to distinguish people and cultures which are relevant to the situation. When speaking of art tradition I frequently use the term *Euro-American* or simply *European* by which I mean the long term stylistic tradition often referred to as "Western Art". It would thus include the Spanish traditions which are to be found in this area. When speaking of persons, I use the well-known Southwestern term *Anglo* for those Americans whose native language is English, and who are the chief purchasers of Navajo crafts.

WEAVING

The uses of fabrics woven by Navajo women have changed with time, as have the stylistic features. If there is a relationship between use and style, examination of these historical changes should provide a useful starting place in a highly complex situation.

The Navajo apparently learned the techniques of weaving from the Pueblo some time before 1800. During the 19th century cloth gradually replaced buckskin for clothing, and by the end of this period trade cloth had replaced hand woven material. About 1900 the weaving of wearing blankets ceased, and the chief product became rugs made for sale, although saddle blankets have been made in considerable quantity, and sashes were made probably to a greater extent than is implied by the lack of attention given them in the literature. Technically, rugs are usually thicker and coarser than blankets. Stylistically, certain changes occurred at the same time as the shift in use, but stylistic features are so varied that the influences are not immediately apparent, although in some cases the stylistic requirements of individual traders are documented. As Adair (1944:135) says concerning silverwork designs, they show "the Indian's idea of the trader's idea of what the white man thought was Indian design". What emerges very clearly from the story of the influence of the traders on style is the variety of tastes in Anglo society, and the variety of ideas as to what Indian design should be. The romantic appeal of the primitive is widespread, but "primitive" is variously conceived. On the other hand, one cannot conclude that Indians were without ideas of their own, and there are many tales of the difficulties of getting a weaver to make a rug to order. Traders were not entirely immune to direct indoctrination as to what is Indian, and historic blankets were widely used as sources of design ideas.

Mills (1959:63) maintains that in spite of the influences of trader and purchaser, the rugs express basically Navajo values. He says: "If the values of an alien culture are expressing themselves in Navajo weaving, I err in drawing conclusions about Navajo values from this art." He surmounts the difficulty of "alien values" by considering only the qualities he finds characteristic of all Navajo art forms. Which is fine as far as it goes, but what about the other qualities? Unless they are also meaningful, the whole idea of form-meaning is greatly weakened.

Whether considered subjectively or in terms of specific qualities, there is great variation in Navajo weaving style, and the interpretive possibilities are correspondingly diverse. This diversity can be illustrated by some examples of the various styles, historical and recent, with brief indications as to context and some interpretive speculations.

HISTORIC BLANKET STYLES

Except for saddle blankets, most of the weaving done by Navajo for Navajo was in the form of blankets to be worn as outer garments. These blankets were replaced by the commercially produced Pendleton blanket at the end of the 19th century. A blanket is worn for protection from the elements and is also worn when the person goes away from home. A blanket symbolizes the excitement of going out among people, and the protection which it affords from people, especially strangers, as well as from the elements. It is also a symbol of Indianness.

The earliest designs were all horizontal stripes. (In discussing weaving, "horizontal" is considered to be the dimension across the width of the piece, i. e., the direction of the weft, as this is the way the weaver sees it as she weaves.) Stripes are, of course, a first step in design in this technique; Pueblo blankets have always maintained the rather simple striped patterns. Striped patterns persisted among the Navajo through the subsequent style phases, and were probably numerically much more common than would be thought from the samples pictured in books and on view in museums, as they were less often preserved or photographed. Reichard (1950:206) says that in a ceremonial context stripes to the Navajo are symbolic of protection because they have a terrifying effect, but the Navajo do not seem to carry over such symbolism to other contexts. Still, the broad black and white stripes of the "Chief" style blankets are very similar to the stripes which often protect Pueblo clowns, and Pendleton blankets are usually striped.

TERRACED

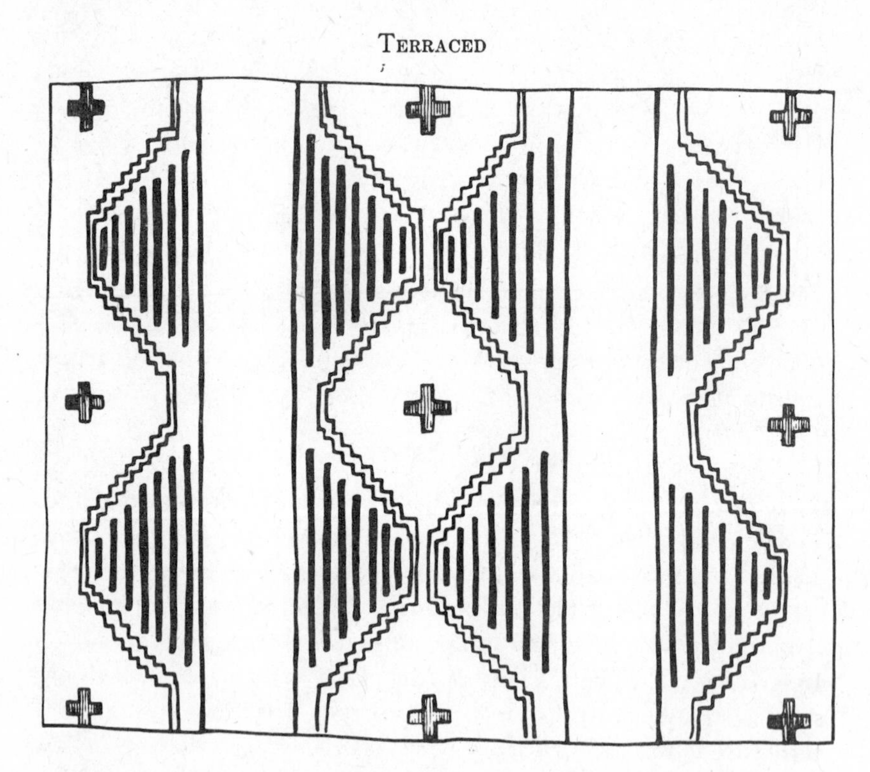

The next period, 1800–1863, produced a style called by Amsden the Terraced style. During this period stripes gradually became more complex, characteristically moving across the blanket in zigzag or diamond forms which were made up of a series of right-angled steps or terraces, i. e., of horizontal and vertical component lines. This is also the period of Bayeta red combined with white, blue (indigo), and black. Patterns of the period are very bold and assured, not very complex, and lack borders and, usually, outlines. The biaxial symmetry is seldom perfect in spite of the technical excellence. The blankets of this period are considered by Amsden (1949:209) "the supreme expression of Navajo skill at the loom", although there are recent prize-winning rugs that equal the fineness of weave and excel in absolute perfection in terms of regularity of design.

DIAMOND

In the period following the Navajo defeat and the captivity at Bosque Redondo (Fort Sumner) from 1863 to about 1900, came the style which Amsden calls the Diamond style, which has also been referred to as the "serrated" or "dazzle" style. Other styles persisted, and it would probably be more accurate to say that certain style qualities increased in proportion, rather than that one style replaced another; many pieces of the period are neither "pure" Terraced nor "pure" Diamond. Blankets of this period were characterized by colors of great variety in hue and of marked intensity, by the use of points in profusion, by careful outlining of these brilliant points, some ambiguity of figure and ground, rhythmic variation achieved by color shifts in repeated elements, moderate complexity, great tension, and a considerable degree of freedom in composition.

These qualities are technically a result of experimentation with new commercial dyes and yarn, and interpretively, clearly suggest very strong emotions and controlled aggression. They also convey a feeling of great vitality. Blankets of this period were worn not only by Navajo, but were widely traded and worn by Indians of other tribes, and were increasingly purchased at first by Mexicans and Anglos as blankets, later to be used as rugs.

RUGS

With the turn of the century came the completion of the transition from the weaving of blankets to be worn to rugs for sale, and the rise of regional styles largely as a result of the influence of the various traders, each with his own ideas as to what Indian design should be. Perhaps the greatest single stylistic change associated with this transition is the use of heavy borders. Amsden considers the borders entirely a result of white pressure; Mills thinks it consistent with Navajo values. I only note that the use of borders developed during the reservation period, that the greatest use of borders came with rugs made for sale (rather than blankets); that such borders are usually found on the bold contrasting types of rugs, but not in the more reposeful, harmonious types. I also note that the Navajo attitude toward boundaries depends on the control—they provide safety for the "life space" if one controls the area within, but may also be constricting and threatening. While the reservation (like the blanket borders) was imposed by others, it is constricting, but also protective. In sum, however, if all this has meaning, the interpretation favors Amsden, because: (1) The change so largely coincides with the switch to rugs, (2) It is the aggressive, barbaric, centrifugal types which are contained, not the peaceful harmonious types which are protected, and (3) The opening or spirit path through the border is not really part of the design, but almost a hidden evasion of it.

Of the styles which have continued to the present, there are, in addition to the regional styles, a number of special types which for the most part may be woven anywhere on the reservation. These include, first of all, the "translations" of Navajo religious art which exhibit a full range of seriousness and sensitivity, and their lack. There are sandpainting tapestries, "Yei" rugs portraying something like the supernatural figures, usually in a variety of garish colors, and the Yeibichai rugs showing masked dancers. Most persons with understanding and sympathy for the Navajo religion dislike all of them heartily, even the better sandpainting tapestries. There are pictorial rugs in generalized folk-primitive style with animals, trains, and the like, in light bright colors. A traditional type which may be produced anywhere is the "Chief" blanket; a style which comes historically at the transition from striped to terraced. Every so often a rug is produced based on an optical illusion, such as rows of diamonds which produce the effect of stacked cubes.

About half the rugs produced each year, however, fall into none of the named categories, according to Maxwell (1963:52). He says: "The General rug is the rug whose design, quality, and color do not distinguish it as being from any particular locale. They may be plain stripes or geometric patterns with or without a border." The regional and special styles are the ones usually bought by collectors and Southwest buffs, and the others by the more casual buyers.

At least a dozen and usually more regional styles are distinguished by experts (Tanner 1964). Four well-known regional types will be briefly described to show the range of variation.

Tec Nos Pos

The Tec Nos Pos looks like a Victorian idea of Indian design. Its most marked feature is a series of elaborate concentric borders, within which elements are symmetrically scattered without strong structuring lines. The number of colors is variable, as is the emphasis on color, and the intensity. Contrasts in hue and values are minimized by the smallness of the elements in the design; this is the style with the greatest emphasis on detail. There is no ambiguity of figure and ground. Outlining of all figures is characteristic. In general the composition is fairly complex (4), neither bold nor delicate (3), high in tension (4), and low in movement (2) and quite formal in effect, although the patterning lacks coherence.

Interpretations suggest an exceptional degree of control, a lack of emotional commitment (to the style? to communicating with it?), busyness, or compulsiveness.

Two Grey Hills

The Two Grey Hills style is most valued by connoisseurs for the highest standards of craftsmanship. Stylistically it is marked by the exclusive use of natural wool colors—black, brown, white, tan, and grey in harmonious shades, used in a moderate degree of value contrast (3–4). Details are quite small (1–2), but combined into quite large units

(4). The structuring lines tend to be diagonal, arranged in the form of one or two large diamond shaped forms with elaborated multiple sides. The whole is strongly contained by heavy and multiple borders. While forms are distributed throughout the field, the arrangement often achieves a strong center emphasis. All the composition qualities are balanced at about the half way point, but the total effect is of much more unity and sometimes drama in the compositions, although some seem "fussy" and the perfection excessive.

The structural diagonals of this style suggests Aaronson's interpretation regarding need for achievement which could refer to the makers. The use of color suggests at the same time closeness to nature and great sophistication.

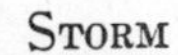

Storm

The Storm pattern associated with the Tuba City area is the most dramatic of rug styles. Colors are limited to black, white, grey, and red, used with great contrasting effect. Small details are rare, and outlining confined to a few figures. While the field is moderately full (4), with contrast of figure and ground, there is a strong center emphasis. Structural lines consist basically of opposed diagonals in the form of a large X, and radiation from the center. Boldness, tension and movement are all high. The whole is controlled by a border which may be strong in contrast and multiple (i. e., black and white), but is not broad. Design is formed of solid areas and heavy lines often in zigzag form.

Interpretively, this style is rather obviously one of "barbaric" vitality, somewhat controlled by formal patterns and a definite border. The name indicates what it probably suggests to the Anglo purchaser, that the primitive means closeness to the elemental and powerful forces of nature (perhaps danger encountered or mastered?). It is of interest that this pattern formally resembles, in its emphasis on radiation from a center controlled by a border, the design of the ketoh and also the drypaintings, although in these more purely Navajo forms the tension is less and the harmony greater.

VEGETAL DYE

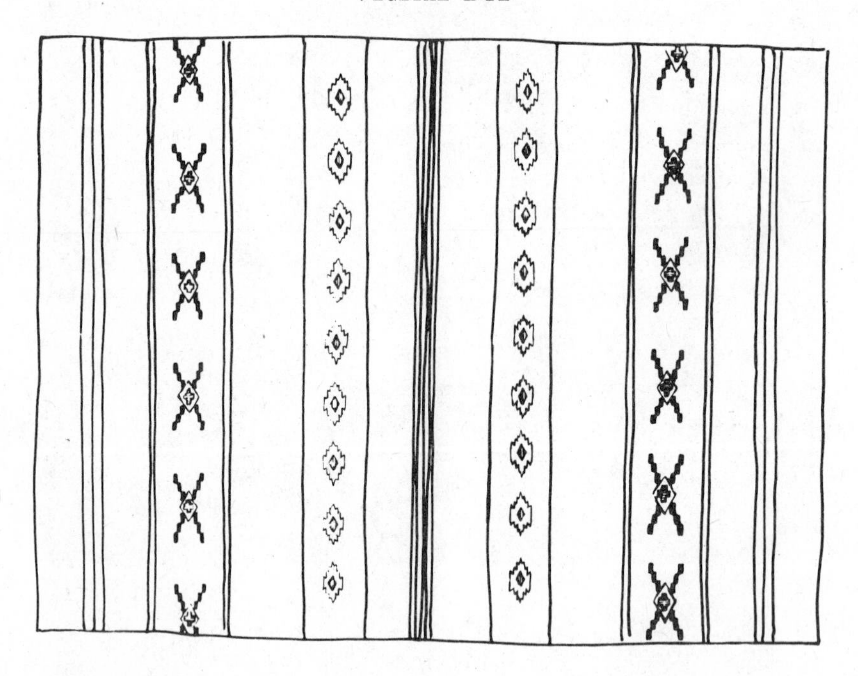

The vegetal dye rugs, particularly from Crystal and Wide Ruins, have but few stylistic elements in common with the detailed and elaborate Tec Nos Pos or the dramatic Storm patterns. In almost every aspect, harmony is stressed rather than contrast. No borders are used. The soft colors, usually warm in tone—(yellows, oranges, and tans), are arranged in bands of parallel stripes rather evenly distributed over the field. There is some use of outlined detail, but in terms of simple figures statically repeated within the bands. Variety is achieved by the number of harmonized hues, often intermingled, and by alternation of patterned and plain stripes, and by some value contrast, with black and contrasting outlines used sparingly.

The appeal of these rugs leans very heavily on values assigned to closeness to nature and self sufficiency. Regardless of any visual effects it is part of the rules that no commercial dyestuffs be used in these rugs; however pleasing the subtlety of the effect such a rug would lose value if the dyes in it were discovered to be commercially obtained. The idea that is important here is that this is the way weaving was done before being corrupted by contact. Interestingly enough, it is probable that very few vegetal dyes were ever used before the "revival" in the 30's. At any rate, interpretations of the formal qualities place the stress on harmony, gentle yet warm emotion, patience and optimism, and a kind of relaxed vitality.

It is my impression that the traders most sympathetic to the Navajo way, especially the Navajo religion, were those who encouraged the use of vegetal dyes. They have always appealed to the more esthetically oriented in Anglo society, as well as to those attracted by the myth of the "really native" form.

General

As to the General rugs, they seem to be of better quality than those described as tourist rugs that were common in the 1930's, although in some cases the colors can still be described as "riotous aniline". Reichard attributes garish hues entirely to the consumer and to the use of aniline dyes, but it seems clear from her accounts that color sensitivity varies in weavers as it does in purchasers.

> It is the use of color secured by aniline dyes that the Navajo rug loses its artistic value. The white tourist is the ultimate consumer. His standards are lax and he knows nothing about Navajo rugs. He sees them hanging from the framework of a roadside shade. They look to him romantic, barbaric. He will take one home to his room. One remark I have often heard made by the more sensitive of his ilk is, "Oh, they are not nearly so nice when you get close to them, are they?".
>
> One reason those he sees are not, is to be laid at the door of his brethern who drive in haste and buy in ignorance. They want something gaudy; they would like it to be large; it must be cheap.

> Since Navajo rugs are usually sold by weight, large ones, no matter how hideous, are expensive. The jarring color combinations are due more acutely to the buyer's taste than to cheapness. It is true that the Navajo, now that so many things are furnished her, must buy such dyes as are available. If left to herself she would, more often than not, use the more quiet colors, of which she has a good variety. Occasionally she would, as she has in the past, come forth with a daring essay at brilliancy which might turn out to be a stroke of genius. (Reichard 1936:26)

Of the 32 General rugs examined, 4 were multicolored aniline, 2 vegetal dyed, and 16 black, white, and grey, usually with red, and 1 in tones of brown. The remaining 9 cases had color schemes which departed from the usual rules followed in fine rugs, where the browns are not found with reds if the number of hues is limited. In these 9 there was a yellowish tan with black, white, grey, and red, which was hardly "riotous," but was disharmonious.

The various named styles, for all their variety, can be considered as a class on the basis of use, since those found reproduced in the sources are all prizewinners, collector's items, and museum pieces. All are characterized by fineness and perfection of weave. In stylistic qualities there are some characteristics which seem to distinguish General rugs from these "fine" rugs. The commercial rugs are simpler, usually lack linear forms and outlining, and tend to be bolder due to larger forms and value contrasts.

For all the variety of stylistic features, there are several differences worth noting between the historical blankets, made for Indian use, and the rugs made for sale to Anglo purchasers. The most noticeable to me is the exactness of the more recent pieces. Deviations from exact symmetry, variations in color are very rare. By all accounts, this is the result of pressure from the traders who sought to "improve the standards". It was largely to check this perfectionism as a general trend that I included the recent commercial sample, and it appears to be as true of run-of-the-loom items as of the prizewinners. This shows up in the ratings of *degree of symmetry* and in *formality*.

Esthetically, the effect is toward a lessening of vitality that is less pleasing than the effect produced by the slight irregularities of the historic blanket styles. In terms of communication, this emphasis on perfection seems to convey the message that a human being is as good as a machine, which is comforting.

SADDLE BLANKETS

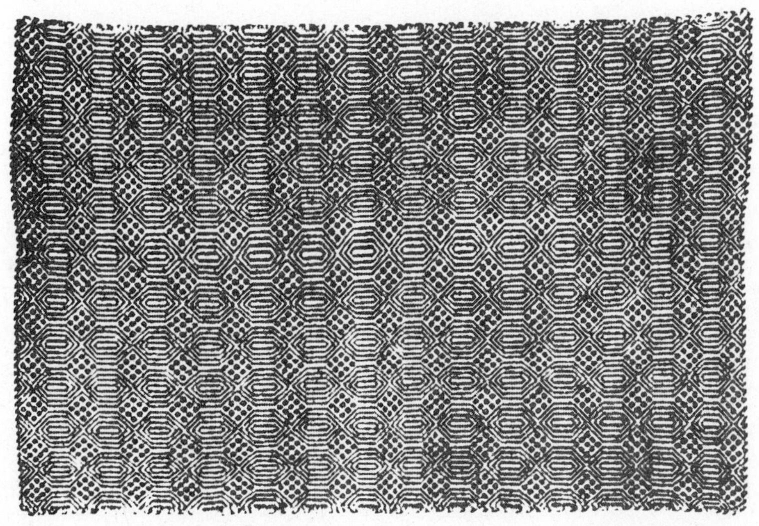
MERA 1943

Since the turn of the century the only pieces which the Navajo themselves use are certain of the saddle blankets, and the stylistic differences between these and the Navajo rug are startling.

The majority of saddle blankets made for home consumption are produced by a different technique than the Navajo rugs (Amsden 1949, Reichard 1936). Instead of the tapestry weave by which solid areas of color and bold patterns may be achieved, these saddle blankets are woven in twill weaves which result in small repetitive geometric patterns. In these patterns, even in the cases where colors contrast in hue and value, the components are so small, (the area of the colors may be only the width of a single thread), that all contrast is minimized, and the effect is quite subdued.

The chief use of these blankets is not only under a saddle when the horse is ridden, but as a seat on the ground when a horseman is visiting. It is these blankets which women weave for their men, and which are tacitly displayed as the work of women of the family when men go visiting. From these circumstances one might conclude that the communication has to do with the kind of women a man likes to think of as related to himself. Quiet repetitive patterns with strong emphasis on craftsmanship are characteristic of "women's art" all over the world. Hoernes-Menghin has expressed the male view of this in its most extreme form:

> The geometric ornament seems more suited to the domestic, pedantically tidy and at the same time superstitiously careful spirit of women than to that of man. It is, considered purely aesthetically, a petty, lifeless and, despite all its luxuriousness and colour, a strictly limited mode of art, but within its limits healthy and efficient, pleasing by reason of the industry displayed and its external decorativeness—the expression of the feminine spirit in art. (Hoernes-Menghin 1925:40, as translated by Goodman in Hauser 1951:23)

Yet when there is an audience which will applaud the more dramatic products of women, they seem quite capable of producing them, and furthermore, to enjoy the work, as in the case of the Navajo rugs made for sale. When Navajo women wove blankets to be worn, those woven for men seem to have been much bolder in pattern than those woven for women. But it is the saddle blankets which convey the full Penelope image of the industrious, capable woman, even tempered and serene, never making herself conspicuous.

BASKETRY

Baskets, like pots, are containers, and are used in much the same way. The uses of containers fall into two main categories: purely domestic, and ceremonial. They may also, of course, be made for sale or trade. However, technological differences in the manufacture of pots and baskets not only have a direct effect on design, as in the matter of curved and straight lines, but make the creative process psychologically different. Painting on a pot is put on afterward for purely esthetic effect. Designs on baskets are part of the manufacturing process and closely related to it. They do not require extra effort in the same manner as pottery painting, and in fact tend to relieve the tedium of the process itself. Designs in all weaving processes are not effected by motor expressiveness except insofar as skill makes for regularity. Because of technological limitations, design in basketry is the least "free" of all Navajo arts.

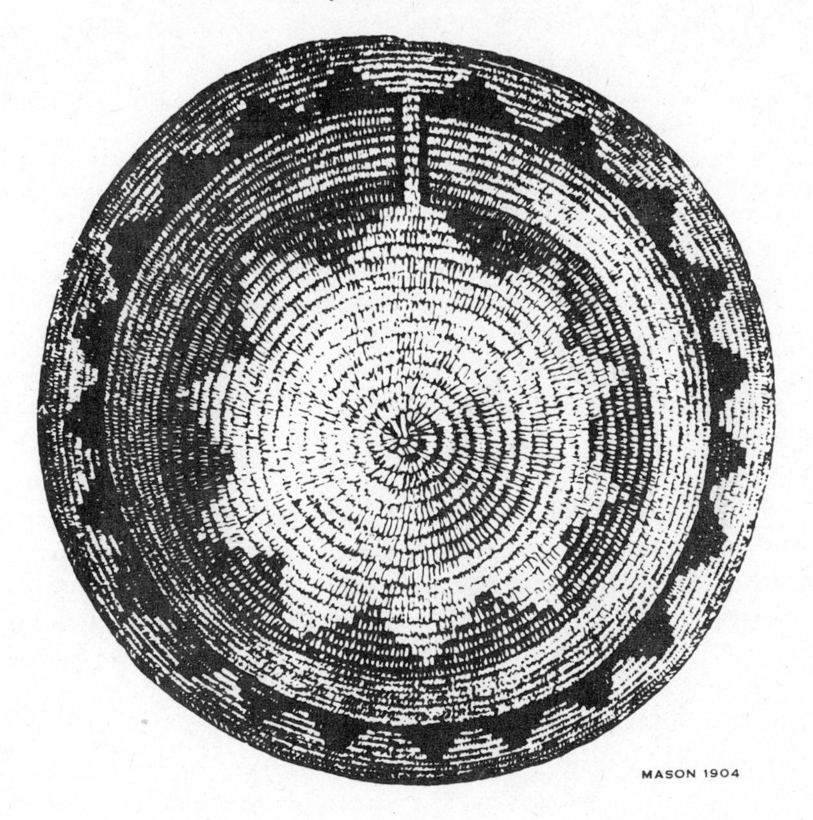
MASON 1904

> . . . Navajo basketry is employed today exclusively in a ritual context. The uses to which baskets are put may be grouped into two categories: (1) in song ceremonials, which have as their objective the curing of disease; (2) in weddings.
>
> In song ceremonials, baskets are used in several different contexts: (1) as a drum; (2) as a container for the ritual bath; (3) as a container for ritual paraphernalia and medicine (rattles, sacred meal, prayersticks and ritually prepared cigarettes); (4) as a food container in certain ceremonials; and (5) as a portion of the mask in certain of the nine-night ceremonials. (Tschopik 1940:447)

Designs on Navajo baskets are quite simple, and although one pattern commonly known as the wedding basket seems to be the most typical, there is a fair amount of variation. Navajo basketry has in recent times been used almost entirely in ceremonial contexts, but Tschopik was told that there was no difference in design between baskets used ceremonially and those for everyday use. Apparently the only ritual requirement of the design is that it provide a means of orienting it to the points of the compass. This is done by means of a break in the pattern which forms a "door" which can be turned to the east (ibid.: 445).

The layout of the design is affected by the way the ritual requirement for an opening is carried out. Emphasis on the "door" beyond the ritual necessity tends to alter the design from a purely radial one to one which is bilateral as well. This path or doorway gives a bilateral quality in which opposition plays no part; in this it is similar to the paintings of Blessing Way. It is interesting to note that in illustrations of these baskets the door is placed at any old position and is neither oriented to the conventional east of the page nor toward the top or bottom to conform to the symmetry. This suggests that to the observer from our culture the line is regarded as an abberation in the symmetry, and therefore an expression of the irrational—mere superstition, not part of the design. To the eye attuned to only simple symmetrical usage, in which a round form has no directional orientation, that is the way the opening appears.

While the radial layout seems to be the most usual, there is sufficient variation in symmetry and in the direction of structural lines to suggest that there is no specific symbolic or form-meaning which relates these designs to specific ritual usage, except in the general sense of order common to all symmetrical forms. However, the lack of border of any kind rather than the incomplete one found on so many drypaintings, together with the radiating quality of the preferred pattern, suggests that the power of whatever sacred material is held in the basket is expected to go forth in all directions. Outlining of figures is not common, so there is little of the feeling of control and containment in this regard either.

The analysis of basketry design was made from black and white illustrations, but it seems clear from the accompanying descriptions that Navajo baskets show relatively little emphasis on color when compared to those made by some of the other peoples in the Southwest. Three colors are used: black, "white", and brown or red. When the baskets are used in wedding ceremonies the contents are blue cornmeal and yellow pollen, which would complete the basic requirements of color symbolism in Navajo ritual, but I do not know if the colors of the baskets and contents were thought of in this way.

The designs, as I have said, are quite simple. According to Barry's hypothesis, this is correlated with lack of severity in socialization. As drypaintings are on the whole rather complex, either his hypothesis does not apply or there is a great difference in the socialization of males and females. If the Rorschach interpretation, W, can be considered as complexity, either the women who weave baskets lack intelligence, organization and drive as personalities, or they do not use these qualities in making baskets. However, the interpretation of the designs on baskets in terms of modal personality projection is complicated by the fact that they are often made by Utes and Paiutes.

As the baskets are all used in ceremonial contexts, it is clear that the style is not determined by this consideration, because the sandpaintings do tend to be complex. The difference seems to be that, to consider the function in terms of communication, baskets simply do not carry much in the way of a message. Applying the terminology of Berstein (1964) in regard to language, one could say that baskets are a kind of "restricted code", whereas the drypaintings with which they are used carry the communication in a highly "elaborated code".

POTTERY

AFTER TSCHOPIK 1941

Pottery is used in the home to store, cook, and serve food. It is sometimes given to other households with food in it. Cooking pots are seldom decorated except for some kind of patterned roughness on the surface which has a useful purpose in making the cooking ware more easily handled. Pots for eating and storage purposes are decorated as part of the housewifely desire to have things "nice". In any culture keeping the home "nice" is compounded of neatness, cleanliness, and attractiveness. While the criteria for each of these aspects varies widely from culture to culture, the components are there and are not often distinguished from each other in the general appraisal. A nice house, which often includes "pretty things" reflects the success of a woman as a woman, her desire to have things nice for her family, and the ability of her husband to provide. Where the woman makes her own utensils, her skill in making them is also a matter of personal pride. Family pride in such a household skill may also be marked, as when techniques are passed down through the matrilineage. There may even be secrecy in this regard.

If formal qualities do reflect or transmit feelings appropriate to the situation, one would expect the painting on domestic pottery to convey this domesticity. In terms of values, it would be the meaning of home, and the characteristics of the respected family. It should convey, in terms of personality, the preferred self-image of the woman who makes it. But, as such painting is also to a degree expressive, in the sense of serving as an outlet for the individual, one would expect that in some degree the fantasy life of the painter would come through the more conventional expression. Desires which affect the family life might be expressed, and these might well be cultural desires which are also seen in religious art, such as the desire for rain and good crops, for health and children. On the whole one would expect that the importance of presenting a picture of a nice home would tend to mute any elements which would be contrary to this expression, or disturbing in any way, because however satisfying it might be to the maker, others would not react favorably.

Among the Navajo, it is clear that pottery was never of great artistic significance. It was simply a minor craft which was earlier subordinated to basketry and probably hide containers, and later supplanted by trade goods.

At first glance the thing which strikes one about the available sample of Navajo pottery is that it is, especially when compared to that of the

Pueblos, very crude and simple. Upon analysis, the striking thing is the extraordinary amount of variety in these few and simple examples. Examination of the analytical data reveals that, aside from complexity, almost every degree of every category is used. There are no strong stylistic features which might yield to interpretation except this diversity and the simplicity itself.

The simplicity would, according to the hypothesis of Barry, indicate lack of severity of socialization, and according to Fischer is correlated with egalitarian societies. These hypotheses are supported, but both these qualities are in contradiction to those in the sandpaintings. It is, of course possible that the society as perceived by women is less hierarchical than that perceived by men, and that socialization is more severe for males than for females. However, comparison with the qualities of the more developed female art of weaving suggests that this difference is not based on sex-determined sub-cultures, insofar as they are reflected in art.

As a vehicle for self-expression, pottery painting, being a relatively free medium, offers the greatest opportunity of any art form available to Navajo women, except, perhaps, solitary song. The taboos mentioned by Tschopik (1941) may account in part for the abandonment of the craft, but they do not explain why the pots which were made seem to have been painted with so little artistic concentration. As seems to have been the case with baskets, their role in communication was probably not important. Furthermore, it seems evident that the possibilities of self-expression did not provide sufficient motivation in the face of the lack of other incentives; but perhaps beyond this the very freedom of the medium made it less attractive than the patterned, controlled quality of the weaving process, which combines many small elements.

The impression one gets is that the potters were not "saying" anything at all, but only trying out the effect of an experiment which occurred to them in a off-hand way. One can see a variety of influences —Pueblo, Mexican, and Anglo on even these simple forms. Had the craft been developed and a real style emerged, the forms would perhaps have become increasingly meaningful as the skill at communicating in this medium developed. The very variety does, however, suggest a degree of artistic potential, and raises the question as to whether the development of a style rests on selection and elimination of basic form-qualities rather than on a process of accretion.

On the other hand, the lack of formality in pottery painting does show stylistic variation from other arts. Household articles are not important as articles of display, and Tschopik finds considerable individual variation, supporting interpretations which assign a social rather than a psychological meaning to the precision of Navajo art.

JEWELRY

Aside from ritual costume and paraphernalia, self-adornment has the obvious function in communicating information in the not unconnected realms of status and sex. Concerning the Navajo, Kluckhohn and Leighton say that one of the attributes of a respected man is the possession of tangible and intangible goods, among which "hard goods" (principally jewelry) are prominently mentioned.

> A good appearance is valued; while this is partly a matter of physique, figure and facial appearance, it means even more the ability to dress well and to appear with a handsome horse and substantial trappings. (Kluckhohn and Leighton 1962:300)

But, as Adair says about jewelry:

> The display of wealth is not a personal matter as much as it is a family matter. It is not "see how much money I have" but "see how much money we have in our family." (Adair 1944:98)
>
> The Navajo's jewelry serves three functions: as decoration, to display his wealth, and as a collateral against which he can borrow at the trading post. (ibid.:99)
>
> The aesthetic function of silver is of a secondary nature. Navajo admire beauty of craftsmanship; a heavy piece of silver, well marked with dies and set with good stones of a dark color, excites admiration. Sloppily made, poorly constructed silver is rarely worn by them although they may sell much of it for white consumption. (ibid.:100)

Insofar as the silver is made for sale, however, Anglo concepts of status and attractiveness influence the forms as well as the quality. In the Anglo display of Indian silver there is evident a conflict of values. In Anglo the sexual attractiveness of a female and her status as a lady calls for a certain amount of fragility and daintiness, and a massive "barbaric" quality has been regarded as deviant until very recently, and is still reserved for the more daring. And, of course, few Anglo women can wear much of the heavy Navajo silver for very long without

ADAIR 1944

WHITEHAIR, NAVAJO

discomfort. On the other hand, a man who wishes to communicate his masculinity is exceedingly sparing in the wearing of jewelry. Hence usually the only Anglos who wear Navajo silver to any extent are those whose desires to exhibit their status as knowledgable Southwest Buffs overcomes the wish to appear as desirable and respectable examples of their own sex and society. So aside from the poor craftsmanship of tourist pieces, silver made for sale often loses some of its stylistic quality by being lighter and smaller. Where the emphasis of the Anglo owner is on authenticity of style, the pieces are likely to be displayed as a collection, and have little to say about the sex of the owner. Antiquity and traditional form are important values.

The fact that Anglos wear less and lighter jewelry than do Indians means that by the wearing of considerable amounts of it the Navajo indicates not only his ability to secure it, but also his pride in being an Indian. I suspect that Indian women know that Anglo females lack the strength and endurance to wear many pieces, even though they obviously admire it and presumably could afford it, and so the Navajo women shows her superiority in this regard.

There are certain limitations on the study of this art form within the present framework. In the first place, the approach calls for consideration of the form within the context, which means a consideration of when, where, and how it is worn. This calls for an analysis centered on the whole matter of dress and ornament, the nature of self and body images, which in turn calls for cross-cultural study to be meaningful. Only by stretching the convention to a considerable degree can we consider the designs as two-dimensional forms, as can be done with other forms of Navajo visual art; hence the descriptive categories of the schema used are less satisfactory for this craft.

In spite of these limitations, certain observations are suggestive of the possibilities in the interpretation of this art form in terms of some applicable form-qualities and the obvious functions of the medium.

I. Layout

In the treatment of silver there are two basic techniques for shaping the piece. One is by hammering, the other by casting. In the former the shape of the whole is of necessity quite simple, and the designs depend on stamped-in elements and some added features such as turquoise and small balls of silver. Cast silver, exemplified by the ketoh (bow-guard) as seen on the wrist of Whitehair in the illustration, permits of more variety and delicacy of shape. While casting as a technique has been known as long as pounding and stamping, the latter seems to have been consistently favored, except for the ketoh and for small elements to be used in necklaces. Hammering is perhaps less tricky, but esthetic preference is surely a factor. This is possibly an example of the Navajo tendency to achieve effects by a variety of combinations of small elements, to which the use of dies gives very great scope.

> The Navajo smith is just as proud of his collection of dies as he is of the silver he makes. To the Zuni, the die is just another tool. (Adair 1944:152)

To the artistically trained Anglo, the creating of new forms in cast silver seems more of an artistic achievement, and the use of dies for stamping designs is likely to be regarded as "mere craftsmanship". But new cast forms are not likely to look Indian enough, and so their sale potential is lessened.

Navajo silver made before World War II is characterized by fairly large design units (4–5) and not a great deal of small detail (3). There is usually a strong center emphasis which is often marked by a set of turquoise. When compared to the Zuni style which frequently involves many stones of equal size, this would seem to suggest an individualistic quality as compared to Zuni communalism. In context, the pieces are worn with other pieces. Necklaces and belts, however, usually consist of a number of units of equal size and the identical design, often marked by a center pendent or buckle of slightly different form.

The field is typically only moderately full (4), but there is considerable variation which, according to Adair, reflects the individual taste of the smith.

II. Repetition, Balance, and Symmetry

Pieces of jewelry are nearly always symmetrical, with an emphasis on the biaxial-radial form. As jewelry in many cultures is so often symmetrical, this would not seem to warrant a great deal of interpretive emphasis. However, the greater use of the biaxia'-radial forms may be of some interest, especially when compared to the greater incidence of bilateral forms in Anglo jewelry and the greater use of bilaterality and two-dimensional repetition in Zuni work. This emphasis is marked in regard to buckles; buckles on concha belts are biaxial-radial in design, which seems to be a strictly Indian development. The contrast with the typical bilateral Western buckle can be seen in the photograph of Whitehair.

Precise symmetry is considered important by the Navajo, and is closely correlated with good craftsmanship in all work.

III. Lines

Insofar as the concept of component line applies, silverwork seems to show no marked trends or avoidances in the various categories of line. Component lines are for the most part made by the use of dies with which they are stamped into the silver. Adair categories the sample of dies used as including 23 crescent shapes, 11 triangular, and three straight edge. From his data (Adair 1944:105), I would consider many of these to have a strong radial component. In layout, straight lines are more often used in radial patterns in the intermediate areas of the design field, while curved lines are very characteristic of the borders. Borders are especially characteristic of the older pieces, and are often scalloped on conchas.

Structural lines comprise or enhance the biaxial-radial layouts.

IV. Color

Although the Navajo use coral and shell as beads, they do not set stones other than turquoise in silver. In this they contrast with the Zuni, who use a variety of colors to produce mosaic effects.

> Silver to the Zuni is primarily a plastic material in which turquoise may be held; silver in itself does not possess the beauty that it does in the eyes of their Navajo neighbors. (Adair 1944:151)

In view of the usual hypotheses regarding color, the implication would be that either jewelry is less important generally in the expression and communication of emotion among the Navajo than the Zuni, or that it concerns a lesser range of emotion, or the color of silver has meaning in itself.

As to value contrast, it is interesting to note that the Navajo prefer silver very shiny to emphasize the beauty of the silver and to make the pieces look new. The Anglo prefers it oxidized to bring out the contrast of the design and to make the pieces look old. In either case, the contrast of values is high, in the one instance within the area of the form itself, and in the other especially as seen against clothes and skin.

VI. Composition

Design of the twenties and thirties has been called "baroque" when compared to the massive forms of earlier work, but this seems justified only in terms of this comparison. On the whole the works of this period are not really complex within a broader frame of reference, and they are substantial rather than elaborate.

In terms of the interpretations relating to status, this is perhaps significant. The message conveyed by the wearing of such jewelry is that the family is composed of substantial citizens, rather than conspicuous consumers. The substantial quality and relative simplicity are consistent with these values.

The Ketoh

From the context in which it is worn, it may be assumed that this form of jewelry has a somewhat more specific meaning than can be postulated for other forms.

> The ketoh is one of the few pieces of Navajo jewelry which has not been commercialized by white men. It alone, of all Navajo silver, remains the exclusive property of the Indian. From the point of view of design, many of the finest pieces of Navajo silver have been ketohs. Many of them are still being worn, and fine ones are still being made by the smiths. (Adair 1944:35)

The bow-guard, furthermore, is not worn by women, so the wearing of the ketoh indicates very clearly that the wearer is a man and an Indian and proud of it.

> Ketohs decorated with openwork produced by casting have a characteristic design, which is built up of the elements which lead from the center to the edges of the ketoh. Frequently there are four shallow *s*-shaped bars, like those found on the buckles. Each of these four bars leads out to a corner. The *x* thus formed is quartered, four bars of silver leading out to the edges, midway between the corners. Very often the bars, in a vertical position and radiating from the center of the ketoh to the midpoints of the top and bottom edges, have small curvilinear bars branching from

> them in a leaflike pattern. The horizontal bars, extending to midpoints on the vertical edges of the ketoh are shorter and simpler in design. This style of composition makes the center of the ketoh the focus of interest. A turquoise is usually set in this area, giving just the accent needed to complete the design. From old ketohs it seems that this design existed before turquoise was set in silver; however, once the art of setting was learned, stones were used.
>
> Silversmiths continue to make bow-guards by fashioning the metal into thin rectangular sheets. The designs which are stamped on these sheets are often very similiar in form and composition to the designs of the cast ketohs. Many times there will be not only the single set in the center, but one at each corner as well.
>
> The Navajo men wear their ketohs today more for decoration than for protection when using the bow. Bow-guards may be seen on dress occasions: at squaw-dances, at sings, and when the men come to town. The silversmiths make ketohs for the Pueblo Indians as well as for the men of their own tribe. During the summer rain-dances in the Hopi villages and at Zuni, the dancers wear bow-guards, which are an essential part of the dress of many of the Kachina dancers. (ibid.:34)

In comparison with other jewelry, the ketoh is usually less massive, and is characterized by reverse curves which are rare in Navajo art forms except for the ketoh and the buckle. If regular form, such as in curves as arcs, can be said to suggest formality, and conformity, then these reverse curves should indicate a greater degree of spontaneity than other art forms. The controlling border is not usually abandoned, however. The sinewy, graceful quality of Navajo cast silver is particularly noticeable in the ketoh, and the dramatic center emphasis seems to convey a masculine quality, especially when compared to the all-over design of the twill saddle blankets.

Changing Fashions in Navajo Jewelry

> Standards of beauty are undergoing a change today, just as they have in the past. Silver judged beautiful forty years ago was very massive and heavy with bold simple designs. Twenty years later jewelry was more elaborate in form and beginning to look baroque. Recently there has been a strong influence from the pueblo of Zuni. At this time most Navajo prefer silver with many sets, and even with bent wire work. (ibid.:100)

This taste for turquoise steadily increased until by 1960 the preferred forms of rings and bracelets consisted of large ovals made up of concentric rings of small stones. This trend is quite clearly not due to influence from the Anglo purchasers, as their taste moved steadily toward simpler freer forms. The Navajo taste in jewelry seems to have moved away from the substantial toward the ornate to the extent that they seem almost to rival the contemporary Zuni in expressing concentrated ostentation. In both cases wearing the jewelry stresses Indianness, yet the form is not entirely consistent with traditional values, such as with the Navajo ideal of everything in moderation, or the Zuni requirement of not calling attention to oneself.

What the latest changes are I do not know, but recent pictures of the Traditional Queen candidates at the Navajo Fair show them wearing many fewer pieces of jewelry than was the case ten or fifteen years ago. Prize winning pieces tend to be very bold, in contrast to the increasing delicacy which has been a trend for the previous 50 years.

As has been pointed out (Sturdevant 1957), clothing and ornament tend to change more rapidly than any other aspects of culture. If the formal visual qualities are related to the function of these items, then one would expect that changes in concepts of status and sexual attractiveness would also be subject to relatively rapid change.

Changing styles in this art form, then, present many complex problems of interpretation. To what extent do the changing tastes represent changes in ideas about the nature of status, wealth, and personal attractiveness? Or does the validation of status rest more on just keeping up with fashion regardless of the form fashion takes? Or are many of these changes due less to functional factors than to universal laws of style sequence?

WATERCOLOR PAINTING

Navajo paintings in opaque watercolor and pastels, etc. are entirely a product of the contact situation. The materials are commercially purchased, the artists were encouraged and aided by teachers, traders, and members of local artists' colonies, and the audience is entirely Anglo. The basic style, which has much in common with modern American Indian painting from other tribes, is probably derived originally from schoolbooks, and is not, as has been implied, an inexplicable, sponta-

LAYOUT OF WATERCOLOR BY TSIHNAHJINNIE

neous phenomenon. On the other hand, it is not simply a portrayal of Navajo subject matter in a primitive and undeveloped version of Euro-American representational techniques. While there is considerable variation in individual styles with great differences in the degree of sophistication, it is the most European ones which are the least assured. On the other hand, departures from European-style realism tend to be in the direction of qualities to be found in the drypaintings or which show relationship to traditional Navajo modes of thought.

In terms of communication, the watercolors may be regarded as translations. In subject matter and in style they are a bid for understanding from the Anglo world. In some cases, and in some ways, the appeal tends to partake of sentimentality, but in other cases, and by some of the formal devices, there seems to be a very real attempt to make Navajo values comprehensible to the Anglo viewer.

I. Layout

Almost all modern watercolors conform to the European tradition in the shape of the whole work, as they are rectangular in format and conventional in proportion. The rectangle is usually, but not always, in the horizontal position.

The relationship of figure to ground is always clear and unambiguous, much more so, in fact, than in representational works of the European tradition, as the Navajo artist seldom covers the whole field with paint, but prefers to use the often colored paper as background. In addition to conveying a clear distinction between figure and ground, this usage suggests an acceptance or appreciation of what exists and is available, rather than upon a desire to master the whole field.

In terms of the ratio of figure to ground, the paintings are characterized neither as empty or full, but as clustering around the halfway point in the scale in this regard. This formal characteristic seems surprising in view of the effect of great space which the works often convey. This impression of space depends on the relation of human and animal figures to the landscape elements (see Perspective, below), and to the use of a single color background. A similar comment may be made about the size of design units, as they are often larger than they seem. Figures are usually quite literally human or animal figures and they range in size from almost the full height of the field to moderately small, apparently depending quite simply on how many of them are to be put in the composition. A single figure or the forms collectively very seldom fill the space, nor does their form ever seem affected by the shape of the whole format, as is the case, for example, in a Greek frieze or a Maya glyph. Figures are usually separated by space, the ground color. The most striking analogy here is that with the Navajo value of respecting the integrity of the individual. Watercolors are similar to drypaintings in the various aspects of the relation of figure to ground.

II. Repetition, Balance, and Symmetry

Balance tends to be symmetrical, and slightly more than half the paintings are rated as symmetrical on the scale, although as the repetition is not exact, the degree of symmetry is usually minimal. There is a tendency, too, to use several kinds of symmetry in the same work, which, because it is often subtle or not technically symmetrical due to a slight displacement of the "fulcrum", does not show in the ratings to the extent to which it seems to affect the various layouts. There is, too, the tendency not to oppose figures, but to have them face or move in the same directions, a quality noted in the drypaintings. The sketch of the layout of a work by Tsihnahjinnie at the beginning of this section shows some of these characteristics.

The use of symmetry, especially in works which are in so many ways representational, sometimes impresses the Anglo viewer as naïveté, but as this characteristic is not found in the drawings and paintings of Navajo children to any great extent, it is more likely a deliberate and mature expression of a significantly Navajo viewpoint. Interpretations of this aspect of layout suggest a persistence of Navajo attitudes toward the nature of the universe, either as an idea or an ideal. The artist apparently is seeking to express, convey, or ask understanding for this form of order in Navajo world view.

Whether or not the arrangement approaches symmetry, there are always many rhythmic elements in the paintings. This is particularly evident in the way features of the landscape are handled. Except for the matter of size, vegetation (usually in the form of small shrubs) is not treated to enhance the perspective effect, nor in terms of light and shade. Each one is placed in relation to the others for rhythmic effect, and each bit of vegetation is in itself a collection of elements repeated with only slight variation of regularity, often in a radial, fanlike, two-dimensional form. In fact, repetition with variation, which I have here defined as rhythm, is used in terms of line, form, color, and interval in most of the paintings, and serves to unify the works which might otherwise be somewhat spotty because of the scattering of units over the field. Rhythmic repetition is as important an element in the watercolors as in the drypaintings, but it is in a much freer, less regular form in the watercolors.

III.A. & B. Line

Watercolors, while showing considerable variation, tend on the whole to place considerable less emphasis on line and more on color than do the drypaintings. Outlining is quite light, often delicate, and as it is often in a closely related hue, seems more to emphasize the form than to bound or control it. As a rule, outlines are not continuous around the whole figure. Vegetation features in a landscape often consist of a series of rhythmically repeated lines, and while such elements often involves lines with free ends, usually the only lines with free ends on human or animal figures are those at the ends of the long freeblown hair favored by some artists. Although free ends are used, the effect is never sketchy, but precise and decorative.

Lines are more often curved than straight, but not to the extent that they could be called "curvy". There is considerable variation in the length of lines. Kinget's interpretation of curved line usage is interesting in connection with this art form, as she says that "curved lines are one of the surest indicators of emotionality, of flexibility, of capacity for adjustment and identification" if the use is not "excessive" (cf. p. 84 above). There is a marked and deliberate use of arcs and circles and incomplete circles, especially in clouds, which give a very formal quality. Where free and reverse curves are used, they are likely to be repeated to form a rhythmic pattern.

There is no marked emphasis in line direction, either in component or structural lines, the preponderance of diagonal lines being well within the limits of the proportion to be expected by chance in a free medium (cf. p. 87 above).

III.C. Borders and Outlines

In terms of the picture plane, watercolors are usually very open. In accordance with the Euro-American tradition, the painting would be supplied at some point with a mat or frame which would be expected to harmonize with the decor of the room in which it was hung as well as with the picture.

In some works the regular curve which forms a cloud or a rainbow arching over the whole suggests the encircling guardian of the drypaintings.

When one thinks of the kind of schoolbook illustrations to which Navajo watercolorists were probably exposed (with their modified Art Noveau lines and flat color) the interesting thing is that black outlines are so rarely used.

IV. Color

Navajo watercolorists are clearly very much interested in experimenting with color, and their work shows great variety in color use. In general, human figures and animals, which are quite representational and only slightly stylized in drawing, are very freely rendered as far as color is concerned; horses, for example, may be blue, pink, green, or any other hue. Elements in landscape which are usually very simple and stylized in form, are more often naturalistic in color. However, although stylized clouds are common, a sky painted blue is rare. There must be some significance to this, for the blue skies of Navajo country are unexcelled, and in other respects Navajo artists show themselves very aware of the beauties of their homeland.

Effects range from works of great delicacy to considerable boldness in colors and from the use of a great variety of hues to a carefully limited palette. A variety of means are used to achieve color harmony, the most obvious of which is the unifying color of the paper, which not only fills the area between figures but tends to give a "tone" to all but the most opaque of pigments. Sometimes this unifying effect is achieved by a tone used throughout the palette. Another favored device is gradation in hue, as when each fold of a woman's skirt is of a slightly different shade.

V. Perspective

Many Navajo watercolorists convey the effect of distance, of great expanses of space and a feeling for the landscape to a far greater extent than seems to be the case with other modern Indian painting, to say nothing of any traditional art form of people with a tribal society. This effect of space is achieved with a great economy of means. The chief devices are size, and position, together with slight indications of overlapping. The latter is found in many works, but is used in a very sparing way. In combination with these usages, the single color background often contributes to the feeling of space. There is usually no shading of forms or any effect of light and shade rendered by the use of shadows.

In terms of content, one of the most important devices for conveying the feeling of the landscape is the placing of distant buttes, often one on each side. They are simply and almost symbolically drawn and may be only an outline. The effect of space as shown in the majority of paintings seems to fit with the interpretations concerning views of space and time, because these landscapes are not momentary images of a particular spot at a given moment. For all the Navajo interest in geography, the painted landscape is a symbolic or generalized one which suggests the enduring qualities of Navajo country as a whole, although it is to be noted that the symbols are most often ones which Anglos associate with the area; the distant symbols are not mountains, but buttes.

If, on the other hand, the watercolor painting can be said to portray "clearly depicted space depth" then the hypothesis of Kavolis (p. 136 above) is relevant. His hypothesis is that this indicates that distant events are still relevant, and that the painter has a past value orientation. It is true that in content the paintings are oriented to traditional Navajo culture. The tradition is not, however, that of a distant or mythological past, but of a fairly recent one, although it cannot be identified with any specific chronological period. Elements are selected for Navajoness in a recreated past which is in some ways very much like the "ethnographic present" of the ethnographer.

Kavolis, however, also has a category "location in front of vaguely recognizable space" and in some ways this might be considered a better description. Kavolis's interpretation of this quality is "superior importance of present over past" which I suppose could indicate the uses of the past in art for very present purposes, namely the success of the artist in the modern world.

Even when overlapping and size are used to approximate linear perspective, there is often an important positional quality. Whenever many figures are used in a Navajo composition, the viewpoint of the observer is raised so that the scene is shown in part from above. This has the effect of making it possible for the figures to be more nearly the same size, and to minimize the overlapping. In the Euro-American tradition great value is placed upon the massing of figures in any composition where a number of them are used; the lack of such massing is regarded as unskilled or naïve. This treatment by Navajo artists may be related to the traditional Navajo way of arranging a number of equal elements in various patterns, or it may be the result of the desire to maintain the integrity of each figure. Of course these two ways of perceiving are consistent with one another.

The fact that these artists are perfectly aware of the uses of size and overlapping indicates that they could well elaborate these devices if they chose, and in fact there are a few works in which figures are massed quite tightly, but in these cases the emphasis is on a decorative pattern in the plane of the painting rather than on space depth.

VI. Composition

Perhaps due to the uniform background, Navajo watercolors often seem simpler than closer inspection shows them to be, but they are not, as a rule, complex. Complexity would not fit very well with the feeling of the free simple life in the great open spaces which gives the works much of their appeal to the purchasers.

The ratings with respect to repose-tension cluster about the midpoint. This is somewhat surprising as an examination of the individual qualities which I assume go to make up this total effect tend to be on the reposeful side.

Movement is stressed, and while it is sometimes circular involving the whole composition, it is more often centered on lines associated with the figures in the form of animals or persons in space. Lines of movement are usually parallel or congruent and are seldom turbulent or opposed, although they may radiate from a point of interest.

Watercolors have a great range of effects in delicacy-boldness as in many other qualities. Many, however, have the combination of areas of strong color with a wealth of fine decorative detail which seems to be the essence of the effect of being bold and delicate at the same time so characteristic of the drypaintings. The greater proportion of curved lines and the less frequent use of strong verticals may be factors in the frequent more delicate effect of the watercolors.

In spite of the various formalizing devices which give the watercolors their "Indian" quality, an effect of freedom is conveyed in this medium. This quality seems to be due largely to the effect of space surrounding the figures combined with a feeling of movement. Streaming hair, which in the psychoanalytic view is a symbol of sexual freedom, adds considerably to this effect. Another aspect of this effect of freedom lies in the minimal use of overlapping forms; each unit or figure tends to be fully separated, not "dominated" by any other.

Human figures and animals are usually much less formal in style than the features of the landscape, as if to say that whatever the momentary qualities and activities of individuals, the universe as a whole retains its ordered, timeless, mechanistic quality.

In conjunction with the feeling of the figure to move about freely in ordered space, (and sometimes the loneliness of such a condition), it is notable that the figures are all under careful control by careful drawing, and, usually, complete outlining. Comparison with the nature of the freedom projected by modern nonobjective painting brings out the essence of this effect. In much modern Euro-American painting, the emotions and personality of the individual are seen as being freed from the bounds of controlling form, while even the most acculturated of Navajo artists show great sensitivity to formal qualities.

Insofar as watercolors differ in their qualities from the dry-paintings, they are also a statement of different values. By the context one would say that they are not just an interpretation of the Navajo to an Anglo audience, but a statement of a new Navajoness, which, however much some old values may be cherished, accepts new elements —especially the technological ones—because use of the media themselves say this. In other words we can see in these paintings an affirmation of traditional values, a nostalgia for former days combined with an acceptance of items of material culture.

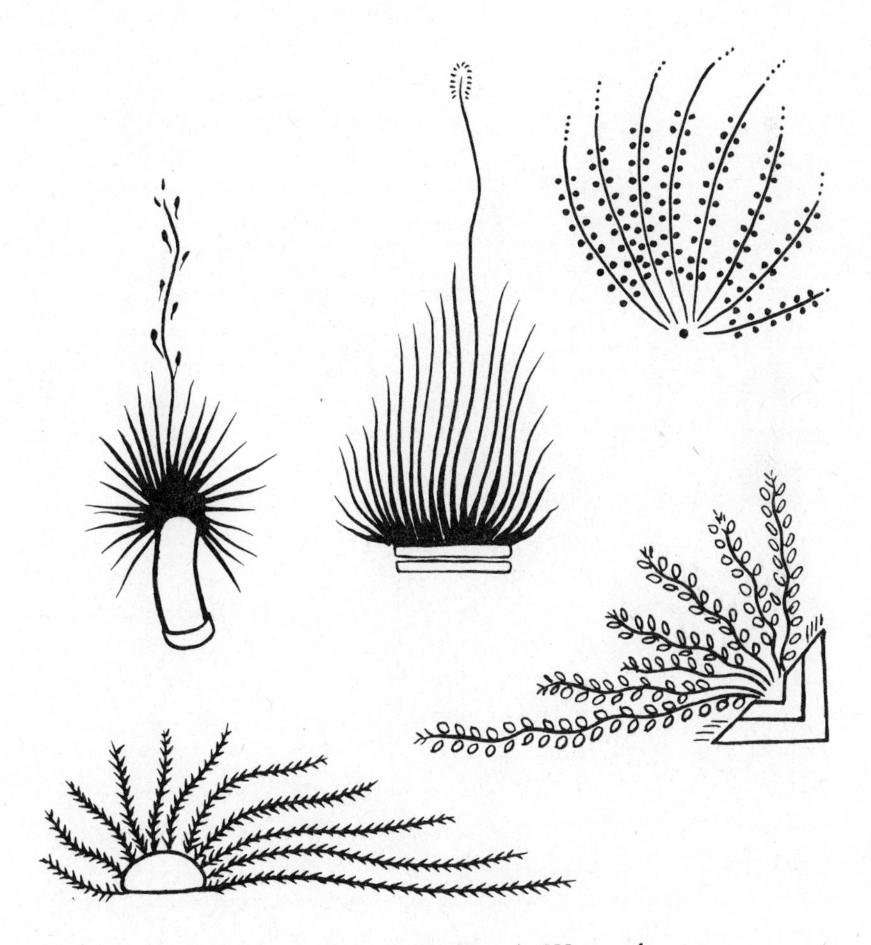

Plant Forms from Navajo Watercolors

NAVAJO STYLES AND THE NAVAJO STYLE

Having surveyed the various arts and crafts of the Navajo and examined the variations in their form-qualities, it is now possible to consider the question as to whether the various art forms are variations of a single Navajo style or whether they are entirely different and convey the idea of Navajoness by association only. In terms of formal description, works of art may be said to be stylistically similar to the extent that they share the same form-qualities. (A more complete description would include content and the relation of content and form.) In this section a summary of the form-qualities of all Navajo arts is presented, examining which qualities are found in all media and which in only some.

The first thing that meets the eye in examining the data (summarized in the Appendix) is the extent of the distribution of most of the form-qualities recorded. This indicates that all the basic categories of form-qualities are available by choice to the artist. Some test samples of arts and crafts from other cultures indicate, however, that the range is not always so great. There are several possible explanations of the diversity in the Navajo case: (1) The schema may be lacking in some formal qualities particularly typical of Navajo art. This is where the process of developing stylistic analysis must proceed from the complementary pole, the study of a style in terms of its own rules and logic, such as Holm (1965) has done for Northwest Coast art. (2) The "reverse halo" effect has made for a greater range; that is I have tended to rate the works in relation to each other rather than against the standard. This may be the case, but not, I think, to an extent which would account for the wide distribution. (3) This variation is in itself an expression of the Navajo Way, and the effect of a strong style is achieved in each medium because most of the works vary from the typical in one or two characteristics only; almost any characteristic may be the one varied. Some art styles are probably relatively "loose", others "tight", and Navajo art falls into the former category.

For the description of a style, the full significance of data presented here cannot be evaluated without comparative material, although certain trends stand out quite clearly regarding Navajo styles and the Navajo style. Among the various media there are certain qualities which vary with the techniques, such as the straightness and direction of lines in weaving. Other qualities seem to vary with the uses and functions of the art form; for example, the highly symbolic drypainting form, having so much to "say" differs from other forms by frequently being more complex. Other tendencies run through all the media and probably impart something of the basic premises of Navajo thought.

I. Layout

The shape of Navajo art and craft works is quite varied, except where technological factors are important and influence a clear-cut tendency. In the ratio of figure-to-ground all art forms vary chiefly within the three middle categories. This does not seem like a very definite characteristic until one compares it with such "full" styles as Maori carving. There is usually no ambiguity between figure and ground in any Navajo medium. The exception—and in Navajo art there always seems to be some exception—it is to be found in some weaving. In measure (size) there is again considerable variability, but the combination of moderately large design units together with small components or details is sufficiently marked to be noted.

II. Repetition, Balance, and Symmetry

Repetition in one form or another is an important characteristic of Navajo art. Symmetry is often to be found in combined forms in the drypainting, and to a lesser extent in basketry, jewelry, and sometimes even in watercolor. Biaxial and radial forms are frequent, and bilateral rare, except in watercolors. Repetition of components, with variation which takes many forms, are important in producing rhythmic effects in all media.

III. Lines

Much has been made of the Navajo use of outlining (Mills 1959), which is especially characteristic of the dry and wet paintings. In weaving and basketry it is associated only with the most technically excellent works, and in pottery painting it is not common. It is interesting that in both styles of painting, figures which are outlined are not characterized by endless lines, as different parts of the figure are outlined in different colors. The use of curved and straight lines varies with the medium. Lines in weaving are straight, lines in jewelry are evenly divided between curved and straight; curved lines are somewhat favored in watercolors, and straight in drypaintings. Lines oblique to each other are about what one might expect through chance, while parallel lines are of considerable importance, and perpendicular relationships minimized.

As to line endings, the most characteristic form is for a line to end where it meets another line. Continuous (endless) lines are rare except in jewelry, where they result from the technique of setting stones, and in the saddle blankets. Lines which end without meeting another are rare in the crafts, but often found in the painting styles. It is interesting that such lines are neatly finished off by terminal markers in drypainting, but usually have free ends in watercolors. The use of pointed forms is not characteristic, but where they are used, as in some drypaintings and weaving, the distribution tends to be bimodal—either the work bristles with points or has relatively few. The rounding or "crispness" of corners does not seem to me to be a very useful descriptive category in terms of Navajo forms. It would be more relevant where many rectangular elements were present, as in Maya art.

The smooth, controlled quality of line characteristic of Navajo work is more readily apparent when compared with the short, sketchy "nervous" lines which are often seen in both traditional and modern Apache drawing.

Structural lines are notable for the absence of opposition. Favored are parallel lines, either horizontal or vertical, and a radial organization.

There is considerable variety in the use of borders and outlines. Traditionally the emphasis seems to have been on either no border, or one with an opening, but in more recent work, especially that for sale, full borders are common. Outlines are found in the fine art and in the more carefully executed craft pieces. Where found, they are usually complete.

IV. Color

Considerable variety is to be found in the use of color. In the sacred arts the number is limited, in weaving the differences are marked between sub-styles, and in watercolor painting there is apparently great interest in experimentation. On the whole, with the exception of the black-on-white pottery and some weaving, the arts are colorful. While the ratings show that contrasts are utilized, they are combined with color harmonies in many ways.

V. Perspective

This quality is, in a sense, not purely formal, but applies only to works with an element of representation, in this case the two kinds of painting. In drypainting space depth is of no importance, except as indicated by slight use of overlapping, but direction, topographic perspective, is. In the watercolors some indication of space depth is indicated in a number of works, but lineal perspective and overlapping are not stressed. Social perspective is conspicuously absent in both forms. By comparison the paintings and drawings of Plains Indians of both the 19th and the 20th centuries show a considerable use of overlapping planes, especially human figures.

VI. Composition

Pottery and basketry are simple in form, as is jewelry. Where the latter has been referred to as ornate, the effect comes from a full format, with repetitive, simple elements. Weaving and watercolors are more variable, but simple compositions are statistically favored. Drypainting is also highly variable in this regard, but differs from the other forms in the frequency of complex works. Except for certain very bold rugs made for sale, Navajo art is marked by a combination of delicacy and boldness which comes out as a moderate rating on the scale. The balance of tension and repose, while fairly variable, tends toward the middle rating in all forms as the contrasts and tensions of elements are harmonized by the over-all order. The crafts are for the most part fairly static in form, whereas the painting styles show a marked feeling of movement. Such movements are smooth and controlled rather than opposed or contorted.

Navajo art is, except for some pottery, all very formal, in that regularity of all kinds is stressed. Even the watercolors, which are so much in the European tradition, have many qualities of regularity and repetition and some even tend toward symmetry of the whole. There is always a certain precision, without sketchy or splashy effects; while the rating is moderate, this formality is marked when compared with representational works in the European tradition to which these superficially belong.

It can be seen from this summary that in one sense Navajo art forms can be considered as a number of styles, because there are stylistic qualities which vary with the techniques, and even considerable variation in certain qualities within the works in any one technique. They are, however, interlocking styles, as there are many qualities to be found in all forms. Kroeber says:

> The basic reason for the concentration of productivity seems to be that for things to be done well they must be done definitely, and definite results can be achieved only through some special method, technique, manner or plan of operations. Such a particular method or manner is called a *style* in the arts. (Kroeber 1948:329)

There are some qualities in Navajo arts which are sufficiently favored to be considered a definite manner in this sense. Usually, and in any medium, a Navajo artist seems to go about his artistic problem by arranging, against a given background, a variety of small elements or components into very formal and symmetrical patterns with parallel or radial structural lines. He prefers that the design units be unambiguous, separate from each other, and carefully outlined.

While this analysis had tended to bring out cultural similarities and overlook differences between individual artists, it by no means should be taken to conclude that such differences are negligible. The same techniques applied to a comparison of the works of different artists would bring out the nature and extent of individual variation within the style.

As for the attempt to test the interpretive hypothesis on the basis of Navajo material, the drypaintings present some fairly clear results. In most categories the descriptive terminology and the hypothesized form-meanings derived from Euro-American sources seem to fit the case of the Navajo drypainting very adequately.

A summary of the interpretations which seem to apply include: need for achievement, driving force and ardor, power in a controlled form, respect for individual autonomy, tension directed outward from the life space, harmony between individuals, emotions controlled by balance and moderation, warm emotions, a desire to analyze, to explore and adapt within limits, and a pervading emphasis on vitality and harmony and control. Perhaps equally significant is the absence of qualities which are interpreted to mean oppositional tendencies or ambiguity regarding social environment, feelings of isolation, suppressed emotions, and interpersonal conflict. The expression of anxiety is limited to a form which suggests relief from it, and aggressive forms appear only in some contexts, where they have the symbolic meaning of protection.

These interpretations seem entirely plausible when considered in terms of Navajo values and ideals, but as an expression of Navajo modal personality they do not fit very well with the accepted analyses in the literature. In terms of the functions of the art form, these interpretations would be very much in accord with what the medium could be expected to convey if it serves to communicate appropriate import to the viewers in the ceremonial situation.

There are, however, two categories of form-quality which resist application of the hypothesized form-meanings because of basically different artistic and presumably cultural viewpoints. The first concerns symmetry and repetition, the second the method of space projection. Both qualities have been discussed above with reference to possible meanings in the Navajo artistic and cultural contexts. The Navajo use and interpretation of these categories of form cannot really be considered to disprove or contradict the hypothesized form-meanings based on Euro-American traditions; they simply go beyond the possibilities that had been considered. There are probably other canons in the Navajo esthetic and the means by which they are achieved that are not apparent to me. Perhaps only Navajo artists and critics can make them explicit.

On the whole the use of the term Navajo style seems justified only in a very loose sense. Analytical procedures, such as cross-cultural consideration of particular form-qualities must either specify the medium or be limited to qualities shown to exist in all media.

9

Ends and Means

This study was conceived primarily as an investigation to test the idea that form-qualities are interpreted similarly by all human beings. To an extent, I feel that the idea is supported. But, in exploring the similarities in interpretation of graphic forms, I have brought out a number of differences. The well-known phenomenon that a work of art is perceived differently by different individuals, and by people with different cultural backgrounds, seems to be a dilemma that is intensified by evidence that people do find similar form-meanings in form-qualities.

An explanation is to be found in the fact that even the simplest form has a number of qualities. Any work of art, then, has a very great number of form-qualities if we analyze it completely. It is the viewer who selects out certain ones as more significant. And so different people will perceive differently the relative importance of the various form-qualities of a work, based on what seems to them as the organizing idea. Possibly the same circular drypainting seems essentially static to an Anglo and full of movement to a Navajo.

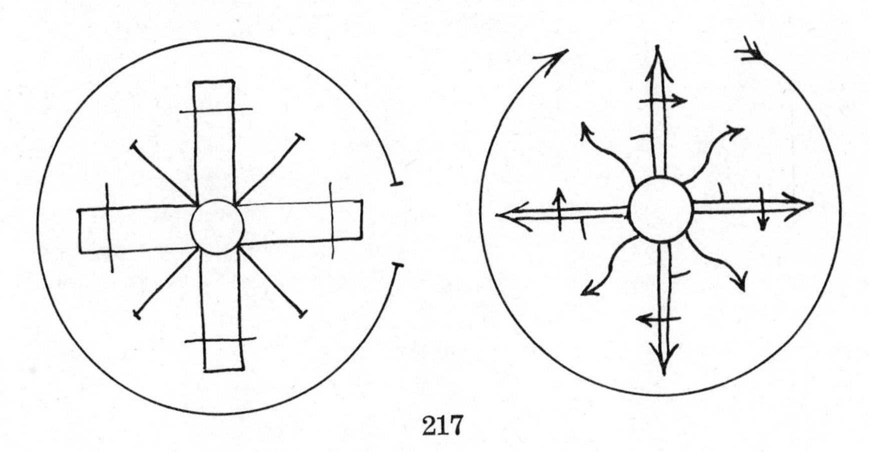

Training in art routinely involves learning to analyze in various terms, such as figure and ground, light and dark, arrangement of planes or structural lines, utilizing the favorite organizing principles of the instructor. It is very difficult not to organize the form-qualities one sees in terms of the principles with which one is familiar, consciously or otherwise. Indeed, one looks at a visual communication in very much the same way in which one hears an utterance—in terms of one's own phonemic pattern.

The linguistic analogy makes clear why I believe the effort to develop more precise descriptive techniques for visual material is important. To carry the analogy further, and assume that if form-qualities are analogous to phones, then the ones customarily used in a style form a system, comparable to a phonemic system, and there are other systemic levels in the way the elements in this system are combined. Consider the different levels of abstraction of the customary terms used descriptively with regard to art styles. Aside from those involving technique or iconography, and looking solely at formal qualities, this is a distinction seldom made explicit—between what I have called form-qualities and the combination of such qualities that I have put under the heading of composition. These latter are more subjective, more a matter of interpretation than the former. "Delicacy" or "complexity" or any of the words used in description nearly always imply a comparison. The comparisons in the viewer's mind of these combination qualities vary widely, so that we get contradictory descriptions—some persons, for example, have described Navajo sand paintings as complex, some as simple; some have emphasized static qualities, some movement. I have tried to define these combination qualities more objectively, but they are best considered as a separate level, or even possibly a separate system, from the primary form-qualities.

There is a still more abstract level: words such as "vitality" and "harmony", which I at first had included under composition, I have finally decided are not formal artistic terms so much as esthetic ones. They refer to esthetic ends rather than artistic means, and perception of how they are achieved varies still more widely than the perception of compositional qualities. This category, while it involves a perception of how form-qualities are combined, is most usefully conceived as of a quite different order than the form-qualities, and involves the esthetic, rather than formal, iconographic, or the technical systems.

If we are to explore the possibilities inherent in the concept of systems at various levels of abstraction, the lowest level must be tackled first. In the previous chapters I have gathered together and systematized a set of terms to fulfill this need. The first requirement is that it is useful descriptively. By using it for a variety of styles in addition to the Navajo styles reported here, I find that the descriptive schema, for all its over-simplification when applied to a particular work, has proved a useful tool in distinguishing styles in a wide range of media. It might be improved by the use of a seven point scale where qualities are scaled, in order to make the distinction between complete absence of a quality and some slight use, or at the other extreme, qualities which are never absent and those that are frequently present. The list of form-qualities will tend to expand as different cultural styles are analyzed, qualities being added which do not occur in art of the European tradition, as indeed happened in examining Navajo works. But a systematic approach should be maintained, as a number of advantages have emerged from the use of a logical outline that can be expanded rather than merely added to in a quantitative sense. The most important of these is a clearer understanding of the alternatives, and the nature of the selection which the artist had made. In addition to expanding and improving this schema, other sets of defined terms are needed in a variety of system categories, the most obvious being the need for a set applicable to three-dimensional works, which correspond, insofar as possible, with the one proposed for graphic arts.

The esthetic terminology, which is so largely a matter of perception and interpretation, such as harmony and vitality, needs to be exp'icitly developed as a separate system—a statement of the basic esthetic ends of art. I suggest that it is useful to postulate that there are universal criteria (since cross-cultural comparisons of esthetic ratings make this a reasonable assumption), and to use a set of esthetic concepts to explore the nature of artistic means and esthetic ends in various cultural contexts. The six canons of Hsieh Ho, which have survived a great variety of interpretations, probably make a good starting place, if they are defined broadly. To these I would add "freshness", the illuminating term suggested by Margaret Mead, which clarifies the quality too often thought of as a need for novelty.

If we take into consideration the different levels of abstraction that are used in describing the formal qualities of art styles, problems of interpretation are also illuminated. At the lowest level of abstraction, such as the quality of wholeness of a circle, or the aggressive nature of points, or the stimulating effect of red-orange, form-meanings assigned to form-qualities seem to have a good deal of consistency in various cultural contexts.

On the other hand esthetic qualities such as harmony, vitality, and freshness seem to be universally valued, and to be related to cultural values, in both terminology and import, by a number of peoples. Interpretations which rest on this level of abstraction seem uncomfortably obvious, so that when we examine such values as harmony and order, expressed so clearly in Navajo art, we are faced with the fact that harmony and order are always valued in art in some way and to some degree, and they are also valued in society—indeed they are necessities of biological existence. It is then hardly surprising that art expresses the cultural values on this level!

It is when we examine the ways the basic forms are selected and combined to achieve these desired ends that the diversity of visual strategies is found, and it is at this level that we can hope to find correspondence between ways of solving artistic problems so as to achieve the esthetic ends and ways of solving problems of living in terms of ethical ideals.

The most clear cut hypotheses that have emerged are those having to do with spatial arrangements, because it is here the metaphors seem most obviously applicable to societal strategies regarding order and the handling of opposition. The Navajo avoid the direct opposition of bilateral symmetry, utilizing the harmony of similar (never exactly the same) units going in the same direction; they avoid the overlapping forms in a way which suggests the value of non-interference; units are not arranged in any kind of hierarchial order with regard to size, overlapping, or by being placed above or below each other; they are more likely to be multiple than paired.

In Fang esthetics, as described in penetrating works by Fernandez, the problem is perceived very differently. Their single figure statuettes are to our eyes very harmonious in their smooth surfaces and complete bilateral symmetry, yet Fernandez says:

> In both aesthetics and the social structure the aim of the Fang is not to resolve opposition and create identity but to preserve a balanced opposition. This is accomplished either through alternation as in the case with complementary filiation or in the behavior of a full man; or it is done by skillful aesthetic composition in the same time and space as in the case with the ancestor statues or cult ritual. This objective is reflected in interclan relations. The

> Fang, like many nonliterate people, lived in a state of constant enmity with other clans. However, their object was not that of exterminating each other or otherwise terminating the hostility in favor of one clan or another. The hostility was regarded as a natural condition of social life, and their concern was to keep this enmity in permanent and balanced opposition. So in their aesthetic life, they aimed at a permanent and balanced opposition. In this permanent tension between opposites lay the source of vitality in Fang life. (Fernandez 1966:64)

In the metaphors of Christian tradition duality often becomes a trinity as the two opposing elements are harmonized, balanced, yet often separated by a dominating third element. Note that the symbolism embodied in the iconography is not entirely the same as the metaphor communicated by the form-meaning:

The style by which conflict is reconciled, and harmony maintained, is symbolized in European tradition by the scale:

and in the tradition of Euro-American art the "balance" is conceived in terms of variations of this kind of relationship. When compared to the esthetics of the Navajo or the Fang, it becomes apparent that the fulcrum is an element of tremendous importance and the triangle is a very fundamental structuring device.

Perhaps this is so because duality is seen in terms of strong opposition, an either/or adversary form of duality, different from the complementary conception of Yin and Yang, or the male-female or good-bad dualities of the Navajo and the Iroquois. Such opposition can be held in check only by perfect symmetry, as in the Fang case, or by a third and often dominating form.

There are a number of ways to order and classify experience, and no form is so simple that it has only one form-quality. A work of art is an orchestration, which may be simple or complex, and which may be perceived in many ways. There may be, however, a limited number of very basic organizing means which people tend to use. The means which has worked most satisfactorily in the past for making sense out of the multiplicity of sense data will tend to be primary. Some tend to organize what they see in terms of the unity in multiplicity, like Navajo or functionalists; some order first in terms of duality, like structuralists and the Fang, and some in terms of a vertical hierarchy, as do, apparently, evolutionists and the Haida.

Within any society there may be differing views as to the nature of the important opposition and the ways considered important to achieve harmony, although beauty and harmony are not necessarily the goals in each work of art. Much misinterpretation about the arts of other peoples has resulted from the assumption that what we regard as ugly is worshipped or admired by the makers. Many of these works deliberately express the wicked, the ugly, and in context are to be contrasted to the good, the true and the beautiful. Art may convey the values of the makers, but not necessarily directly on all levels. Alternate statements may be made and new ways of achieving the values proposed. Values stated at one level may even be contradicted at another level in the same work, so as to call attention to evil.

In the history of European art, there has been a strong trend away from symmetry—obvious balance with a central fulcrum—toward more and more subtle forms of balance. This trend historically parallels the changes in political ideas concerning the structures to achieve order and handle opposition. The changes in art and in society have not been easily accepted, and it seems naïve to assume that the same thing has not happened in other cultural settings. There is no reason why art should always reflect traditional values, or, on the other hand, always be an expression of the effort to change them. If we were as aware of the esthetic canons and artistic traditions and history of non-literate societies as of literate ones, we should in all probability find similar dialogs with regard to changing values which are true of the Orient and the West.

There have been unstated assumptions that the arts of primitive peoples reflect the traditional values, whereas in our civilized society artists are prophets of change. Related to these assumptions is the idea of a complete destruction of artistic expression of traditional art in contact situations, possibly to be replaced by art in the European tradition. The Navajo have adopted a number of new media and new idioms in contact with other peoples, and have made them distinctly their own. Navajo art forms have communicated and are communicating a variety of messages in a variety of ways which I have not included in this essay. Not all Navajo artists are interested in communicating traditional Navajo ways of achieving Navajo values. They think it is more important to protest, and use the devices of art which makes this kind of statement in one of the idioms of the dominant society. Other artists may seek to translate, or to restate traditional values in new forms. They may attempt to return to the forms of the past, yet as in all nativistic movements, incorporate newer ideas.

Art communicates values in the sense that it communicates what is valued, which is important to the artist, whether it is his own inner turmoil, his social protest, or the traditional religion of his people. He will employ the means, the language, which he has learned in his cultural context. His viewers will perceive it in terms of their needs, their values and their language. Communication will be more or less complete, depending on how congruent these factors are. Yet beneath these diversities lie many similarities of perception common to all human animals, and beyond these diversities lie common human dreams.

In interpretations, then, I suggest an explicit distinction: between *ends*—the ideal esthetic values and the ideal social values, and the *means*—the artistic forms and the social forms that are the cultural devices for achieving these ends. In this framework we can better understand questions of universality and cultural relativity in both ethics and esthetics. Just as it can be said that the problems peoples have are more alike than the solutions they find, and the ethical ideas more alike than the way they are defined, so esthetic preferences are more alike than the way *they* are defined, and similar esthetic problems have different possible formal solutions.

Universal ethical principles, which rest on bio-social imperatives, are subject to cultural variation in (a) the definition of what constitutes the society of real human beings to whom they apply, and (b) the different means by which they may be achieved. Similarly, the universal esthetic values, which also rest on bio-social imperatives, are subject to variations which depend on different definitions as to where they apply, and the different means by which people seek to achieve them. In neither case are perfect, permanent, solutions to be found.

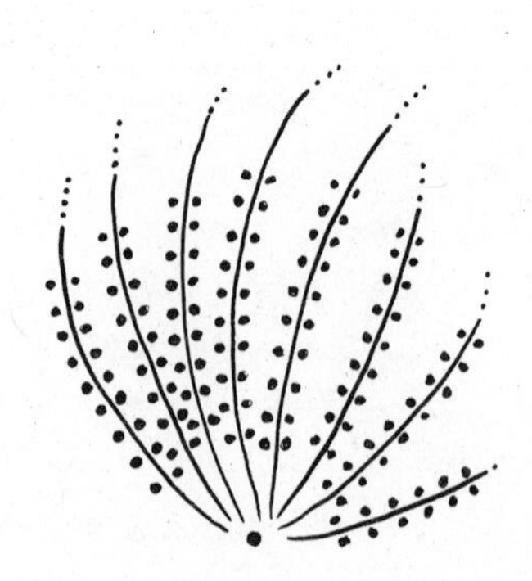

Appendix

SUMMARY OF ALL DESCRIPTIVE DATA FOR ALL NAVAJO MEDIA

Descriptive Data for All Navajo Media

This appendix consists of a summary of the form-qualities of each medium (in terms of percentages), and where this seems appropriate, the overall percentage for all media.

The size of the samples in each medium are given under the first heading, I.A. Shape. The percentages are based on the actual sample where the particular form quality could be observed and tallied.

Where the percentage figure is followed by a question mark (as 40?) the rating has been estimated, on the basis of information not evident or reliable from the reproductions, such as the estimates of color intensity of drypaintings. Such information is based either on direct observation or verbal descriptions of the medium.

0 indicates that less than ½% of the sample displayed this quality.

\- indicates that the category does not apply, or a rating could not be obtained. The "All Media" average is based on the remaining sample.

The sources of the material from which the data was obtained are:

Drypaintings: Newcomb and Reichard (n.d.), Reichard (1939), Wheelwright (1942), and Wyman (1960).

Weaving: James (1914), Amsden (1949), Reichard (1936), Maxwell (1963), Tanner (1964), and a sample of 32 Navajo rugs for sale at the "Mille Lacs Trading Post", a shop attached to the Mille Lacs Indian Museum in Vineland, Minnesota.

Basketry: Mason (1904) and Denver Art Museum Leaflet No. 88 (1939).

Jewelry: Adair (1944), Bedinger (1936), Tanner (1954), Christensen (1955) and Woodward (1938).

Watercolors: Dunn (1968), Hannum (1946, 1958), Mills (1959), Underhill (n.d.) and Arizona Highways (December 1951, August 1954).

The data were taken from published sources with two criteria in mind: 1) that the ethnographic present be considered approximately the 1930's, because the written ethnographic material is mainly from this period, and 2) that the sample be from sources available to those who wished to check the reliability of the rating instrument when tried by other persons. The first criteria could only be approximate, as investigation to establish exact dating would have involved an extensive research effort in itself, and would perhaps have made the second objective more difficult. The exception to both criteria are the blankets, where a more historical treatment seemed interesting, and where samples reproduced are clearly either of historical interest or selected for unusualness, excellence, or unusual excellence. The samples of paintings are called "watercolors", although some are actually pastel drawings. I do not think distinguishing between them would affect the ratings.

Hatcher Art Analysis—Summary Sheet

Scale B ——— Two Dimensional Works

Tally Sheet Nos. All - Expressed as percentages

I. Layout

A. Shape of whole

Sample, Medium		ROUND	OVAL	SQUARE	RECTANGULAR	IRREGULAR	OTHER
82	Drypainting	32	2	17	21	28	0
123	Weaving	0	0	2	98	0	0
16	Basketry	100	0	0	0	0	0
40	Pottery	40	0	0	0	0	60
49	Jewelry	2	30	4	43	6	15
59	Watercolor	0	0	5	90	5	0

B. Distribution of forms

	CENTER	OFF-CENTER	INTERMEDIATE	PERIPHERY	WHOLE
Drypainting	21	0	5	1	73
Weaving	6	1	2	2	89
Basketry	6	0	88	0	6
Pottery	18	0	7	20	55
Jewelry	67	0	2	33	33
Watercolor	27	23	14	0	36
	24	4	20	10	49

C. Relation of figure to ground

1. Contrast

	CONTRASTED	DISTINGUISHABLE	REVERSIBLE	POSITIVE	NEGATIVE
Drypainting	100	0	0	100	0
Weaving	29	43	28	-	-
Basketry	62	25	13	100	0
Pottery	100	0	0	100	0
Jewelry	70	30	0	-	-
Watercolor	100	0	0	100	0
	77	16	7	100	0

C. Relation of figure to ground

2. Ratio	EMPTY 1	2	3	4	5 FULL
Drypainting	0	10	35	49	6
Weaving	0	6	29	42	23
Basketry	0	38	56	6	0
Pottery	8	50	40	2	0
Jewelry	2	18	31	35	14
Watercolor	2	28	40	20	10
	2	25	38	26	9

D. Measure (size)

1. Largest design units	1	2	3	4	5
Drypainting	2	20	25	35	18
Weaving	7	25	39	19	10
Basketry	0	0	25	19	56
Pottery	5	15	30	32	18
Jewelry	2	2	2	12	82
Watercolor	3	17	29	32	19
	3	13	25	25	34

2. Smallest details	1	2	3	4	5
Drypainting	50	35	11	4	0
Weaving	17	34	30	17	2
Basketry	6	50	25	13	6
Pottery	2	23	37	25	0
Jewelry	12	26	37	25	0
Watercolor	22	29	27	20	2
	18	33	28	17	4

II. Repetition, Balance, and Symmetry

HAA–B–SS–2

A. Symmetry

1. Type

a. Bilateral

	SIMPLE	BIAXIAL	RADIAL	ROTATIONAL	DYNAMIC REPETITION
Drypainting	13	0	0	12	22
Weaving	6	0	0	2	3
Basketry	0	0	0	0	0
Pottery	15	0	2	0	0
Jewelry	4	0	0	0	2
Watercolor	29	0	0	5	7
	10	0	0	3	5

b. Biaxial

	BILATERAL	SIMPLE	RADIAL	ROTATIONAL
Drypainting	0	0	0	0
Weaving	0	66	7	2
Basketry	0	0	0	0
Pottery	0	5	0	0
Jewelry	0	27	35	0
Watercolor	0	0	0	0
	0	16	7	0

c. Radial

	BILATERAL	BIAXIAL	SIMPLE	ROTATIONAL
Drypainting	0	0	4	39
Weaving	0	0	0	0
Basketry	81	0	0	0
Pottery	0	0	20	0
Jewelry	0	29	0	0
Watercolor	0	0	3	0
	13	5	5	7

A. Symmetry
1. Type

d. Rotational	BILATERAL	BIAXIAL	RADIAL	SIMPLE	BIFOLD
Drypainting	12	0	0	10	0
Weaving	0	0	0	0	1
Basketry	0	0	0	19	0
Pottery	0	0	0	3	0
Jewelry	0	0	0	0	0
Watercolor	5	0	0	2	0
	3	0	0	5	0

e. Circular	BILATERAL	BIAXIAL	RADIAL	ROTATIONAL	SIMPLE
Drypainting	0	0	0	0	0
Weaving	0	0	0	0	0
Basketry	0	0	0	0	0
Pottery	0	0	0	0	0
Jewelry	0	0	0	0	0
Watercolor	0	0	0	0	0
	0	0	0	0	0

2. Degree	1	2	3	4	5
Drypainting	0	6	20	70	4
Weaving	0	0	7	39	54
Basketry	0	0	12	50	38
Pottery	12	30	27	28	3
Jewelry	0	0	2	12	86
Watercolor	46	30	20	4	0
	10	11	15	34	31

HAA–B–SS–3

II. B. Repetition (Infinite Repetition and Rhythm)

2. Type of repetition
a. One dimensional

	STATIC	DYNAMIC
Drypainting	85*	85*
Weaving	47	24
Basketry	0	0
Pottery	15	32
Jewelry	33	43
Watercolor	65	46
	41	38

b. Two dimensional

	STATIC	DYNAMIC
Drypainting	0	1
Weaving	11	4
Basketry	0	0
Pottery	0	0
Jewelry	2	2
Watercolor	0	0
	2	1

*Estimated, not tallied.

III. Treatment of Lines

A. Component Lines

1. Linearity

	1	2	3	4	5
Drypainting	4	18	32	44	2
Weaving	19	16	24	20	18
Basketry	50	13	13	6	18
Pottery	12	18	12	12	45
Jewelry	30	18	33	16	2
Watercolor	14	3	3	2	5
	21	14	19	17	15

2. Size

a. Weight

	1	2	3	4	5
Drypainting	8	60	30	2	0
Weaving	4	30	40	24	2
Basketry	0	10	46	22	22
Pottery	3	20	32	34	11
Jewelry	0	18	57	18	7
Watercolor	41	37	15	7	0
	10	29	37	18	7

3. Shape of line

a. Degree

	STRAIGHT 1	2	3	4	CURVED 5
Drypainting	10	44	29	15	2
Weaving	97	2	1	0	0
Basketry	75*	0	6	13	6
Pottery	22	28	28	15	7
Jewelry	6	12	41	33	8
Watercolor	0	3	37	51	9
	35	15	24	21	5

*Lines following coils are considered straight here.

HAA–B–SS–4

A. Component Lines

4. Relation of lines to each other

a. Oblique

	1	2	3	4	5
Drypainting	3	13	33	46	5
Weaving	20	16	22	25	16
Basketry	38	19	19	19	5
Pottery	7	5	15	48	25
Jewelry	10	55	23	12	0
Watercolor	0	13	30	48	9
	13	20	23	34	11

b. Parallel

	1	2	3	4	5
Drypainting	3	17	57	18	5
Weaving	3	14	26	37	20
Basketry	25	19	44	12	0
Pottery	30	15	30	22	3
Jewelry	2	14	35	49	0
Watercolor	6	23	51	19	1
	11	17	41	26	5

c. Perpendicular

	1	2	3	4	5
Drypainting	17	41	29	12	1
Weaving	45	15	17	16	7
Basketry	25	12	38	25	0
Pottery	63	12	15	7	3
Jewelry	24	41	27	8	0
Watercolor	36	33	27	1	3
	35	25	25	13	2

A. Component Lines

5. Relation of lines to edges

a. Diagonal

	1	2	3	4	5
Drypainting	7	26	33	30	4
Weaving	32	17	19	22	10
Basketry	32	19	12	25	12
Pottery	8	13	32	30	17
Jewelry	22	27	29	22	0
Watercolor	1	11	35	40	13
	17	18	26	29	10

b. Horizontal

	1	2	3	4	5
Drypainting	21	38	34	5	2
Weaving	18	10	19	40	13
Basketry	13	19	56	12	0
Pottery	32	23	30	12	3
Jewelry	10	39	39	10	2
Watercolor	22	27	40	11	0
	20	26	37	14	3

c. Vertical

	1	2	3	4	5
Drypainting	6	23	33	33	5
Weaving	44	18	21	17	0
Basketry	31	13	44	12	0
Pottery	40	20	27	13	0
Jewelry	10	20	41	29	0
Watercolor	24	32	32	12	0
	26	21	33	19	1

A. Component Lines

HAA-B-SS-5

6. Line endings

a. Endless

	1	2	3	4	5
Drypainting	67	15	10	7	1
Weaving	53	13	11	15	8
Basketry	81	0	6	13	0
Pottery	60	12	15	8	5
Jewelry	29	18	41	12	0
Watercolor	86	11	1	2	0
	63	11	14	10	2

b. Meet others

	1	2	3	4	5
Drypainting	1	7	20	22	50
Weaving	15	7	21	19	38
Basketry	69	0	6	6	19
Pottery	17	15	25	20	23
Jewelry	0	10	29	61	0
Watercolor	3	3	18	64	12
	17	7	20	32	24

c. Terminal markers

	1	2	3	4	5
Drypainting	19	22	27	30	2
Weaving	93	2	4	1	0
Basketry	100	0	0	0	0
Pottery	91	3	3	3	0
Jewelry	76	10	6	8	0
Watercolor	86	10	0	4	0
	77	8	7	8	0

A. Component Lines

6. Line endings

d. Free ends

	1	2	3	4	5
Drypainting	45	23	20	12	0
Weaving	65	17	15	2	1
Basketry	82	6	6	6	0
Pottery	40	20	22	15	3
Jewelry	61	4	14	21	0
Watercolor	14	22	19	39	6
	50	16	16	16	2

7. Meeting of lines

a. Use of points

	1	2	3	4	5
Drypainting	22	44	6	15	13
Weaving	28	17	10	24	21
Basketry	56	32	0	6	6
Pottery	45	20	12	10	13
Jewelry	74	16	10	0	0
Watercolor	45	32	18	3	2
	45	26	10	10	9

b. Corners

	SHARP 1	2	3	4	ROUNDED 5
Drypainting	79	21	0	0	0
Weaving	74	20	4	2	0
Basketry	62	38	0	0	0
Pottery	20	17	35	15	13
Jewelry	-	-	-	-	-
Watercolor	-	-	-	-	-
	59	24	10	4	3

HAA–B–SS–6

B. Structural lines

	H/V	H=V	V/H	D/V	D/H
Drypainting	3	6	7	0	0
Weaving	0	4	7	2	3
Basketry	6	0	6	0	0
Pottery	6	9	6	0	0
Jewelry	5	0	0	18	0
Watercolor	15	6	7	8	3
	6	4	5	5	1

	H/D	V/D	D×D	D‖D	V‖V	H‖H
Drypainting	0	0	1	0	25	0
Weaving	12	9	12	9	0	39
Basketry	0	0	0	13	0	0
Pottery	20	14	18	3	0	0
Jewelry	0	0	0	0	0	0
Watercolor	15	8	14	0	0	0
	8	5	8	4	4	9

	∽	⌒	O	O+*	*
Drypainting	0	1	13	10	34
Weaving	0	0	0	0	3
Basketry	0	0	6	25	44
Pottery	0	0	6	0	18
Jewelry	0	0	12	18	34
Watercolor	2	5	11	2	8
	0	1	8	9	24

C. Borders and Outlines

1. Borders

	NONE	LIGHT	MEDIUM	HEAVY	MULTIPLE	COMPLETE	INCOMPLETE
Drypainting	32	0	2	12	65	2	66
Weaving	64	3	13	11	23	30	6
Basketry	88	0	12	0	6	0	12
Pottery	7	32	0	22	41	93?	0?
Jewelry	25	6	22	44	28	72	3
Watercolor	98	1	0	0	0	1	0
	53	7	8	15	27	33	14

2. Divisions

	NONE	LIGHT	MEDIUM	HEAVY	MULTIPLE	COMPLETE	INCOMPLETE
Drypainting	71	2	0	0	27	0	29
Weaving	90	10	6	2	9	6	4
Basketry	88	12	0	0	0	12	0
Pottery	85	0	15	0	0	0	15
Jewelry	87	5	0	0	8	13	0
Watercolor	100	0	0	0	0	0	0
	87	5	3	0	7	5	8

3. Outlines

	NONE	LIGHT	MEDIUM	HEAVY	MULTIPLE	COMPLETE	INCOMPLETE
Drypainting	4	63	0	3	25	91	5
Weaving	63	20	13	3	12	32	5
Basketry	94	0	0	6	0	6	0
Pottery	93	0	7	0	0	7	0
Jewelry	-	-	-	-	-	-	-
Watercolor	7	82	6	5	7	93	0
	52	33	5	3	9	46	2

IV. Color

HAA–B–SS–7

A. Emphasis

	1	2	3	4	5
Drypainting	0	9	24	67	0
Weaving	4	19	19	30	28
Basketry	0	0	100?	0	0
Pottery	100?	0	0	0	0
Jewelry	0	0	40?	60?	0
Watercolor	0	2	8	27	63
	17	6	32	30	15

B. Number of Hues

	1	2	3	4	5 & +
Drypainting	0	0	4	9	87
Weaving	0	6	27	27	40
Basketry	0	100?	0	0	0
Pottery	100?	0	0	0	0
Jewelry	-	-	-	-	-
Watercolor	0	0	2	14	84
	20	21	7	10	42

C. Intensity

	1	2	3	4	5
Drypainting	0	0	100?	0	0
Weaving	4	14	22	37	23
Basketry	0	100?	0	0	0
Pottery	0	100?	0	0	0
Jewelry	0	0	0	40?	60?
Watercolor	6	17	29	29	19
	2	38	25	18	17

D. Value contrast

	1	2	3	4	5
Drypainting	4	37	37	18	4
Weaving	2	7	12	33	46
Basketry	0	0	0	100*	0
Pottery	0	0	0	0	100?
Jewelry	-	-	-	-	-
Watercolor	2	19	19	39	21
	2	13	13	38	34

E. Hue contrast

	1	2	3	4	5
Drypainting	0	8	62	30	0
Weaving	9	29	24	25	13
Basketry	0	100*	0	0	0
Pottery	-	-	-	-	-
Jewelry	-	-	-	-	-
Watercolor	4	6	26	34	30
	4	36	27	22	11

*Estimated for new; decreases with age.

HAA–B–SS–8

V. Perspective

A. Illusional

	LINEAR	OVERLAPPING	SIZE	COLOR
Drypainting	0	9	0	0
Weaving	-	-	-	-
Basketry	-	-	-	-
Pottery	-	-	-	-
Jewelry	-	-	-	-
Watercolor	11	44	12	4

B. Geometric

	POSITIONAL	DIAGONAL
Drypainting	0	0
Weaving	-	-
Basketry	-	-
Pottery	-	-
Jewelry	-	-
Watercolor	20	0

C. Conceptual

	MULTI-VIEW	SOCIAL	TOPOGRAPHIC
Drypainting	10	0	48
Weaving	-	-	-
Basketry	-	-	-
Pottery	-	-	-
Jewelry	-	-	-
Watercolor	1	0	0

VI. Composition

A. Complexity

	1	2	3	4	5
Drypainting	2	18	21	25	34
Weaving	21	37	25	15	2
Basketry	44	56	0	0	0
Pottery	46	42	10	2	0
Jewelry	47	47	6	0	0
Watercolor	7	38	30	22	3
	28	40	15	11	6

B. Boldness

	1	2	3	4	5
Drypainting	12	29	39	15	5
Weaving	7	13	19	28	33
Basketry	0	0	31	56	13
Pottery	12	20	29	27	12
Jewelry	0	12	63	25	0
Watercolor	4	28	50	15	3
	6	15	39	19	11

C. Tension

	1	2	3	4	5
Drypainting	0	28	47	20	5
Weaving	8	21	25	24	22
Basketry	6	62	19	13	0
Pottery	10	20	25	27	18
Jewelry	6	60	24	8	2
Watercolor	9	30	32	23	6
	7	37	28	19	9

HAA-B-SS-9

D. Movement

	1	2	3	4	5
Drypainting	3	23	20	30	24
Weaving	25	36	20	14	5
Basketry	31	44	6	13	6
Pottery	20	30	20	15	15
Jewelry	39	37	16	8	0
Watercolor	7	16	23	29	25
	20	31	18	18	13

E. Formality

	1	2	3	4	5
Drypainting	0	1	6	18	75
Weaving	0	9	26	34	31
Basketry	0	0	6	69	25
Pottery	15	25	27	25	8
Jewelry	0	0	4	37	59
Watercolor	4	26	36	28	6
	3	10	18	35	34

Bibliography

BIBLIOGRAPHY

Adair, John
1944 The Navaho and Pueblo Silversmiths. University of Oklahoma Press, Norman.

Adam, Leonhard
1949 Primitive Art. Penguin Books, Hammondsworth, Middlesex.

Adams, Wm. Y.
1963 Shonto: A Study of the Role of the Trader in a Modern Navaho Community. Bureau of American Ethnology, Publication No. 188, Washington.

Albert, Ethel M.
1956 The Classification of Values: A Method and Illustration. American Anthropologist 58: 221–248.

Alcock, Theodora
1963 The Rorschach in Practice. Tavistock, London.

Alschuler, Rose H. and Hattwick, LaBerta W.
1943 Easel Painting as an Index of Personality in Preschool Children. American Journal Orthopsychiatry 13:616–25.
1947 Painting and Personality: A Study of Young Children. University of Chicago Press, Chicago.

Amsden, Charles Avery
1949 Navaho Weaving. University of New Mexico Press, Albuquerque.

Arnheim, Rudolph
1954 Art and Visual Perception. University of California Press, Berkeley. Reprinted paper back 1965; page references are to this edition.

Aronson, Elliott

1958 The Need for Achievement as Measured by Graphic Expression. *In* Atkinson 1958, *q.v.*

Atkinson, John W.

1958 Motives in Fantasy, Action and Society. D. Van Nostrand Company Inc., Princeton.

d'Azevedo, Warren

1958 A Structural Approach to Esthetics: Toward a Definition of Art in Anthropology. American Anthropologist 60:702–714.

Barron, Frank, and Welsh, George S.

1952 Artistic Perception as a Possible Factor in Personality Styles. Journal of Psychology 33:199–203.

Barry, Herbert, III

1952 Influences of Socialization on the Graphic Arts. Unpublished undergraduate honors thesis, Department of Social Relations, Harvard University.

1957 Relationships between Child Training and the Pictorial Arts. Journal of Abnormal and Social Psychology 54:380–383.

Barrow, Terry, *cf.* Buehler, Alfred

Beals, Ralph L. and Hoijer, Harry

1965 An Introduction to Anthropology, 3rd Edition. The Macmillan Company, New York.

Beam, Philip C.

1958 The Language of Art. The Ronald Press Company, New York.

Beck, Samuel J.

1952 Rorschach's Test, Vol. III, Greene & Stratton, New York.

Bedinger, Margery

1936 Navajo Indian Silver Work. John Vanmale, Denver.

Bell, John Elderkin

1948 Projective Techniques. Longmans, Green and Co., New York.

Bender, L.

1938 A Visual Motor Gestalt Test and its Clinical Use. Research Monograph No. 3, American Orthopsychiatric Association.

Berlyne, D. E.

1966 Curiosity and Exploration. Science 153:25–33.

Bernstein, Basil

1964 Elaborated and Restricted Codes: Their Social Origins and Some Consequences. American Anthropologist 66 no. 6 pt. 2:55–69.

Bethers, Ray
1963 The Language of Paintings. Pitman Publishing Corporation, New York.

Boas, Franz
1927 Primitive Art. Harvard University Press, Cambridge. (Reprinted 1955, Dover, New York; page references are to this edition).

Bohannan, Paul
1964 Africa and Africans. The Natural History Press, Garden City, New York.

Brain, Thomas
1971 Style in Maori Art, unpublished ms.

Buehler, Alfred, Barrow, Terry, and Mountford, Charles P.
1962 The Art of the South Sea Islands. Crown Publishers Inc., New York.

Bunzel, Ruth L.
1930 The Pueblo Potter. Columbia University Press, New York.

Campbell, Donald T., *cf.* Segall, Marshall H.

Chapman, Kenneth M.
1939 The Pottery of Santo Domingo Pueblo. Los Angeles Museum, Los Angeles.

Child, Irvin L., *cf.* Whiting, John W. M.

Christensen, Erwin
1955 Primitive Art. Bonanza Books, New York.

Collingwood, R. G.
1938 The Principles of Art. Oxford University Press, New York. (Reprinted 1958, Oxford University Press, Galaxy Books; page references are to this edition).

Dark, Philip J. C.
1967 The Study of Ethno-Aesthetics: The Visual Arts. *In* Helm 1967, *q.v.*

Devereux, George
1961 Art and Mythology. *In* Kaplan 1961, *q.v.*

Diamond, Stanley
1964 Primitive Views of the World. Columbia University Press, New York.

Disselhoff, H. D. and Linné, S.
1960 The Art of Ancient America. Crown Publishers, Inc., New York.

Douglas, Frederic H.

1939 Types of Southwestern Coiled Basketry. Leaflet No. 88, Department of Indian Art, Denver Art Museum, Denver.

Dunn, Dorothy

1968 American Indian Painting of the Southwest and Plains Areas. University of New Mexico Press, Alberquerque.

Eitner, Lorenz

1961 Introduction to Art—An Illustrated Topical Manual. Burgess Publishing Company, Minneapolis.

Elkish, P.

1945 Children's Drawings as a Projective Technique. Psychological Monographs 58 #1.

Enciso, Jorge

1958 Design Motifs of Ancient Mexico. Dover Publications Inc., New York.

Fernandez, James W.

1966 Principles of Opposition and Vitality in Fang Aesthetics Journal of Aesthetics and Art Criticism 25:53.

Fischer, J. L.

1961 Art Styles as Cultural Cognitive Maps. American Anthropologist 63:79–93.

Fontana, Bernard L., Robinson, William, Cormack, Charles, and Leavitte, Ernest E.

1962 Papago Indian Pottery. University of Washington Press, Seattle.

Fraser, Douglas

1966 The Many Faces of Primitive Art. Prentice-Hall, Inc., Englewood Cliffs, New Jersey.

Gardner, Martin

1965 The "Superellipse": a Curve that Lies Between the Ellipse and the Rectangle. Scientific American 213: 222.

Gishin Begay, *cf.* Haile, F. Berard

Gotshalk, D. W.

1947 Art and the Social Order. University of Chicago Press, Chicago.

Haile, F. Berard (recorder) Gishin Begay

1949 Emergence Myth According to the Hanelthnayhe or Upward-Reaching Rite. Navajo Religion Series, v. III, Museum of Navajo Ceremonial Art, Santa Fe.

Halpern, Florence
1951 The Bender Visual Motor Gestalt Test. *In* Anderson, Harold H. and Anderson, Gladys L. 1951: An Introduction to Projective Techniques. Prentice-Hall, New York.

Hamilton, Augustus
1896 The Art Workmanship of the Maori Race in New Zealand. University of Otago, Dunedin, New Zealand.

Hannum, Alberta
1946 Spin a Silver Dollar. The Viking Press, New York.
1958 Paint the Wind. The Viking Press, New York.

Haselberger, Herta *et al*
1961 Method of Studying Ethnological Art. Current Anthropology 2:341–383.

Hatcher, Evelyn
1967 Navaho Art: A Methodological Study in Visual Communication. PhD Thesis, Department of Anthropology, University of Minnesota.

Helm, June (ed.)
1967 Essays on the Verbal and Visual Arts. Proceedings of the 1966 Spring Meeting of the American Ethnological Society. University of Washington Press, Seattle.

Henry, William
1961 Projective Tests in Cross-Cultural Research. *In* Kaplan 1961 *q.v.*

Herskovits, M. J., *cf.* also Segall, Marshall H.
1948 Man and His Works. Alfred A. Knopf, New York.

Hill, Edward
1966 The Language of Drawing. Prentice-Hall Inc., Englewood Cliffs, New Jersey.

Hoebel, E. Adamson
1966 Anthropology: The Study of Man. McGraw-Hill Book Company, New York.

Hoernes, H. and Menghin, O.
1925 Urgeschichle der Bildenden Kunst in Europa, 3rd edition, as translated in Hauser, Arnold, 1957: The Social History of Art, vol. 1. p. 23. Vintage Books, Random House, New York.

Hoijer, Harry, *cf.* Beals, Ralph L.

Holm, Bill
1965 Northwest Coast Indian Art: An Analysis of Form. University of Washington Press, Seattle.

James, George Wharton
1914 Indian Blankets and Their Makers. Reprinted 1937, Tudor Publishing Corporation, New York; page references are to this edition.

Jopling, Carol F.
1971 Art and Aesthetics in Primitive Societies. E. P. Dutton and Co., Inc., New York, N. Y.

Jung, Carl G., et al.
1964 Man and His Symbols. Doubleday, Garden City, New York.

Kaplan, Bert
1961 Studying Personality Cross-Culturally. Harper and Row, New York.

Kavolis, Vytantas
1965 The Value-Orientations Theory of Style. Anthropologica Quarterly 38:1–19.

Kent, Kate Peck
1961 The Story of Navaho Weaving. Heard Museum, Phoenix.

Kepes, Gyorgy, ed.
1965 Education of Vision. George Braziller, New York.

Kinget, G. Marian
1952 The Drawing Completion Test. Grune and Stratton, Inc. New York.

Kissell, Mary L.
1916 Basketry of the Papago and Pima. Anthropological Papers of the American Museum of Natural History, 17:115. New York.

Klah, Hasteen *cf.* also Wheelwright, Mary C.
1942 Navajo Creation Myth, (recorded by Mary C. Wheelwright). Navajo Religion Series, v. 1. Museum of Navajo Ceremonial Art, Santa Fe.

Kluckhohn, Clyde, *cf.* also Romney, A. Kimball
1942 Myths and Rituals: A General Theory. Harvard Theological Review 35:45–79.
1949 The Philosophy of the Navaho Indians. *In* Northrop, F.S.C. 1949: Ideological Differences and World Order. Yale University Press, New Haven.
1962 Culture and Behavior. The Free Press, New York.
1964 Navaho Categories. *In* Diamond, 1964 *q.v.*

Kluckhohn, Clyde and Leighton, Dorothea
1962 The Navaho, revised edition. Doubleday and Company, Inc. Garden City, New York.

Kluckhohn, Florence R.
1955 Dominant and Varient Value Orientations. *In* Kluckhohn and Murray 1955: Personality in Nature, Society, and Culture. Alfred A. Knopf, New York.

Kluckhohn, Florence and Stroudtbeck, Fred L.
1961 Variations in Value Orientations. Row, Peterson and Co., Evanston.

Kris, Ernst
1952 Psychoanalytic Explorations of Art. International Universities Press, New York.

Kroeber, A. L.
1948 Anthropology. Harcourt, Brace and Company, New York.
1957 Style and Civilization. Cornell University Press, Ithaca.

Ladd, John
1957 The Structure of a Moral Code. Harvard University Press, Cambridge.

Langer, Susanne J.
1953 Feeling and Form. Charles Scribner's Sons, New York.
1957 Problems of Art. Charles Scribner's Sons, New York.

Leach, E. R.
1954 Political Systems of Highland Burma. Beacon Press, Boston. Page numbers refer to the Paperback edition of 1964.
1961 Aesthetics. *In* Evans-Pritchard and others 1961: The Institutions of Primitive Society. Basil Blackwell, Oxford.

Leighton, Dorothy, *cf.* Kluckhohn, Clyde

Leuzinger, Elsy
1960 Africa: The Art of the Negro Peoples. Crown Publishers, Inc., New York.

Lévi-Strauss, Claude
1955 Tristes Tropiques. (English Edition 1964, translated by John Russel. Atheneum Publishers, New York. Page references are to this edition.)
1963a Structural Anthropology. Basic Books, Inc., New York.
1963b Totemism. Beacon Press, Boston.

Lewis, Albert Buell
1924 Javanese Batik Designs from Metal Stamps. Anthropology Design Series No. 2, Field Museum of Natural History, Chicago.

Lewis, Phillip H.
1969 The Social Context of Art in Northern New Ireland. Anthropological Series of the Field Museum of Natural History, v. 58. Field Museum, Chicago.

Linné, S. *cf.* Disselhoff, H. D.

Lomax, Alan
1967 Special Features of the Sung Communication. *In* Helm 1967, *q.v.*

Longman, Lester D.
1949 History and Appreciation of Art. Wm. C. Brown, Dubuque, Iowa.

Machover, Karen
1949 Personality Projection in the Drawing of the Human Figure. Charles C. Thomas, Springfield, Illinois.

Mason, Otis T.
1904 Aboriginal American Basketry. Annual Report, 1902, U. S. National Museum, pp. 171–548, Washington, D. C.

Matthews, Washington
1887 The Mountain Chant: A Navajo Ceremony. 5th Annual report, U. S. Bureau Ethnology, Smithsonian Institution, Washington, D. C.

Maxwell, Gilbert S.
1963 Navajo Rugs: Past Present and Future. Desert-Southwest Inc., Palm Desert.

McAllester, David P. *cf.* also Wheelwright, Mary C.
1954 Enemy Way Music. Peabody Museum, Harvard University, Cambridge.

Mead, Margaret
1935 Sex and Temperament. Morrow & Co., New York. Reprinted 1968, Dell Publishing Co., New York.
1949 Age Patterning in Personality Development. American Journal of Orthopsychiatry 17:231–240.

Mera, H. P.
1942 The Chinlee Rug. Bulletin No. 13, General Series, Laboratory of Anthropology, Santa Fe, New Mexico.
1943 Navajo Twilled Weaving. Bulletin No. 14, General Series, Laboratory of Anthropology, Santa Fe, New Mexico.

Merriam, Alan P.
1964 The Anthropology of Music. Northwestern University Press, Evanston, Illinois.

Mills, George
1954 Navaho Art and Culture. Unpublished PhD Thesis, Harvard.
1957 Art: The Introduction to Quantitative Anthropology. Journal Aesthetics and Art Criticism 16:1–17.
1959 Navaho Art and Culture. The Taylor Museum of the Colorado Springs Fine Arts Center, Colorado Springs.

Minetta
n.d. Tea-Cup Fortune Telling. W. Foulsham & Co., Ltd., London.

Morris, Desmond
1962 The Biology of Art. Alfred A. Knopf, New York.

Mountford, Charles P. *cf.* Buehler, Alfred

Mumford, Lewis
1934 Technics and Civilization. Harcourt Brace and World, Inc., New York.

Mundt, Ernest
1952 Art, Form, and Civilization. University of California Press, Berkeley.

Munn, Nancy D.
1966 Visual Categories: An Approach to the Study of Representational Systems. American Anthropologist 68:936.

Naumberg, M.
1947 Studies of the "Free" Art Expression of Behavior Problem Children and Adolescents as a Means of Diagnosis and Therapy. Nervous and Mental Disease Monographs No. 71.

Newcomb, Franc J.
1964 Hosteen Klah: Navaho Medicine Man and Sand Painter. University of Oklahoma Press, Norman.

Newcomb, Franc J., and Reichard, Gladys
n.d. Sandpaintings of the Navajo Shooting Chant. J. J. Augustin, New York.

Notes and Queries
1951 Notes and Queries on Anthropology, Royal Anthropological Institution, Sixth Edition. Routledge and Kegan Paul Ltd., London.

Otten, Charlotte M. ed.
1971 Anthropology and Art, Readings in Cross-Cultural Aesthetics. Natural History Press, Garden City, N. Y.

Payne, Edgar A.
1941 Composition of Outdoor Painting. Seward Publishing Company, Los Angeles.

Pearce, Cyril
1947 Composition: An Analysis of the Principles of Pictorial Design. B. T. Batsford, Ltd., London.

Piotrowski, Zygmunt A.
1957 Perceptanalysis. The Macmillan Company, New York.

Pollenz, Philippa
1950 Changes in the Form and Function of Hawaiian Hulas. American Anthropologist 52:225–234.

Pope, A.
1949 The Language of Drawing and Painting. Harvard University Press, Cambridge.

Preusser, Robert
1965 Visual Education for Science and Engineering Students. *In* Kepes, 1965, *q.v.*

Proskouriakoff, Tatiana
1958 Studies on Middle American Art. Middle American Anthropology, Social Science Monograph V, Pan American Union, Washington, D. C.

Read, Herbert
1931 The Anatomy of Art. Faber and Faber, London. Republished 1949, reprinted 1959 as: The Meaning of Art, Penguin Books, Harmondsworth, Middlesex. Page numbers refer to this edition.
1955 Icon and Idea. Cambridge. Reprinted 1965, Schocken Books, New York. Page numbers refer to this edition.

Reichard, Gladys A., *cf.* also Newcomb, Franc J.
1936 Navajo Shepard and Weaver. J. J. Augustin, New York.
1939 Navajo Medicine Man: Sandpaintings and Legends of Miguelito. J. J. Augustin, New York.
1944 Prayer: The Compulsive Word. J. J. Augustin, New York.
1950 Navaho Religion, A Study of Symbolism. Pantheon Books, Random House, New York. References are to the 1963 one volume edition.

Robbins, Michael C.
1966 Material Culture and Cognition. American Anthropologist 68:745–748.

Romney, A. Kimball and Kluckhohn, Clyde
1961 The Rimrock Navaho. *In* Kluckhohn and Stroudbeck 1961 *q.v.*

Schapiro, Meyer
1953 Style. *In* Kroeber, A. L. 1953: Anthropology Today. University of Chicago Press, Chicago.

Schiller, Paul H.
1951 Figural Preferences in the Drawings of a Chimpanzee. Journal of Comparative and Physiological Psychology 44(2):101. *In* Otten, 1971.

Schmidl-Waehner, T.
1942 Formal Criteria for the Analysis of Children's Drawings. American Journal Orthopsychiatry 12:95–104.

Schuster, Alfred B.
1959 The Art of Two Worlds. Frederick A. Praeger, New York.

Segall, Marshall H., Campbell, Donald T., and Herskovits, M. J.
1966 The Influence of Culture on Visual Perception. Bobbs-Merrill Co., Indianapolis, Indiana

Shepard, A. O.
1948 The Symmetry of Abstract Design, with Special Reference to Ceramic Decoration. Publication 574, Carnegie Institution of Washington, Washington, D. C.

Sides, Dorothy Smith
1961 Decorative Art of the Southwestern Indians. Dover Publications Inc., New York.

Smith, Marian W.
1962 The Artist in Tribal Society. The Free Press of Glencoe, Inc., New York.

Spencer, Katherine
1953 Mythology and Values, PhD thesis, Department of Anthropology, University of Chicago. Published 1957, Memoir of the American Folklore Society, v. 48, American Folklore Society, University of Pennsylvania, Philadelphia.

Sternberg, Harry
1958 Composition. Pitman Publishing Corporation, New York.

Sturtevant, William C.
1966 Seminole Men's Clothing. *In* Helm, 1967, *q.v.*

Tanner, Clara Lee
1954 Navajo Silver Craft. Arizona Highways Vol 30, No. 8:16–33.
1964 Modern Navajo Weaving. Arizona Highways Vol 40, No. 9:6–19.

Taylor, John F. A.

1964 Design and Expression in the Visual Arts. Dover, New York.

Thompson, J. Eric

1954 The Rise and Fall of Maya Civilization. University of Oklahoma Press, Norman, Oklahoma.

Tschopik, Harry Jr.

1940 Navaho Basketry: A Study of Culture Change. Amerian Anthropologist 42:444–462.

1941 Navaho Pottery Making. Papers of the Peabody Museum of American Archeology and Ethnology, Harvard University, Cambridge, Massachusetts.

Underhill, Ruth

n.d. Here Come the Navaho! U. S. Indian Service, Ft. Defiance, New Mexico.

Waehner, Trudes

1946 Interpretation of Spontaneous Drawings and Paintings. Genetic Psychology Monographs 33:3–72.

Wallace, Anthony F. C.

1950 A Possible Technique for Recognizing Psychological Characteristics of the Ancient Maya from an Analysis of their Art. American Imago 7:239–258.

1956 Revitalization Movements. American Anthropologist 58:264.

Watkins, Frances E.

1943 The Navaho. Southwest Museum Leaflet #16, Southwest Museum, Los Angeles.

Wheelwright, Mary C., *cf.* also Klah, Hasteen

Wheelwright, Mary C. (recorder)

1946 Hail Chant and Water Chant (Klah). Navajo Religion Series v. 2, Museum of Navajo Ceremonial Art, Santa Fe.

Wheelwright, Mary C. (recorder) and McAllester, David P. (ed.)

1956 The Myth and Prayers of the Great Star Chant and The Myth of the Coyote Chant. Navajo Religion Series v. 4, Museum of Navajo Ceremonial Art, Santa Fe.

Whiting, John W. M. and Child, Irvin L.

1953 Child Training and Personality: A Cross-Cultural Study. (Reprinted 1962: Yale University Press, New Haven. Page references are to this edition.)

Wilson, John A.
1946 Egypt. *In* Frankfort, Henri, Wilson, John A., and Jacobson, Thorkild, 1946: Before Philosophy. Penguin Books, Harmondsworth, Middlesex.

Wingert, Paul S.
1962 Primitive Art. Oxford University Press, New York.

Wolfe, Alvin W.
1966 The Complementarity of Statistics and Feeling in the Study of Art. *In* Helm, 1967, *q.v.*

Wölfflin, Heinrich
1915 Principles of Art History. Translated by H. D. Hottinger, 1932. Reprinted, n.d., Dover, New York. Page references are to this edition.

Woodward, Arthur
1938 A Brief History of Navajo Silversmithing. Bulletin #14, Museum of Northern Arizona, Flagstaff.

Wyman, Leland C.
1952 The Sandpaintings of the Kayenta Navaho. University of New Mexico Press, Albuquerque.
1957 The Sandpaintings of Beautyway. *In* Wyman, Leland C. 1957: Beautyway: A Navaho Ceremonial. Bollingen Series LIII, Pantheon Books, New York.
1960 Navaho Sandpainting: The Huckel Collection. The Taylor Museum, Colorado Springs.
1965 The Red Antway of the Navaho. Navaho Religion Series, v. 5. Museum of Navajo Ceremonial Art, Santa Fe.

Indexes

INDEX OF DEFINITIONS USED IN THE ANALYSIS IN THE SCHEMA-OUTLINE FORM

AUTHOR INDEX

SUBJECT INDEX

END OF VOLUME